MONEY HAS NO COUNTRY

MONEY HAS NO COUNTRY

BEHIND THE CRISIS
IN CANADIAN BUSINESS

Ann Shortell

Macmillan Canada
Toronto, Ontario, Canada

Canadian Cataloguing in Publication Data
Shortell, Ann
    Money has no country

Includes index.
ISBN 0-7715-9144-6

1. International business enterprises – Canada.
2. Investments, Foreign – Canada.   3. Canada –
Economic policy – 1971-   .* I. Title.

HD2809.S56 1991   332.6'7371   C91-094523-3

Jacket design by David Montle

Macmillan Canada
A Division of Canada Publishing Corporation
Toronto, Ontario, Canada

1 2 3 4 5 JD 95 94 93 92 91

Printed and bound in Canada by John Deyell Company

TABLE OF CONTENTS

To Herb

A man's homeland is wherever he prospers.
Aristophanes
Frogs, 405 B.C.

Acknowledgments

Money Has No Country was born as a proposal in 1989. The midwife was my agent and friend, the late Peter Livingston. His exuberance and enthusiasm inspired me to set down an outline; his excellent editing skills sharpened my concept, leading to Macmillan's interest in the book. Peter was a wonderful agent and an even better person; I sorely miss him, as do his many friends and clients. Peter's former partner and close friend David Johnston has done an admirable job of stepping into the breach for me and so many other writers.

Denise Schon bought the book for Macmillan, and has remained a strong supporter of the idea. I must also thank Ron Besse, Bob Dees, and Carmel Shaffer at Macmillan for their enthusiasm and hard work, and freelancer Wendy Thomas for an admirable copy-editing job.

An editor makes all the difference to any writer's work. With keen discernment of stylistic problems and an eye for the meaning behind the story line, Philippa Campsie made that difference in these pages.

I traveled to Japan in March 1990 as a recipient of the Japan Assignment Award, sponsored by the Asia Pacific Foundation of Canada and the Japan Foreign Press Center. Thanks go to the Foreign Press Center's able liaison, Mr. Seiichi Soeda, as well as to managing director Fumio Kitamura, and the center's president, Teruji Akiyama. My guide, Momoko Manon, was as pleasant as she was efficient. Since that trip, the Asia Pacific Foundation has provided me with introductions, set up interviews, and dug out research materials on a number of occasions, for which I thank the tireless Susan Phillips and her staff.

A supportive network of family and friends is a blessing and a necessity for any writer. Mine begins with my parents, Iris and Vincent Shortell, and my sisters Gail, Susan, and Maureen. My sister Carol played a special role in this book: she was chief organizer, research assistant, and cheering section.

Many thanks also to my strong phalanx of friends, especially Harold Burke, Cherllyn Ireland, Marci MacQuarrie, Bob Parkins, Anne Marie

Smart, Brenda South, Cathy Stevulak, Theresa Tedesco, Marianne Tefft, Steve Trumper, and Kathy White.

Roberta Grant and Theresa Butcher doubled as friends and valued resources. A vote of thanks to Jennifer Osther and Scott Kortje at the *Financial Times* library and to Scott Maniquet and the rest of the staff at the *Financial Post* library.

Angela Ferrante, Peter Herrndorf, Len Hill, John Lute, John Macfarlane, Doug Robson, and others provided essential aid and support when I needed it most.

I owe a particular debt to Patricia Best, my partner in my previous two books. Writing with Pat was often, to use one of her favorite phrases, like "cooking with oil." At times in this solo effort I sorely missed her elegant way with words and her ability to cut through the complications to the essence of a situation.

Carol Goar, Doug Kennedy, Terry Shaughnessy, Richard Siklos, and John Stackhouse patiently and kindly offered criticisms on particular chapters in the book. Their advice and guidance gave me confidence to make necessary and valuable changes in approach and content.

I also benefitted on a number of occasions from reading the thoughtful perspectives of Peter Cook, Terry Corcoran, and Edith Terry at the *Globe and Mail* and David Crane at the *Toronto Star*, as well as the thorough reportage of many other fine journalists.

The *Financial Times* of Canada provided me with an opportunity to explore some of the subjects in this book as a senior staff writer and as a columnist. My thanks to publisher Barbara Hyland and editor Steve Lawrence.

Many sources bent over backwards to help me ensure that this book is both accurate and insightful. Bob Blair, Brian King, Pierre Jeanniot, Richard Li, Dick Thomson, Hugh Wynne-Edwards, and many others willingly answered questions and openly debated points of contention.

And finally, thanks most of all to my companion, Herb Solway, for instilling in me the determination to complete this book.

Ann Shortell
Toronto, July 1991

Not in Our Stars

We has met the enemy and it is us.
— Walt Kelly (1915-1973)

W e have been lying to ourselves about money for a long time in this country. Of course, that's not the only matter about which Canadians have been afraid to face the music. We are in a serious crisis of confidence in Canada because we've been avoiding the hard truths about our political makeup and economic future for decades.

We don't work hard enough; we don't think we should have to work harder. In fact, we claim we have a right to social programs that other countries have not instituted because of their enormous cost. We see ourselves as a rich nation, able to support people who choose to remain in their home regions; but we are billions and billions of dollars in debt. We've been too generous with money we've never had. Profligate, even. This book is called *Money Has No Country*, to reflect the international forces buffeting our economy; but it could as easily be called *Country Has No Money*.

We expect too much of our government and too little of ourselves. We turn on our politicians almost on a whim, then expect them to have the guts to risk their careers by formulating and executing tough policies that show leadership. In recent times, the struggle between our demands on government and our expectations of it has intensified. And, fatally, we are turning inward as the rest of the world rushes by.

Whenever we run out of excuses for our sorry state, we can always point to the United States, whatever the problem may be. Our vision is skewed by the existence of the United States in so many ways that we can't grasp the natural links between our two nations. Or the natural, logical differences. We strike out at the specter of free trade because we are afraid for our lives.

Yet we continue to delude ourselves about our importance in the world. The best example is the comical idea that Canada is a first-rank nation, a "world-class" country. We seem to have the idea that since we have whined our way into the Group of Seven meetings (still called the G-5 in most places outside of Canada), we are somehow on a par with the major powers. Actually Italy, the other late addition, deserves to be there on the basis of economic performance. We don't.

But we can't keep our heads in the sand any longer. This nation is in serious trouble. It's not just that we're in debt for so much money that most of us can't begin to grasp the numbers. It's worse than that, much worse. Our natural resources, the strengths upon which Canada was founded, are now a serious weakness. Miners and drillers and lumberjacks are out of work; the world won't pay our prices, and our coal and oil and trees are being bargained away. We still view these resources as money in the bank and expect them to set us up for the future. This is willful blindness, because the international markets have shown that we can't count on them. We are clinging to frontier-era solutions in a post-industrial world.

There are plenty of places to lay the blame about all this. Let's start with government, since that's where most Canadians place their expectations for prosperity. For fifteen years we had in Pierre Trudeau a prime minister who was openly contemptuous of forming policies that were founded on economic necessity or tied to economic theory. The policies of his era, to borrow a phrase, haunt us still. The present federal government is aware of our problems but has done little to solve them. Instead, after seven years of sitting on their hands about issues such as research and development and the need for committed long-term money to help companies build technological capabilities, the Conservatives are preparing to run their third election campaign in good measure on their vision of Canada's economic future. Would that they had the accomplishments to back up their ideas.

The business community has fared no better. With all its jargon and slogans about globalization and international competitiveness, its strategies have for the most part been nothing more than a jumble of polysyllabic words. Canadian business is viewed by those outside the country as generally unprepared to cope, let alone compete, without trade barriers or other forms of government protection.

But how do we get beyond pointing our fingers and talking, talking, talking about solutions to our economic disasters? How do we take this country in hand and make it work economically? First, there must be a national consensus that we need to change our approach to our economy.

And we must develop a strategy that will be implemented by government, business, and labor—and supported by the voting public.

In order to plan for our future, however, we must agree on our present position as a nation. We must take a good, hard, honest look in the mirror. That's what I'm providing here: a series of stories that reflect our economic choices, each one from a different angle. I'm not an economist, but a story teller. My stories explore such issues as the effect of open competition on our companies, our attitude toward foreign investment, our willingness to build companies here, our ability to compete. At the end, I won't pretend to provide all the answers—but I will share my view of how we must shake up this nation's approach to business and the economy. Opinion, after all, is the beginning of dialogue. And we need to talk frankly about our future while we can still plan for one.

I caught my first, startling glimpse of the fractures in our economic landscape while visiting a Bay Street brokerage house in early 1987. That was back when the deals were flowing as smoothly as single malt Scotch and a lot of people thought brokerage houses were the hub of the economy. Michael Sanderson, the American who for a time headed the Canadian branch of New York securities firm Merrill Lynch, was ruminating about the way Bay Street was changing. Everything, he told me, hinged on the effect of the foreign companies coming to Toronto to take over the local financial business. He kept repeating the same phrase over and over again, "Nomura Securities is coming to Toronto," like a mantra.

The phrase had a hypnotising effect: as I rode the subway back to my office, I couldn't get it out of my mind. Nomura was dazzling enough on its own; after all, the giant Japanese broker has more money behind it than the entire Canadian securities industry. But the aspect that stopped me short was that from the point of view of all these giant international firms, we were just an insignificant secondary market. A place for them to expand their reach because the stock market was roaring and they could make a few extra bucks. They could take us or leave us, without giving the local brokers much thought. It was so dismissive, this international surge of money. Not just of Bay Street, but of our country.

Shortly after, I had a second glimmering of what that new buzzword of the 1980s, globalization, meant for Canada. I was working on a book on the Brascan group, dealing with Trevor Eyton and the Bay Street elite.[1] These

---

1 *The Brass Ring*, by Patricia Best and Ann Shortell, Random House, 1988.

guys all talked about Canadians in a somewhat disparaging way, as if they knew some very basic fact about life that most Canadians hadn't yet discovered. I realized after a while that they did indeed have a different perspective on the world from that of the average Canadian.

In 1987, most Canadians, for example, still felt some pride of ownership when talking about a crown corporation such as Air Canada. To the business community, Air Canada was an inefficient company that should be sold by the government and allowed to compete with foreign airlines for the customer's dollar. If it didn't survive, too bad. A cold, clinical dismissal of a national talisman, yes. But very much the tone business used to discuss any company, whether it was Canadian Pacific or Connaught Biosciences. It sounded as if the business community simply didn't care about the country. It only cared about the almighty dollar.

This explanation wasn't completely accurate, although it had more than a grain of truth in it. The greed decade made anyone in business focus on all the lovely money to be made, and quickly. Longer-term goals were left by the wayside. But that didn't mean that the more typical emotional response to Air Canada and other unprofitable companies was the correct alternative. After all, Canadians had paid to keep Air Canada aloft for years and the government couldn't afford that expense any longer. Besides, the same people who felt all tingly about sighting the maple leaf on an airplane wing wouldn't hesitate to go to Buffalo or Seattle to board an American airplane if the airline offered a cheaper fare. It didn't make sense to protect Air Canada, or the other crown corporations like it.

The airline conundrum, however, forced me to acknowledge the noticeable rift between ordinary Canadians—described by business with derisive distaste as "left of center"—and business leaders—described by many Canadians with envious contempt as "to the right of Genghis Khan." It was as if we were living in two different countries. In a sense, that is true.

In order to build the country, we erected barriers protecting our nascent banking system, our airline, many of our manufacturers. Even after these companies were established, we saw little reason to tear the barriers down. Those barriers also fostered a branch-plant mentality when multinationals, particularly American companies, set up subsidiaries to distribute to, and at times manufacture for, the Canadian marketplace. We began to believe that we had a right to demand these "made in Canada" products—even when it made no economic sense to have separate production facilities to serve such a small marketplace or to truck items across the country instead of across the border.

At the beginning of the 1980s, this cosy little protected enclave was for the most part still intact. It fit well with the traditional Canadian psyche as a country that likes to be governed. In social terms, this meant national health care. In economic terms, it often meant government-regulated monopolies, such as Bell Canada, or government-supported industries, such as coal mining, or government-subsidized regions, such as the Maritimes, or government ownership of crown corporations. Yet the sad truth was that we didn't have the money to pay for much of this grand social and economic architecture. And by borrowing to build, we were weakening our hold on the land. We were left vulnerable to any sudden shifts in our economic fortunes because we could no longer buy our way out of bad times.

The 1980s swept away many of our barriers, in the process irrevocably altering our core of economic values. The motive behind the transition to laissez-faire attitudes was that the fewer the rules, the easier it would be to make money. The fortunes being made in the stock market and real estate market in Canadian urban centers fueled the mighty-dollar mentality, of course. And the Progressive Conservative Party, which formed the government from 1984 on, mirrored the dollar-first mores of business. The Tories believed in less-is-more government, selling crown corporations, letting banks and brokers compete.

This theory of economic minimalism was worldwide and in large part based on Conservative ideology. Margaret Thatcher in Britain and Ronald Reagan in the United States were the movement's main proponents. But like almost everything on the world economic stage, it was also based on common sense and the recognition that government could not afford to subsidize so many economic sectors and could not control economic forces. After all, deregulation of the United States airline industry and the savings and loans companies took place during the presidency of Jimmy Carter, not Ronald Reagan.

Even earlier, the linchpin planners behind many of the world's leaders had started thinking this way. Former German Chancellor Helmut Schmidt built a friendship with former Secretary of State George Schultz in the 1970s based on their common commitment to a market economy and free trade; the two were part of an informal elite think-tank called the Library Group—named after the location of their first meeting in the White House in 1972—which also included Paul Volcker (at that time Schultz's assistant, later Federal Reserve Board chairman), Anthony Barber from the United Kingdom, France's Valéry Giscard d'Estaing, and Japan's Takeo Fukuda.[2]

---

2 For more on this group, see Schmidt's book, *Men and Powers—A Political Retrospective*, Random House, 1990, translated by Ruth Hein.

Deregulation, unfortunately, proved disastrous to the United States financial sector. There, greed led to an unconscionable abuse of a loosened regulatory system. But in other industries in the United States and elsewhere, deregulation has proven successful—particularly since barriers between countries have been toppling and companies must be efficient to cope with new foreign competition. Companies that have already fought for their lives in their home countries are ready to take on all comers. Of course, along the way they have fired thousands of workers and made once-comfortable communities into ghost towns. The economic tides of the 1980s left many innocent victims. But their plight was inevitable, given the increase in global trade since the Second World War.

Canada was playing a defensive game throughout most of the 1980s—catching up to American or other foreign trends, deregulating to allow companies to prepare for global competition. In its recognition of this need to be in sync with its trading partners, the Conservative government was a friend to business. For those who disagreed with its policies, it was seen as the puppet of business. There was even a conspiracy theory making the rounds from 1987 or so: the Tories and the business elite, by pursuing the Free Trade Agreement with the United States, were selling out the country. However, equating flawed policies with deliberate treachery was going a bit too far.

As I toured the country during the autumn of 1988, I was struck by Canadians' fear and distrust of a more open-market arrangement with the United States. The Tories won the election that year and we now have free trade, but most people neither voted for it nor wanted it. Canadians preferred to turn inward for shelter, looking for protection from economic challenges. And when free trade collided with a recession and questionable monetary policies, the disaster that resulted was blamed on the United States trade deal. It isn't surprising that there should be so much opposition in Canada to broadening the deal to include Mexico.

Free trade polarized Canadians. Those for and against free trade live in two different theoretical lands. The "pro-Canada," anti-free trade group believes in government subsidies, crown corporations, protection of industry, barriers to foreign money. In other words, control. The open-borders group subscribes to laissez-faire economics, deregulation of industries, privatization of government companies, encouragement of foreign investment. In a word—competition.

Actually, both pro- and anti-free trade groups are wrong, but for different reasons. The control group ignores the fact that we are a trading nation. More than three million Canadians work in businesses that in 1989 sent $137 billion in goods or services abroad. One-third of our gross national product comes from foreign trade.

The go-global set was also off base, however, because we weren't yet ready for the real world. Free trade, of course, brought to almost every sector of Canadian business the same foreign competition that Bay Street had already been facing. And some of the same business types who had pushed so hard for open borders and scoffed at the rest of the country's fear were knocked around pretty badly when the American players arrived in town.

The governments, both federal and provincial, didn't help at all. In fact, the federal high-dollar, high-interest-rate policy badly damaged Canadian companies' ability to compete at a crucial juncture in our economic future. It's widely acknowledged that most of the jobs we have lost won't be replaced. We didn't need to lose all of them. But even those who blame all Canada's problems on the demon free trade must acknowledge that we needed to lose a good number. Those jobs were being subsidized by the entire country through prices that had been too high for decades. Tax policy at both federal and provincial levels also became the bane of business, dramatically illustrated by the truckers' convoy on Parliament Hill and on Toronto's highways in May 1991.

Events following the Free Trade Agreement showed clearly that many of the forces shaping Canada's economic future are beyond Canadians' control. Whether for or against free trade, most Canadians would agree that in recent years our economic links have brought with them a definite loss of sovereignty on our part. And since national power is now determined by economic might, we feel ourselves diminished among nations. Since we've always depended to a certain extent on international trade for our prosperity, the blow is mainly psychological. That doesn't, however, diminish its effect on a Canada undergoing a painful redefinition of its nationhood.

Free trade, however, is not the most important element of our economic policy, nor is it the focus of this story. It is rather one result of a natural evolution of the other forces of the 1970s and 1980s. Overspending and government excess created a desperate need to sell crown corporations. The inability to continue supporting industries indirectly through restrictions on competition led to domestic deregulation and finally the lifting of international trade barriers. And the realization that stifling competition and encouraging inefficiency were holding back both companies and nations, while others were advancing into new realms of automation and technological innovation, made free trade inevitable. Choosing free trade means choosing open markets in order to force change, and free trade has become a way to draw Canadians' attention to the failure of this country to adjust to economic and political changes that have already swept and are still reshaping much of the world.

This redrawing of the world map does not mean, however, that members of the business elite of a country like Canada can live apart from their nation, in some special transnational stratum that allows them to take advantage of our standard of living while withdrawing from our social fabric. For a while I was dismayed by the disintegration of values that I saw in this nation. It seemed possible that we would end up with a small coterie of "haves" who operated without regard to nationalism and didn't much care about the country.

I regained some of my native optimism after reading the startling conclusion of the seminal book on the state of our world, *The Competitive Advantage of Nations* by Harvard business expert Michael Porter.[3] Porter, who believes that the health of individual industries is at the heart of a vigorously successful economy, is convinced that those industries need their homelands in order to grow and prosper. He rejects any argument that international competition reduces the importance of the nation-state. "Globalization," counters Porter, "makes nations more important, not less."

This is admittedly one side of a heated debate on sovereignty and business. But it's nonetheless heartening to think that before they can become internationally competitive, there is a valid argument that our industrial giants need to be on the same wavelength as workers, consumers, and policy makers.

The pace of change we all face sent me in a number of different directions during the preparation of this book. When I began my planning, the Canadian economy was still surging, although the stock market crash of 1987 had demonstrated the fragility of the boom. The year 1989, when I began my research, witnessed the cataclysmic revolts and rebirth of Eastern Europe and the Soviet Union. It seemed that the entire world as we had

---

3   Published by The Free Press, a division of Macmillan, Inc., New York, 1990.

known it was gone forever. At the same time, we in the West recovered from our fascination with junk bonds and designer everything and began to care more about saving the planet and the health of our own communities. The era of glitz and expense-account voyeurism had been replaced by peace and community activism.

During 1990, however, the hopes for peace were offset by the growing realization of the suffering the Soviet Union and Eastern Europe would face in grappling with their reinvention. War loomed in Iraq and there was a series of economic shocks. The American financial system was in crisis; the Japanese stock market crashed hard; the Canadian recession was followed by one in the United States as well, and by the autumn of 1990 there were global fears of depression. Americans were distracted from their financial anxiety by the display of their crushing military might during the Gulf War. Canadians, with a worse economic picture and a minor military involvement, didn't experience the same euphoria.

The recession, in fact, colored my view of our prospects for too long, since it hit hardest in my adopted home of Toronto. I grew weary and depressed listening to outraged business types say they were sick of the taxes and government policies and the bickering and negativism among Canadians—mainly about taxes—and were packing up and heading for Florida. I can only conclude that now they've done so, the rest of us can get on with the reshaping of Canada.

The urgent need for political change was set off by the failure of the Meech Lake Accord, but there was already an underlying dissatisfaction with the established state of affairs in the country. In addition to an outbreak of violence by native Canadians in Oka, Quebec, there was a widespread reaction to the goods and services tax, the truckers' convoy, even a march on Queen's Park by blue-suited radical conservatives. The nation has been playing political brinksmanship, with Quebec separation a real possibility.

That possibility loomed large during the spring of 1990, when I was conducting interviews in Tokyo on Japanese plans for investment in Canada. On my last day in the country, I discussed the subject with an experienced Japanese foreign correspondent (who had visited but never covered Canada). He was sanguine. Why did it matter so much that Canada might be reshaped because of the demands of its regions? he asked. Weren't countries all around the globe redefining their sovereignty? He was right on one score: Canadians were looking upon Quebec's separation as tragic while cheering on regional movements in other parts of the world.

Finally, I realized that what bothered me most was that Canadians have
been fighting about their varied definitions of our country without being
willing to admit that these visions all carry with them certain assumptions.
And that those assumptions carry a price. Whether it's higher air fares or
lower-quality goods, higher taxes or higher interest rates, we pay a price for
our quality of life in a nation of 26 million people spread over thousands of
miles of territory. Former Air Canada chief executive Pierre Jeanniot is
blunt about that: "There is a price to being Canadian," he warns. "Most of
us are quite willing to pay it, but let's face facts."

And while some of the sacred cows in this country are still sacred, others
are simply beef cattle. We need to sort out our priorities. Do we need a
Canadian airline? If so, are we willing to support it with government policies
that will foster its growth? This is the type of question dealt with in the
following chapters. For although this is a book about our need to deal with
the rest of the world, we must turn our gaze inward in order to decide how
to cope with the challenges of the new international economic order.

The cruel world outside certainly isn't going to wait for us to get our act
together. The economic changes of the past decade have been radical, far-
reaching, and irreversible—and almost totally beyond our control. There is
a struggle between the open-trade policies of the 108 nations that subscribe
to the General Agreement on Tariffs and Trade (GATT) and those nations
that are forming trading blocs that supersede all other trading arrangements. With the GATT talks stalled, the focus of our attention has been on
the North American market. For Canada, the Free Trade Agreement was
prompted by the fear of being shut out of key trading patterns with the
United States. Our aggressive move to open our borders was part of a chain
reaction, since the United States was waving the threat of protectionism
because of its inability to compete with Japan, the one nation whose power
it fears. Once we had dropped our protective barriers to the United States,
however, we had no choice but to negotiate with the Mexicans when the
United States decided to look at free trade on its southern border as well.

Beyond industry deregulation and trading blocs, however, lies an even
more fundamental change in the shape of the world economy. We now live
in a post-industrial age, the age of computer-based knowledge. This has cut
away the basic economic notions of transportation costs and, to some
extent, the need to group suppliers and customers. American futurist Peter
Drucker says that, as always at a time of sweeping historical upheaval,

"almost everyone has a sense of deep unease with prevailing political and economic policies . . . things somehow don't fit." People don't understand the new rules, but they know the old just don't apply any more. His words strangely echo those of a 1987 Japanese think-tank report: "Rich, developed nations are experiencing a . . . loss of purpose, identity and values."[4]

For Drucker, "The significant thing is that we are in a post-business society." Post-business. Post-industrial. Knowledge society. Information overload. Whatever the words, the effect is devastating, particularly for a country still relying on cheap resources to offset disadvantages in labor costs and taxes, with a black hole where research and development should be, and a proven inability to translate technological dynamism into thriving high-tech-based industries capable of both innovation and execution.

Canada has auto parts firms, textile manufacturers, furniture companies, and others that surely won't survive the effects of the 1990-91 recession. We will be a nation effectively facing deindustrialization—the loss of industries without their replacement—unless we act soon to push our businesses out of the dark ages and into the information-based renaissance.

The academics have been having a field day with these very real and telling problems. There have been more studies on trade, investment, and competitiveness than the average newspaper reader can keep track of, let alone absorb. Much of value has come from these studies, and I am not in competition with any of them.

Instead, I explore a few of the nation's fondly cherished beliefs and open them for public scrutiny and debate. Take the belief that we need a national airline. Or that a Canadian owner is always better than a foreign owner. Or that we have something to offer the Japanese when we approach them about partnerships in developing technology. Or that a so-called national treasure such as Connaught Biosciences was a real loss to the nation when it was absorbed by a French company a couple of years back. I deal with the Canadian banks' determined North American business strategy, but I could be dealing with packaging companies or beer companies. I talk about our attitude toward Hong Kong investment, but I'm really talking about the cost of closed minds.

In some of the stories I tell in *Money Has No Country*, you could change the name of the company without changing the point of the story. I chose Connaught, but I could have examined high-technology company

4 *Report on Internationalisation and Cultural Friction* by Japan Economic Research Institute, December 1987.

Lumonics, sold to the Japanese in 1989, or Leigh Instruments, purchased by a British company in 1988 and shut down in early 1990.[5] I could have written (but I didn't) about Varity Corp., the old Massey-Ferguson tractor company, which received millions in government grants and is moving to the United States without paying any of it back. Or about Canada Packers, recently purchased by a British firm; or de Havilland, sold by the government to Boeing Co. of Seattle a few years back, which also took millions in public money and then decided the company couldn't work (a sale to a European group was under discussion as this book went to press), or the steel or lumber industries. The list goes on; every day in the paper we see a host of new names and buyouts and failures that, on further reflection, are somehow part of the painful adaptation of Canada to the world around it. It's as if the entire puzzle has been thrown into the air and we're waiting to see where all the pieces land.

I also didn't write about Northern Telecom or Bombardier or the few other Canadian companies that have made a success of their businesses abroad. Nor am I concerned with the entrepreneurs who, like Paul Desmarais, have become fed up with Canada and are concentrating their energies on expanding abroad. I also have not dealt directly with Canada's role in Eastern Europe. (At present, it is only as a government giving aid, or through individual efforts to make a difference through investment or initiative.) This is not a book about "going global" in that narrow, business-hero sense of the term. Rather, it is about all the elements that are coming into play as Canada deals with international business forces. The same issues of foreign investment, deregulation, privatization, or research and development surround every question we face regarding trade, investment, and national well-being.

It would be impossible to tell all the foreign investment stories; there were 688 foreign takeovers and 213 new businesses set up by foreigners in 1990 alone. And this is not a "free trade book" per se, although there is a chapter on our reaction to the United States-Canada agreement and the proposed North American deal, and one on competitiveness. Yet every chapter in this book is about more open trade and investment; every chapter deals with the question of competitiveness.

I want to provoke discussion about how Canada has handled its place in the world. How some sectors of our economy have prepared to handle foreign competition, or have decided they couldn't, or haven't been given

---

5   Leigh was purchased by Plessey PLC, which in turn was bought by General Electric Co. of Great Britain and Siemens AG of Germany in 1989. The new owners shut down Leigh.

the choice. How we are perceived elsewhere in the world, and how we can best take advantage of that perception. Finally, how we have dealt with opening our borders. In all of this, there are times when Canada has precious little control, and it's best to realize that. In other instances, there are things we can do to greatly improve our position, should we choose.

Money Has No Country outlines the economic choices we have faced in recent times and how business and government has responded to those choices. It also considers the price we must pay for our nationhood in the future, and how we will structure our country to make that payment. Through these tales of great achievement and human error, strongly held beliefs and sheer opportunism, that is a question I pose again and again.

Ultimately, this must be a positive book. Because no matter how badly we've botched an initiative or misunderstood our position in the world or simply missed our cue in competitive terms, in the autumn of 1991 there is finally a full-fledged debate under way in this country about Canada's economic future. It is being led by a federal government desperate to capitalize on an image of national prosperity and leadership in national unity, but in a sense the government's motives are beside the point. People are being prompted, in good part by the daunting conditions of the past two years, to look at our image of ourselves. From here, we can do great things, if we have the will. I see this book as a part of that debate.

CHAPTER ONE

The Best Defense

Steven Shindler and I have been shoehorned into an arid, featureless cubicle at Toronto-Dominion Bank's United States headquarters, high above West 52nd Street in Manhattan. Every available meeting room is stuffed with bankers coddling clients and cutting deals with fellow financiers. Trouble is, there are more financial workouts on the table than there are new loans. In the winter of 1991, corporate America is coping with the recession and the Gulf War. A foreign bank like TD is simply playing the angles, trying to pick up some of the choicest pieces of business as a financial crisis spreads from the United States savings and loan companies to the New York banks. Twenty-eight-year-old Shindler is a director of communications finance at TD. Four years out of school and too young to have ridden the roaring 1980s Wall Street bull market, he is luckier than many of his former Cornell MBA classmates: he still has a job. But Shindler's intense energy makes all this harsh reality seem almost beside the point. Unscarred by the vicissitudes of the money decade, he still weaves dollar-sign dreams.

Shindler is telling his war stories, something more experienced investment bankers are too embarrassed to do these days. During his time at the bank, he has developed a close and warm relationship with the chief financial officer at client McCaw Cellular Communications, who is himself a former investment banker. Shindler takes particular pride in TD's front-line participation in McCaw's financings—U.S. $4.75 billion during 1990 to fund a takeover of its rival, LIN Broadcasting. As he details his own and his bank's victories in the arena of United States communications company finance, however, I'm having trouble fitting together his TD and my TD. The place I bank is the home of Green Machines and yellow-brick branches scattered throughout southern Ontario. The smallest of the old Big Five

Canadian banks, it has also traditionally been the least international in emphasis.[1]

Shindler grew up with his own, very different American banking system. While a child in New York, he banked at a small institution with the home-grown moniker Apple Bank; later, J.P. Morgan and Bankers Trust epitomized finance for the commerce student. Now, this young American banker was sitting in a soulless office in Manhattan outlining with almost religious fervor TD's key role in financing a giant American telecommunications company.

I knew before I arrived that morning that TD had essentially sidestepped corporate Canada as a major source of business growth; that half of its corporate loans were now in the United States, and the balance would soon tilt in Manhattan's favor; that its strategy dovetailed with the plans of every one of the large six Canadian banks. But I also knew that most Canadians would be shocked to realize that the epicenter of Canadian corporate banking has already shifted south. Today, the big Canadian banks all think of themselves, not as Canadian, but as North American banks with headquarters in Toronto.[2]

This revolution in the Canadian financial system can't simply be attributed to free trade. The forces that drove this change were in place by the 1981-82 recession. By that point, large Canadian businesses didn't turn to Canadian bankers when they needed money. Instead, they raised money abroad or through the stock markets. Following their clients, the banks spent much of the decade transforming themselves into companies that could operate abroad and in the investment banking world. Canadian historian and business commentator Michael Bliss pegged that fundamental shift in finance in a 1990 review of two books that dealt with the Wall Street decade.[3] Bliss talked of "the broader truth about the so-called golden age of greed. It was really the impersonal evolution of financial markets in the 1980s—strings pulled by an invisible hand—that jerked the dancers into spectacular new contortions." Canadian bankers, realizing early on that it was jerk or be jerked, decided to take the offensive. But at times the strings

1 Canada's banks rank, in terms of size: Royal Bank of Canada; Canadian Imperial Bank of Commerce; Bank of Montreal; Bank of Nova Scotia; Toronto-Dominion. Recently, the National Bank has been added at the bottom and the slogan altered to Big Six.
2 The exception is Montreal-based National. It has recently expanded beyond Quebec and defines itself as a Canadian bank. It is also, however, expanding in the U.S.
3 The review, in the May 1990 issue of the *Report on Business* magazine, praised *Barbarians at the Gate*, the story of the RJR Nabisco leveraged buyout, and criticized *Liars' Poker*, a broker's account of trading house Salomon Brothers.

were well beyond their grasp; the bankers were burned by overblown visions of global financial empires and by expensive purchases of Bay Street brokers.

Still, by the end of the decade the bankers' aggressive game plan had equipped them to compete in the increasingly dangerous realm of international finance. It had also separated them from their country. They aren't playing the game solely from Bay Street because that center of Canadian finance is now a mere way station for corporate lending. Most of the old-line brokers not already bought by the banks have been swallowed by foreign firms or nickeled and dimed into obscurity. This evisceration of Canada's native financial core is invisible to the average citizen, but it is an integral part of the country's changing definition of sovereignty.

As for TD, it proved itself throughout the 1980s to be the best Canadian bank, with the leanest management and the ability to build the strongest capital base. Its executive suite jumped the right way in both of its crucial decisions: to build a brokerage operation rather than buy a Bay Street broker; and to concentrate on the United States rather than spread its operations too thinly through Europe and Asia. It's a good thing that chairman Richard (Dick) Thomson and his team were so smart through the 1980s, though, because the 1990s promises to be a real killer of a decade for banks.

TD was already finding that out by the time of my Manhattan tête-à-tête with Shindler. Its loan losses were shooting up in Ontario, and two credit agencies were about to knock the bank's debt rating down a notch. Ironically, it was hurt because the credit raters had frozen the bank at a point of transition. The punishment, however, would only reinforce TD's decision not to be caught again with a narrow regional lending base. I realized with a start that by looking through the eyes of a young Manhattan banker, Steven Shindler, I was seeing the future of Canadian corporate finance. And it had very little to do with anything Canadian.

For the TD bankers, as for their counterparts, the 1980s had meant facing a major shakeup of their long-term relationship with corporate Canada. Multinationals with Canadian branch operations began making more and more decisions at home, which meant less financing by Canadian subsidiaries at Canadian banks. Worse still, all companies were financing more and more through securities markets rather than through their bankers. The banks needed to boost their corporate lending business by winning back old customers and finding new ones. For TD, that meant two things. Expand into the United States, and expand into investment banking.

An investment broker acts as a middleman, raising money for a client by arranging to sell the company's debt or stock for a fee. Toronto-Dominion chairman Dick Thomson has never accepted the dividing line between brokerage and corporate banking, where the client borrows money and is charged a rate of interest by the bank. "There's no logical reason for it to be done by investment dealers," he says. "It could better be done by banks. It's just that there was a licensing arrangement that kept us out of that business."

It's natural that Thomson would see matters that way; he's been surrounded by the bankers' viewpoint all his life. He learned about Canadian banking's roots from his father, Harold, a banker at the pre-Commerce-merger Imperial Bank of Canada. When Dick, after getting an engineering degree from the University of Toronto and a fresh Harvard MBA in 1957, decided to follow his father's path, Thomson senior advised his son that the smaller TD would provide better opportunities. Today, the six-foot, two-inch Thomson appears a banker's banker, down to the crinkly graying hair and standard steel-rimmed glasses. His thought patterns are austere and focused, well balanced by the more wide-ranging philosophies of his diminutive counterpart, TD president Robert (Robin) Korthals.[4]

Even Thomson knows, however, that permission to enter investment banking was no small license. The exclusion of bankers from the investment brokerage business in North America was sealed by the stock market collapse of 1929. The United States government, shaken by the financial debacle that followed, was also fearful that banks would be tempted to arrange stock issues in order to provide clients with money to pay back bank loans. It passed the 1933 Glass-Steagall Act, excluding banks from underwriting or trading stock on any client's behalf. At that time, much of the money used in Canadian business was invested by foreign interests; the government back in those years was not a big borrower and the domestic business was quite small. And the Scots who had founded the banks in Canada had always steered clear of investment banking. They defined themselves strictly as commercial lenders, following a Scottish financial

---

4 A more iconoclastic character, Korthals didn't hesitate to wear his bathrobe to the 1990 Writers Development Trust charity dinner in Toronto, in honor of the evening's "Come in What You Write In" theme. He was embarrassed, however, that the robe was "Commerce maroon." Trust a banker to reinterpret the palette in terms of competitors' colors.

tradition of separating commercial banks and merchant or investment banks.

Until the 1970s, that restriction was fine with Canadian bankers: they made loans to corporations and handled their payroll. But they didn't advise them on business plans or raise money to finance their projects. During the 1970s, however, banks pushed into the project finance and advisory areas, cutting into the investment dealers' territory. And once they began expanding their foreign operations, the banks became even more of a threat to the smaller, more locally oriented dealers. In a sense, foreign expansion and the move into investment banking were intertwined. "Corporate banking in the U.S. led into the investment banking," Thomson confirms, "because it was such a logical progression."

"You can start it with the computer and telephone communications," says Thomson of the shift in financial markets toward international investment banking. "That's what made it possible. Instant communications. Reliable communications. And a huge market of sophisticated people evolved." The first step for the Canadian banks was the foreign exchange desk. The banks needed to ensure that their short-term lending arrangements were competitive with foreign lending rates; that meant finding the least expensive sources of money. They also needed to be able to supply customers with cash for foreign operations. "Currencies fluctuate, so that today your short-term money might come from the United States or tomorrow it might come from Japan. It's all enmeshed into one funding pool," explains Thomson. "You can't sit here on Bay Street and operate in Canadian dollars only and be competitive."

To be involved with foreign exchange markets, he adds, financial companies need offices abroad and enough customers and orders to make the offices pay. They also need capital so that they can commit themselves to large international deals. It was this growth of international trade in money, particularly the currency-swap markets, that overwhelmed Bay Street brokers.

"As long as you could sit right here on Bay Street, everybody dealt only in Canadian dollars," recalls Thomson. "Then there crept in over the 1960s and 1970s the idea that we could deal in U.S. dollars, and then it came ultimately to be yen, deutschemarks and sterling, and U.S. dollars." Often, this borrowing would be done on the booming Eurodollar debt market, with companies borrowing in one currency from, say, a German bank, then swapping the loan into another currency through a different financial institution—and hedging against a change in the relative value of the two currencies through a British broker. There were several important players in this international game of currency juggling: Germany, Japan, the United States, Britain, France, and Switzerland. Canadian banks were large relative to their American counterparts, and the Canadian currency quite stable, so Canada could play too. But this new sophistication left many brokers out in the cold. More and more often, Thomson says, "a corporate treasurer didn't want to get a quote from some guy who only dealt in Canadian dollars."

Make no mistake, the bankers were motivated to muscle in on the brokerage business by fear. They had been steadily losing business since the 1982 recession as clients avoided high-interest-rate loans and opted to raise money by issuing stock. The only ones more scared than the bankers were the brokers. Canadian companies issuing stock realized there was a big world out there, and they had been steadily grasping more power in their relationships with brokers. They demanded lower fees and price guarantees on stock issues. That led to innovations such as the so-called "bought deal," which was actually a brokerage guarantee to pay the client the money, charge a minuscule fee, and assume all the risk of selling the stock. Even with this aggressive deal making, however, stock trading was shifting outside the country. By the time the bank-broker dance began, almost half of the trading in large stocks interlisted on American exchanges was being done in the United States. Canadian brokers were still making many of these trades, but they realized they had no real hold on their clients.

Bankers and brokers were united in their terror of the foreigners set to arrive on their turf. As the bull market roared through the 1980s, American firms looked north. Canada was the fourth largest capital market in the world, although well behind the big three of Tokyo, New York, and London. In these heady times, however, it was considered worth conquering. Merrill Lynch already had a big operation in Canada, and it became rapaciously aggressive. Prudential Insurance's brokerage subsidiary Prudential-Bache Securities arrived with big money to buy brokers and woo clients. Goldman Sachs, Morgan Stanley, Salomon Brothers were all setting up offices or simply scooping business from New York.

Even more daunting was the specter of the Japanese brokerage firms. Singly, any one of the largest was bigger than the entire Canadian brokerage industry. "Nomura Securities is coming to Toronto" was the chant on Bay Street. Says TD vice-president Charlie Baillie: "We all thought the foreigners were going to be big factors." For the brokers, that meant run for cover. For the bankers, it meant step in first before the competition took the field. "You had the power of the bank's capital and the flexibility of the dealer," reasoned Bank of Nova Scotia vice-chairman Peter Godsoe. "They meshed. And if you were going to protect your home base and make it grow in a universal sense, you had to be strong at home to compete out there, or people were going to come in and just take you. Like the Japanese did with ships and cars."

With the banks awakened to the potential in the brokerage business and the dangers of limiting their own growth in the go-go financial world of the day, the result was inevitable. By autumn 1986, London had just deregulated its financial services sector (the "Big Bang"), and Ontario was preparing to let foreigners and banks own minority positions in brokerages.[5]

Two banks had already taken important steps in that direction. Back in 1983, TD had taken advantage of a legislative loophole that allowed banks to trade stock on clients' instructions, as long as they only took orders and didn't offer any advice. In a move that shocked Bay Street, it opened a discount brokerage operation. That was not something that the other banks wanted to emulate at this point, however. They were much more intrigued by a more recent maneuver by Bank of Nova Scotia. Quebec, broadly interpreting its own powers in order to promote local business development, had announced it would let banks register to trade stock under provincial securities legislation. Scotiabank promptly signed on.[6]

That changed everything. Brokers began approaching bankers about selling out. TD was approached by one brokerage firm looking for an offer for a control position, says Charlie Baillie. It said no, but "every two weeks after that we had conversations" with someone or other on Bay Street. But the bankers needed the OK from Ottawa before they could plunge into the brokerage world. In October 1986, they decided it was time for a no-holds-barred conversation with federal finance minister Michael Wilson.

Canadian banking used to be a fraternity. The bankers socialized regularly, they all knew each other and each other's wives (the only role for women in

---

5 In Canada, the provinces regulate stockbrokers and the federal government regulates banks. The two levels of government share regulation of trust and insurance companies.
6 Royal Trust also registered, but since it wasn't a bank, its move didn't have the same impact.

the banking world in those days) and families, and each knew where the others stood on the issues facing the industry. Originally strictly commercial lenders who would take individual deposits, they moved into the consumer finance business and into the residential mortgage market in 1967 and soon came to dominate both. They steamrolled into the credit card business, the mortgage market, and credit insurance sales, and in the 1970s and early 1980s funneled money into technology to dominate multi-branch banking and, later, automated banking machines.

But while they seemed a juggernaut, by the mid-1980s they really were no longer that tight with one another. Oh, the Canadian Bankers' Association still held its predictable annual meetings, full of tired speeches aimed at the nightly newscasts. And the chief operating officers of the Big Six still met with the governor of the Bank of Canada a couple of times a year to discuss monetary policy, just as the CEOs and the Bank of Canada governor met in turn, spring and fall, with the finance minister of the day for a private dinner of financial chatter. But the bankers weren't presenting a completely united front to Ottawa any more. They were more competitive and their corporate strategies were more closely guarded. An American, Bill Mulholland, headed the Bank of Montreal; the TD had broken ranks publicly when it set up the discount brokerage operation. They were all concentrating on their individual agendas.

As a result, the Canadian Bankers' Association, which had traditionally worked hand-in-glove with the federal finance department to shape the entire financial industry, was having trouble dealing with financial institutional reform. With insurers, trust company chieftains, and brokers all lobbying for different types of change as well, Ottawa's plans kept getting shot down. In autumn 1986, as Ottawa's finance department worked on its third blueprint for new financial legislation in as many years, Michael Wilson's office let the bankers know privately that the politicians and bureaucrats would be better able to consider the banking industry's proposals if the various banks would get their act together and agree on a strategy for their industry.

The bankers privately agreed. They knew they needed to protect their turf—and that meant aggressively cutting into the brokerage business. It would be a good idea, the bankers decided, to hammer out a united front the way bankers had in the good old days—over a couple of days of golf and tennis in the refreshing atmosphere of a private club.

Golf and tennis, in fact, were key factors in the choice of Chateau Montebello, in the Gatineau region of Quebec, as the location for the bankers' cabal. The chateau agreed to keep its courts and links open until the weekend after Thanksgiving, when the bankers and their guests descended. It was also the sentimental favorite as the site where the bankers used to meet back in the halcyon 1950s. As one senior banker recalls wistfully, "We decided we'd have another meeting like we used to hold." (He hadn't, of course, attended the meetings of thirty years before, but he was sure life had been much easier back then.)

There were about forty participants; three or four executives from each bank, ranking bureaucrats from the finance department and the Bank of Canada. Michael Wilson, Gerald Bouey and Deputy Inspector General of Banks Donald Macpherson all attended.[7] TD's contingent included Thomson, president Robin Korthals, and executive vice-president Charlie Baillie. The organizational details were left up to Canadian Bankers' Association president Robert (Bob) MacIntosh. The former Scotiabank executive recalls assigning the seats on the bank jets: everyone wanted to be on Royal's deluxe model; no one wanted to travel with TD chairman Dick Thomson.[8] "I got the short straw," recalls an executive from another bank ruefully. "Because Dick [Thomson] runs a lean, mean bank—it's an old plane." Any such indignity was balanced by the line of limos at the airport in Ottawa, waiting to transport the precious cargo to their weekend retreat. The same banker chuckles about the decidedly conspicuous display: "It was either a gathering of Mafia chieftains or bankers."

The bankers had planned to discuss the international financial community's Third World lending problems—which were particularly worrisome to a few of the Canadian banks—and the recent failure of two western Canadian banks. But they were so preoccupied with survival plans, that other items were pushed off the agenda. "The focus on the securities business became more urgent as the weekend progressed," recalls Paul Cantor, CIBC's president of investment banking. When Michael Wilson arrived by helicopter for a special CEOs-only luncheon, there was only one topic: Ottawa must help the banks muscle into the brokerage business.

As the bankers expected, Ottawa saw it their way. The deal was sealed at Montebello. Wilson, a former broker himself, had no ammunition. "The

7 Bouey was replaced by John Crow in 1987.
8 In the late 1960s, several executives of Quebec-based Brinco were killed in an airplane crash; New York investment banker Bill Mulholland was brought in to head Brinco as a result, leading to his eventual ascension to the top of Bank of Montreal. After the Brinco crash, Canadian companies instituted strict rules about their executives traveling on separate flights.

government saw that the investment dealers were so small they were either going to be taken over by the New York investment dealers or by the major U.S. banks," recalls Thomson. Even Ottawa and the provinces couldn't use the Canadian dealers for their own foreign financings any more. The banks had Canadian nationalism on their side, and they used it. "Why should Canadian governments be using foreign dealers? That was the question that was being talked about," Thomson says. "No other country needs foreign dealers. And of course the problem was our dealers were too small. And therefore when Ontario went to the United States, they used Salomon Brothers. Now Wood Gundy would be along too but would be a small player in comparison to Salomon."[9]

The bankers had ample proof, then, that "the dealers here in Canada needed to expand rapidly. They were privately held corporations, so it was hard for them to raise the capital to do it," says Thomson. For the investment dealers, "it was a Catch-22. That's how the decision was made." Once Ottawa was onside, the rest was easy. Ontario, where most of the brokerage firms were headquartered, was furious that its years of careful studies on the issue were hastily pushed aside by Ottawa's new resolve, but it had no choice but to fall into line. Financial institutions minister Tom Hockin, Wilson's junior minister, made a deal with provincial financial institutions minister Monte Kwinter in Ontario, and the brokerage watchdog, the Ontario Securities Commission, was among the last to know. In December, Ontario announced that banks could buy up to 100 percent of brokerage firms. Foreign firms could buy into brokers in stages. As of June 1, 1987, the field was wide open to all comers. It was called Little Bang, a takeoff on London's Big Bang the year before. But for the brokers on Bay Street, it was nothing short of cataclysmic.

Now everyone was out to cut the best possible deal. For the dealers, there was the potential for money, lots of money. For the bankers, there was the business they had been lusting after—and the danger that they would blow it by making the wrong choice in a partner. The bankers hired American brokers as advisers and traveled to Europe to look at universal banking in action. "We normally aren't a great study place, but it was really back to business school planning, basics," says Scotiabank's Peter Godsoe. The two dangers were paying too much for a broker, and making the brokers into unmotivated millionaire employees. Godsoe voiced the banker's nightmare: "You buy it, you destroy it, what have you got?"

---

9 Ottawa and the provinces still use foreign brokers for sales outside Canada; but without more capital, Canadian brokers eventually would have been completely cut out of the large government issues.

During the next year or so, the bankers made up their minds—and then most of them changed them. June 30, 1987, the day they were allowed into the brokerage business, turned out to be just about the peak of the five-year bull market. Some of the deals weren't cut until after the stock market crash, but most of the decisions were made under the influence of the 1987 market euphoria. By January 1988, when CIBC bought 63 percent of Wood Gundy, four of the big five banks had bought brokers. Bank of Montreal owned 75 percent of Nesbitt Thomson Deacon; Scotia bought 100 percent of McLeod Young Weir; and Royal Bank purchased 68.5 percent of Dominion Securities. That jumped to 74 percent in 1991. Only TD made the less exciting but potentially far less costly choice—to build its own brokerage firm.

"We didn't see October 19 coming," says TD senior vice-president Charlie Baillie. "We weren't that smart." Baillie, a puckish man with wisps of silver hair and a permanent twinkle in his eye, had set up TD's New York operation in 1979 and five years later returned to move the bank into the fringes of investment banking. His group did mergers and acquisitions work, private placements of corporate debt with institutional clients, and ran the bank's own money market operations. He was in at the ground floor of the 1987 decision-making rounds, and these days he sounds smug about TD's decision to enter the brokerage business by building its own shop. He should. Given that the decision was made during the weeks preceding the October 1987 stock market crash, it was an incredibly lucky call.

TD thought building was the better route than buying from the start. But they still talked to brokerage firms. And every time another deal was announced, they looked at the idea of buying all over again. But they never wavered from their initial instinct. They felt that the brokers, who owned stakes in their own businesses, wanted to charge too much for the companies. The public brokerage companies were trading in the United States at 70 percent of their book value; Canadian brokerage firms were asking for double their book value. And TD, even without the crash, believed that more and more Canadian business would be channeled to international firms. The banks entering the business could only hurt the hefty traditional fees the brokers took in. "The banks may not be good in the securities business," Baillie says, "but whatever business we've gone into, the margins have gone down."

The other bankers also knew that it was much cheaper not to buy existing brokers. Scotiabank's Godsoe says his bank figured building would cost half as much as buying. But they had to balance that cost against the time and effort it would take to build from scratch. By buying, they gained the people who knew the business, which relied much more on instinct and intuition than banking. And they were gaining a retail business as well as the ability to do investment banking for corporate clients. Retail brokerage is much more personalized than the bank's traditional retail branch business. That's where TD had an advantage. It had already opened its retail discount-brokerage operation. In fact, the existence of its Green Line Securities was a good reason not to buy a full-service retail broker, which provides advice but charges a higher fee for the same trading service. On the corporate side, TD was very concerned that there would be a clash between its commercial bankers and any investment bankers brought in. Baillie says that the executive suite believed no matter how it tried to reassure them, the bank's corporate finance people would be sure they were losing business to any dealer it might buy. There would be, Baillie believed, "a Damocles sword hanging over both as they worried about it." In the end, the group decided that "even if we weren't that successful, building would probably be a better decision than buying."

This meant, of course, that they were going into a new business without any experienced people. When they had entered the consumer finance and mortgage businesses in previous decades, the banks recruited from those industries. This time, Thomson, Korthals, Baillie, and Ernest Mercier, executive vice-president of corporate banking, drafted the blueprint for the new business. Then Baillie and Mercier were told to reshape the corporate and investment lending departments, combining their people and operations. For example, TD's corporate coddlers, or "relationship people," were renamed corporate finance experts. And every team that went after new business included an equal number of investment bankers and corporate bankers — "whether we needed them or not," Baillie says. "It was partly for morale and partly educational." It worked. By 1989, the new area was renamed the corporate investment banking group, with Baillie and Mercier ruling in tandem.

Of course, since they started from scratch, they couldn't move everywhere at once. TD is still the leader in the discount brokerage business, with

60 percent of the market's annual $100 million in revenues. Ironically, the other banks, even with their full-service brokerage companies, have all entered the discount business as well. Still, TD is only an order-taker for stock trades, and only for small investors. It still doesn't have much capacity to underwrite stock issues, unless they're huge new issues with a guaranteed retail demand such as the Air Canada or Petro-Canada privatizations. It also can't compete for the bought deals for stock, where the brokerage buys stock and warehouses it until it can resell it. Still, says Baillie, "We've exceeded our expectations on the results."

And it already operates in a number of areas of the business. It does foreign currency swaps. It offers mutual funds and pension fund management—but hires outside advisers to do the management for all funds except those that are directly tied to the fluctuations of the stock indexes such as the TSE 300. In 1991 it launched a new fund designed for institutions and linked to the TSE index. It's a leader in preferred-share stock issues, including innovative shares called "auction preferreds," with a dividend rate set at a monthly auction. In concert with American broker Goldman Sachs, the bank has even arranged these special stock issues for sale to foreign companies, such as a three-country sale of preferred shares for Britain's Cadbury Schweppes.

It raises money for small companies, particularly for companies with a net worth of $50 million to $200 million, by arranging private placements of their debt. For instance, in 1990 it raised $42.5 million for tug and barge operator SeaSpan International. In fact, the bank has built this into one of the largest private placement departments in the country. By 1990, after three years in operation, the group had raised more than $1.5 billion in twenty-seven separate deals. Among the most noteworthy: it organized Canada's first leveraged buyout fund, a U.S. $107.5-million financing for Genstar Capital Corp.; and the country's first high-yield subordinated debt fund, $157 million for Canadian Corporate Funding Ltd.'s CCFL High Yield Fund and Company, Limited Partnership. It also raised money for one of Canada's first arbitrage funds, U.S. $82 million for Lancaster Financial Inc. of Toronto.

Some niches have worked better than others. Baillie cites the bank's money market operation, which in winter 1991 he was calling the most profitable in the business. Commercial paper is a natural, he says, since it can be warehoused and sold through the branch system at a higher price. TD, he added, had 22 percent of the commercial paper market in 1990; half of that was sold through its branch system. This territory hasn't been

defended by the brokers the way the fixed-income—bonds and debentures—area has been, he adds. Baillie freely admits that the bank had real
trouble competing in the bond area at first. Their long-time bond salespeo-
ple were "older, less educated, not computer literate, and didn't read the
papers." Besides, the bank's main customer for debt, "the branch buyers,
don't have the appetite for bonds." In March 1989, the fixed-income area
was merged with the much more aggressive swap group and now consistently makes a trading profit. That's more than can be said for most of the
brokerage divisions at the other banks. "We think the other banks are still
treating their dealers as portfolio investments," says Baillie. "The longer
they leave them separate, the more time we have to become a creditable
player in the market." No matter what the other banks call their brokerage
operations, however, they can't call them good buys.

Stepping off the elevator onto the fifth floor of Toronto's BCE Place tower,
the visitor will notice a strange decorating quirk. Half the hall is tiled, black
and white, in the long-time style of brokerage firm Wood Gundy. Just past
Gundy chairman Ed King's office, however, the tile is replaced by a muted
green carpeting. That's where the CIBC offices begin. It's a small touch, but
telling; when the Commerce decided to integrate the brokerage headquarters with its own investment banking group, it wanted the brokers to
understand that they still had a measure of their own independence.

But only a measure. Paul Cantor, CIBC's president of investment banking, likes to give tours of the new $15-million bank-broker trading floor. It's
the most computerized, most integrated trading floor on the Street. One
day in spring 1990, Cantor shows me the foreign exchange department (run
by the bank) and the currency swap desk (run by Gundy, but registered on
the bank's balance sheet). The 840 monitors and the bankers and brokers
working side by side are impressive. Unfortunately, the results up to then
hadn't been. "I'd like to have made more money," Cantor sighed that day,
"but I'm very pleased with the strategy. And it will pay off." When? His
reply was as optimistic as possible. "In the long run—in the medium term—
maybe even soon."

The Gundy purchase was not in the cards for CIBC. It had planned to
build an investment bank through selective links with brokerage firms
around the globe. In Canada, it chose Gordon Capital, investing in that
aggressive broker's new merchant bank in early 1987. "The link-up with
Gordon," says Cantor, "was intended to get us closer to a knowledge

base." Then came the other banks' purchases, the stock market crash, and the sudden crisis at Wood Gundy. The broker had committed itself to buying stock in a British privatization issue in September 1987. After the crash, it looked like the British government was going to hold it to that promise—at a cost of $60 million to the firm. That was $60 million the firm didn't have.[10] The Toronto Bronfmans stepped in to carry the company on a short-term basis, but it was available for a good price. Or at least, it seemed like a good price at the time. CIBC couldn't resist.

By 1990, it seemed that CIBC should have resisted. The retail market had been dreadful ever since the purchase, and Gundy was losing more money than many of the other brokers. Then the planners at CIBC and Gundy made another risky decision. In January 1990, they bought Merrill Lynch, Canada's retail brokerage. They paid $37.5 million—50 percent above the division's book value—for 20 offices, 685 employees (including 264 retail brokers), and 140,000 accounts. But there were deserters, and too much overlap; offices were closed and the Street felt the bank should have laid off a lot more people than it did. By September 1990, Gundy had a $52-million loss to show on its operations so far that year—and the bank had to swallow $29 million of that.

For months, the Street gossiped about the bank wanting to bail out of the retail side of the brokerage business entirely. And there were also rumors that it had asked Gordon Capital to step in and run the institutional side of the division, hoping still to capture some of the expertise it had admired so much four years earlier. Neither of those events occurred. Cantor says the bank never had any intention of selling the retail operation. As for the Gordon rumor, it "must have been based on history, not current facts. When we were faced with mounting losses, I would brainstorm the widest possible range of solutions. But a Gordon solution really didn't solve the issues." But it was clear that everything that could go wrong had gone wrong. Reflecting on the Merrill purchase, Cantor said in mid-1991 that he stands behind the purchase—and the price. "My definition of 'deep pockets' is the ability to stick to the strategy during adverse markets." He was rewarded, finally, in 1991.[11]

The rest of the bank-broker stories weren't quite as dismal. But they

---

10 It actually lost $20 million.

11 Finally, small investors began using stockbrokers again. Although they weren't as interested in buying stocks, they were looking for alternatives to suddenly lower bank rates. CIBC-Wood Gundy and other brokers began to make money again. "The results of our strategy," says Cantor, "are beginning to bear fruit."

weren't pretty, either. First, there was a lot of truth to the clichés about culture clash. "The investment dealers looked on the banks as being a little slower, but powerful. They distrusted them and fought against them," Scotiabank's Godsoe said in 1988. "In fairness, the real world was somewhere in between." In between didn't turn out to be a terrific place for Scotiabank, however. The bank had bought McLeod in part because it wanted to add to its retail investment network. But the addition didn't add up to profits. By 1990, the brokerage was costing Scotia 5 to 10 percent of its earnings. At that point, Godsoe told a reporter that the bank had paid McLeod's partners too much, and the brokerage had not performed as expected. But he stuck by the decision to buy. "Do we think the strategy was right for this bank? Yes, we still do."

The brokerage was still making money, added his boss, chairman Cedric Ritchie. "They're having a rough period right now. I'm the first to admit that our timing couldn't have been worse. But I take comfort in one fact: the last guy who was perfect in this world was crucified 2,000 years ago." But neither man addressed the rumors circulating that senior brokers at Scotia McLeod were so unhappy under the bank's thumb that they were talking of engineering a management buyback—and hang the consequences of being a nonentity in international terms. Once again, no such event ever occurred. But the fact that it was rumored told a tale of insecurity and angst over a deal gone sour.

Perhaps everyone's expectations were simply too high. It turned out that unless the brokerage firms did very well, the results didn't measure up to what the banks had paid for them. For the Royal Bank, that was two times the book value of Dominion Securities. The renamed RBC Dominion Securities was the star performer among the bank-owned brokerages. In 1989, two years after the purchase, it earned $32 million—its second-highest profit ever. But it was still the bank's worst-performing division. It was only in 1991 that record treasury and securities earning began to shine in comparison to recession-afflicted consumer and corporate division results.

During the bad years, the retail market was the most disappointing. Reduced to zero after the crash, it didn't begin to rebound until 1991. During that time, 60 percent of the trades logged on the Toronto Stock Exchange were made by brokers for the firm's own account—so-called "principal trading." Less than 20 percent was trading by retail clients. Brokers were trading on average one stock a day, filling in time by trying to sell bonds and mutual funds. Paul Taylor, executive vice-president of treasury and investment banking for Royal, tried at one point to take solace from the bloodbath by pointing out that not everyone would survive. "If the weak can be driven to the wall, so be it."

Surprisingly, however, some of the "weak" who were driven to the wall in Canada were the giant foreign brokers whose very presence had been feared. A couple of the American retail giants who arrived in style in the mid-1980s left quietly in the early 1990s. Merrill Lynch Canada, which had linked its success to the Toronto Bronfmans' Edper group of companies, found it just wasn't making any money; in 1988 it lost $8 million. The sale of its retail operations to CIBC in January 1990 was the result. Less than a year later, it fired all of its research analysts, equity sales people, and stock and bond traders in both Canada and Australia. Essentially, it was a spent force, its global strategy in tatters. The cause was poor management at home base: Merrill didn't manage to make much money during the bull market. But it only demonstrated that a strong base is needed for any kind of global competition.

Following Merrill out the door, Prudential-Bache sold its retail branches to Burns Fry in June 1990. This was simply part of a general cutback at Prudential. In a memo leaked to employees, American chairman George Ball said it best: "Business stinks." Dean Witter, a Canadian brokerage subsidiary of giant American retailer Sears Roebuck, sold its operation to Midland Walwyn Capital Inc. in July 1991.

Corporate finance specialists fared better. By 1991, there were offices for a few New York firms, such as First Boston, Morgan Stanley, Salomon Brothers, and Goldman Sachs, British firms, including S.G. Warburg,[12] and a hybrid of the British and French Rothschild merchant banks. And they were doing business. Goldman and Warburg were awarded the international Edper group financings, elbowing aside long-time favorite Gordon Capital. Morgan Stanley has been particularly successful; its deals include the 1988 purchase of Polysar Energy & Chemical Corp. by Nova Corp. and Nova's subsequent sale of Polysar's rubber division; the 1988 Inco Ltd. poison pill; and the Reichmann family business restructuring, including the 1990 sale of the Reichmann family's GW Utilities to British Gas PLC.[13] But these foreign companies didn't really need their local branches to do business. Morgan Stanley's counterpart on two of its deals, J.P. Morgan, represented British Gas on the Consumers purchase and Bayer on the Nova

12 Warburg bought control of local firm Alfred Bunting and Co. The firm is now called Bunting Warburg Inc.
13 The Nova deal is described in Chapter Six and the British Gas deal in Chapter Five.

rubber division purchase—with brokers from other offices operating in
Toronto out of its affiliate, Morgan Bank of Canada.

The Japanese, on the other hand, never really got started. During 1988,
five Japanese brokers opened offices in Canada. The smallest, Sanyo Securities, shut up shop in early 1991. The four giants—Nomura Securities,
Daiwa, Yamaichi, and Nikko—barely made money on their minuscule
bond portfolios and steered clear of the stock market. Yamaichi was more
venturesome in the bond market, but quickly bailed out when it began to
lose money in a big way. One Japanese bank, Sanwa, did buy control of
Toronto brokerage McCarthy Securities in autumn 1990, but this was long
after most securities firms had sold out to either a bank or a foreign owner.
The much-feared Japanese presence didn't alter the structure or power
lines of the finance community one iota. Canada was too small for the
Japanese to spend much time on it. Especially since they had made a mess of
their plunge into New York and were concentrating on cleaning that up
rather than bothering much with more peripheral markets.

As for the rest of the Canadian brokerage industry, it limped along for
three years without the support of its small investor base. Retail broker
Richardson Greenshields of Canada Ltd., controlled by the Richardson
family of Winnipeg, tried to find a buyer in 1988, but gave up after months
of fruitless searching. A retail-based firm, Richardson made its staff cuts
early, however, and was profitable again well before some of the competition. Midland Doherty and Walwyn Stodgell Cochran Murray, the other
two large retail firms, eventually merged in a pool of red ink.[14]

The losses were larger on Wall Street, but comparatively the much
smaller TSE fared far worse. In 1990, according to the Securities Industry
Association, American brokerage firms lost a total of U.S. $500 million; it
was only the second time ever that the Street as a whole lost money, and the
1973 loss of U.S. $72 million paled in comparison. In Canada, our five stock
exchanges lost 22.4 percent of their value on shares traded during 1990. Bay
Street firms lost a total of $230 million. The mergers, including Merrill-
Gundy, accounted for much of the money down the drain. Nevertheless,
more mergers are predicted, especially on the retail side of the business.

However, the first half of 1991 raised profits and brokers' spirits. Brokers
were making money again. Bankers began to hold up their heads about the
purchases.

*

---

14 The firm is now called Midland Walwyn Capital Inc. With the Dean Witter purchase, it
now has the country's largest retail brokerage operation.

A revolution like this had never before been experienced by Canadian business. But Canada was ill-equipped to cope with the new Bay Street. In fact, throughout these years of boom and bust, buying and selling, trading and investing, competing and failing, Ottawa had been working and re-working the same set of legislative changes that had prompted the drones at Finance to tell the bankers to get their act together at Montebello. Finally, in late September 1990, yet another junior finance minister announced yet another blueprint for reform. Minister of State for Finance Gilles Loiselle unveiled Ottawa's fourth attempt within a decade to revise financial laws — the third by the Tories. Loiselle proposed that financial companies be allowed to do all kinds of business, in effect creating a universal banking system.[15] Banks could own insurers and sell insurance through the mail to credit card customers. But Loiselle wouldn't let them sell insurance from their branches because of a powerful insurance brokers' lobby. In response, the bankers continued their own lobby as the proposals slowly moved through parliamentary committees.

The proposals ground their way through committee meetings for much of 1991. First the trust bill. Then the insurance bill. There were four bills on line, in fact — banks and credit unions would come later.[16] The reforms were widely viewed as allowing more power to fall into the hands of the banks — but in reality they only confirmed the situation that existed, with a few minor changes. In fact, the world had long since passed these changes by.

Some of the bankers might now regret that they had ever heard of Montebello. "No one is better off for having spent hundreds of millions of dollars," declares TD's Baillie. Although the markets finally picked up in 1991, he doesn't think the industry will ever be profitable enough to allow a decent return on the purchase price tags. "I would have a tough time being in my position," he adds, "at a bank that bought a broker."

But the basic decision to move full steam into the investment banking business was sound. In fact, it was the only way to go. Thomson confirms that had the industry remained a collection of small brokers without international connections, "Canada would have lost that business to the major New York dealers. Now, it wouldn't have happened quickly.

15 Bankers don't like to use the term universal banking, because Germany's universal banks are allowed to own stakes in commercial business. Canada's bankers are against any links between banks and the commercial sector.
16 Loiselle hoped to see the package passed by Parliament by September. Instead, he was shuffled upward to Treasury Board. His successor, John McDermid, began to talk of having all four bills passed by January 1992.

Through restrictive legislation, we would have been able to keep the dealers out by giving a monopoly." Eventually, however, the customers would simply have headed south, looking for cheaper money. Bay Street would have lost the investment banking business, and the Canadian banks would have risked losing their local customers entirely.

It was the price the banks paid and their timing that make it seem to some observers that they took the wrong path. The only fear the banks don't have, ironically, is that the brokers will leave—their three-year golden handcuff contracts expired in the spring and summer of 1991. There isn't anywhere for them to go—in this country at least.

By working for the banks, however, they could choose to practice their trade just as easily in New York as in Toronto. In fact, a good portion of Baillie's investment banking crew is located in New York. And that side of the business was looking considerably brighter for Canadian bankers in the spring of 1991.

When I first met him, Arthur English was eager to talk pipelines. The stocky, sanguine head of TD's United States operations enthused that this would be a great example of a Canadian bank like TD taking on the United States financial establishment. After all, the proposed TransCanada PipeLines (TCPL) Iroquois pipeline is a Canadian style of operation: public-sector transportation of natural gas over the wide expanse of Canada to light kitchen stoves on Long Island. And TD, with its partners Union Bank of Switzerland, First Chicago, and Prudential-Bache, was about to blow away the competition on the financing bid—big international competitors such as Citibank, Barclays, and Bankers Trust. TD's group was already one of seven finalists from twenty-three syndicates invited by TCPL project manager Morgan Guaranty Trust to bid on the U.S. $750-million project. And English assured me that it planned to go all the way.

A number of New York types were at TD headquarters in Toronto for meetings, and English had already arranged for the two women leading the pipeline bid to drop in on our interview. Debra Gaffney-Gravenese, as director of utilities and project financing, was English's captive industry expert. Amy Miller, as director of the bank's United States syndication group, was the financing mind behind TD's pipeline bid. Both had joined TD from American banks, with impressive credentials and contacts. And the story was intriguing. We all agreed to meet in New York and go over the pipeline project in detail. English was confident of the result; after all, his people had built one of the top three utility financing groups in the United States.

A couple of weeks later, when I arrived in New York for the briefing, English dismissed the pipeline with an expansive wave of his right hand. He'd just returned from a swing west, so he wasn't sure who was free to chat or about what. But he was sure there were other things to talk about around the office. "The issue isn't Iroquois, the issue is being a leading player." Yes, TD had been one of the two banks left in the running for the pipeline deal. But it had lost, or more accurately, had backed away when it realized the deep discounting the competition was willing to do for the client. In fact, that was one of two big bids the bank had backed away from at the last moment just in the past week. Barclays Bank of Britain scooped both. That was fine by TD, English assured me. It's great to be a winner, but not at just any price. Still, we agreed that while there has to be both in life and business, "losing is never as good a story as winning."

There are actually plenty of wins ranged on a five-shelf glass cabinet tucked just inside the entranceway to TD New York. Most are just the usual boring Lucite "tombstones" that mark the bank's participation in equity or (more often) debt financings for companies or public utilities.[17] Sometimes TD is listed as one name among many, but more often as the number three or number two name or as co-manager of the financing. Sometimes the bank is right on top, with names from all over the world ranged below. There are Canadian clients operating in the United States, such as long-time client Rogers Communications (Ted Rogers is on the TD board) and the Belzberg family's First City Financial Corp. But more often American companies are the clients: Southwest Virginia Cable—U.S. $37.5 million; Cable Utilities; Tembec; Pacific Corp.—U.S. $30 million.

TD is also at the top of the list as co-agent or organizer or manager of a few plum Wall Street financings: Turner Broadcasting—U.S. $1.4 billion; Cable Vision—U.S. $1.15 billion; Metro Mobile—$300 million; General Electric Capital—U.S. $750 million; Peachtree Cable—U.S. $250 million; American Cable Systems California—U.S. $190 million. TD is ranked eleventh in the United States as a money raiser through these group financings, or syndicates; much of that money is raised for communications companies.

The catchiest display item is the paper container topped with lacquered

---

17 The name tombstone originates with the ads the companies place in financial papers to trumpet their success. The Lucite versions run $50 a crack, with an average of three dozen distributed for each issue.

popcorn, sporting the news of a recent U.S. $400-million United Artists short-term fund raising. "I've seen that at every office I've been in the last few days," comments a passer-by. But TD is not just another office; it's second in importance only to the Bank of New York on the list of twelve financial institutions participating, including Canadian rival CIBC. The kitschy design was part of English's drive to make the tombstones more interesting—and cheaper than the usual Lucite jobs.

A communication company is also responsible for TD's largest trophy, the U.S. $3.75-billion deal for young Steven Shindler's favorite client, McCaw Cellular. With this type of recent success, it's easy for English to switch from pipelines to the communications sector. After all, this is a real TD specialty, one Charlie Baillie focused on when he opened the New York office, and one president Robin Korthals set the stage for back in 1964 when he agreed to back Ted Rogers's cable operations. TD also took a chance on cellular technology, backing Rogers again with his Cantel Inc.

Rogers has long since sold his United States operations and is back home struggling with a high debt load. But TD has racheted its experience with his and a few other Canadian companies into a significant position as an American cable and cellular financier. McCaw was another relatively early pick; TD became involved with the firm in the early 1980s, well before it showed signs of growing into the world's largest cellular company. That's far from their only communications client, however. TD lends more to the cable industry than any other bank. Communications loans account for 30 percent of the bank's American business, and the United States office has far more outstanding commitments in the area than TD has in Canada.

After changing the topic of the day to the bank's communications lending successes, English quickly finds a few likely bodies for me to talk to. He runs that type of open, flexible, responsive office. Like TD chairman Dick Thomson, an engineer-turned-MBA-turned-banker, English was recruited by Korthals in just such an offhand fashion almost twenty years ago. As a University of Western Ontario grad, English was waiting for a potential employer who never showed. So instead, he began chatting up a banker waiting for another student at the regular round of meet-the-students interviews. Korthals's interview never turned up either, but he arranged for English to come to head office for a second meeting.

English held a number of positions at head office and moved to New York to replace Baillie in 1984. Back then, according to English, United States operations consisted of Baillie and "two dozen low-tech calling officers with big checkbooks" who would take orders on approval from

Toronto. They set up ten offices in nine cities. But in the 1980s that strategy was reversed, and operations were centered in New York, with branches in Chicago, Houston, and Los Angeles. The bank began to pursue a policy of heavy MBA recruiting and raids on other banking specialists.

Steve Macdonald, the head of TD's communications group, is sky-hooked by English into our meeting. Macdonald, in turn, arranges for me to chat with William Glasgow, chief financial officer at Prime Cable, based in Austin, Texas. (Macdonald cautions English before Glasgow arrives: "William. He can't stand being called Bill.") Glasgow happily launches into the details of his relationship with TD. Prime is an important client, about the same size as Ted Rogers's American cable operations once were. The relationship actually predates Glasgow. Prime became a client in 1980, but took on a more important role with the bank during the last recession. TD and former junk bond broker Drexel Burnham Lambert asked Prime in late 1983 to help turn around a bad cable investment in Atlanta. By 1988 TD and Drexel had their money back, and Prime had made a few dollars on the arrangement as well. These days, TD is Prime's number-one money lender—ranking ahead of GE Capital and Bank of Boston.

It's "troublesome" the way U.S. banks "go hot and cold on an industry," Glasgow complains. "From a business standpoint that's very, very hard. You build relationships with banks. You build relationships with people, and then boom! So from my vantage point it would appear Canadian banks are much more stable than American banks." In fact, as the United States financial system undergoes a shakeout, Glasgow thinks the Canadian banking system might be the superior one. Still, Glasgow says nationality does matter when he looks for bankers. It's just that he doesn't consider Canadian banks as foreign. "Language is a very big barrier; customs are a very big barrier." But that doesn't affect Canadian relationships. Funnily enough, while TD is busily doing a sales job to convince clients that it is a North American bank, Glasgow definitely considers it Canadian—and prefers dealing with Canadians there. He feels they have the ear of head office.

The Japanese banks were hot to make loans to companies like Prime last year; then, stung in the United States leveraged-buyout market, they pulled back. A few European banks are still pushing their services. The same week that he visited TD, Glasgow breakfasted with representatives from Britain's National Westminster Bank. Crédit Lyonnais and the ever-aggressive Bar-clays are also around, although Macdonald believes that "even they have been retrenching some." In fact, he claims that in recessionary 1991, competition for business is "non-existent." (By mid-year it was picking up, but only for very conservative transactions.)

Last year's mega-deal for McCaw Cellular wouldn't fly this year, either. The reasons are easy to list. The recession has resulted in the reduced use of portable telephones, and thus of McCaw's cellular transmission service. The United States government has also imposed stiffer regulations on how banks can categorize loans to industries such as cellular communications.[18] Another reason is the very serious problems in the banking business worldwide.

That same international crisis in banking, however, was a boon for the Canadian banks' operations in the United States. The Canadian banks had been hard hit by the investment banking meltdown during the late 1980s. But they were well-positioned to profit from the blows that were knocking down the American banking system. TD's offices were all full during January 1991 because American companies were looking for money. The Canadian banks could be seen as vultures, picking and choosing among the remnants of the American financial system. In some instances, they might be better compared to grave robbers. No matter what, it was clear that the Canadians had the luck of timing on their side. They moved into the United States; a few years later, hundreds of American financial institutions fell apart. This left the Canadians with plenty of room to establish themselves in their adopted territory.

George Bush's son Neil has been castigated and humiliated for his role as a director in the failed Silverado Banking, Savings & Loan. But in fact he was just taking advantage of a policy that his father publicly smiled upon as vice-president during Ronald Reagan's two-term presidency. Reagan was Mr. Deregulation, and he allowed the S&L industry to move into just about any type of lending it chose, curbing the risk with a blanket government guarantee for depositors. By 1990, this policy had already cost the United States government U.S. $500 billion; estimates pushed the eventual tally up as high as U.S. $3 trillion. By the time Bush's secretary of the treasury, Neil Brady, appeared before a Senate committee in February 1991 to explain his proposed United States financial reforms, Washington was running 330 S&Ls and had already sold or liquidated another 99. In total, more than half

---

18 The cellular industry must be placed in a riskier loan category and there are limits on the amount a bank can lend to that category of company.

the nation's S&Ls were in trouble. As Brady put it, "We let S&L owners go to the casino with Uncle Sam's checks in hand."

The American banking industry was not so reckless in its lending policies, and it would be unfair to lump them with the moribund S&Ls. But it is tempting to do so. In 1989, the banks had piled up more losses on bad loans than at any other time in the past fifty years—and that total rose sharply through 1990. The Federal Deposit Insurance Corp., the United States equivalent of the Canada Deposit Insurance Corp., booked U.S. $4.8 billion in losses that year by paying off depositors in 169 failed banks. In 1991, there were 1,000 banks on the federal regulators' watch list, and they estimate there will be another 180 to 230 bank failures before all the problems are discovered and cleaned up. And this year, the banks going under will be much larger institutions; FDIC could pay another $5 billion. The FDIC has joined with the Federal Reserve Board, the United States counterpart of the Bank of Canada, to demand that banks increase their capital. The cause of this implosion of the American financial system is bad debt. Poor lending policies led to risky real estate loans, high-debt leveraged buyout loans, and good old Third World loans (now better known as "less-developed country" or LDC debt). The stock market collapse, the recession, and the real estate crisis all hit at once. Washington is very worried, though, because usually bad debts don't show up so early in recession. And traditionally they double during a downturn.

In part, the banks made these risky loans because their old corporate clients had turned to foreign markets or the stock market for money. Banks that had never lent on real estate before found they had no other takers for their money. As a result, real estate loans almost doubled as a percentage of banks' assets during the 1980s. And all that money fueled the historic boom in the real estate market—leading inevitably to the equally historic bust.

Of course, American banks aren't quite as sacred as Canadian banks. There are more than 12,000 banks south of the border; almost 2,500 are national banks. The top fifty control 60 percent of the industry's assets. Those are the ones, however, that everyone is really worried about.

For months, there was talk of mergers or foreign acquisitors among the CEOs of the large New York money-center banks, sacrosanct names such as Chase Manhattan Corp., Chemical Banking Corp., Manufacturers Hanover Corp., Citicorp. Chase fired 5,000 people in one go; Citicorp fired 8,000. Problem loans at the four banks were up 26 percent during 1990. American real estate loans and LBOs at these and five non-New York money-center banks were more than three times as much as their equity.

Finally, in July 1991, the penny dropped. Chemical and Manufacturers announced a $2-billion merger to create the country's second-largest bank. Said one analyst, "We think this is the harbinger for things to come." The banks explained that they needed the strength to compete internationally.

In the past, the United States banks have been big losers in the global arena. One American analyst described them to *Time* magazine as "retreating from the global marketplace with their tails between their legs." Another said, "U.S. banks are pygmies in a world of giants."

Treasury secretary Brady's reforms were designed to address these two very real problems. He proposed to strengthen the system and make it internationally competitive at the same time, with the most wide-ranging financial system restructuring since the Depression. Accounting rules would be changed to help the system cope, and FDIC would get more money. Meanwhile, healthy banks could move into the insurance and securities business and have nation-wide branches.

Brady isn't moving a moment too soon. The banks need his help; they also believe they need to switch to universal banking, which is practiced in most of Europe and even in Canada. A couple of banks were ready to jump the gun on the securities business. J.P. Morgan and Co. won approval from the Federal Reserve Board to underwrite United States equities in September 1990. Bankers Trust followed with a push both to underwrite and trade securities. After all, it argued, through its foreign branches it already makes 70 percent of its income from fee-related business as opposed to more traditional banking. Chase and Citibank, despite their loan problems, have also applied for entry into the investment banking business.

One proposal in United States law varies quite dramatically from Canada's approach. For the first time, industrial companies will be allowed to own banks. Some analysts see this as a way to keep the banks in American hands, rather than passively allowing foreign financial takeovers. In a funny kind of way, it also shows the Americans paying homage to the Japanese *keiretsu* system.[19] The six largest Japanese banks are all tied to *keiretsu*, or corporate industrial groups. Three of them have their own *keiretsu*. When they lost capital during the stock market crash in Tokyo in 1990, the related companies lent them money. Americans now seem to feel they also need these friendly corporate faces when their banks are in trouble.

As for the Japanese, it's a good thing they had that support system. They

---

19 *Keiretsu* are families or networks of companies. They have interlocking directorships and shareholdings and buy one another's products. Often, one company supplies parts for another.

had been aggressively attacking foreign markets through the late 1980s, cutting margins in the wholesale banking business, and gaining 40 percent of the world's market share. But their lending ability was backed by their Japanese stock portfolios. When the Tokyo exchange dived in 1990, they had to back off quickly.[20] In 1991, they had some relief, as the yen rose during the Gulf War. Still, they couldn't play for the same stakes that they were used to.

The Europeans were not paying the price for overaggressive lending the way the United States and Japanese banks were. But they had their own preoccupations, particularly the demand for capital for German reunification and from eastern Europe. And the banks were finding that customers weren't as keen on having all their needs met by one trans-European bank. They prefer to use the best in each business, be it a Japanese broker like Nomura Securities for Euromarket issues; German and French banks for trade financing; or Barclays or Citicorp for treasury management.

This ill wind was all to the good of Canadian banks building in the United States. Still, it was essential to any success that they understand their role in this morality play. Of the hundred-odd international bankers, four Canadian banks ranked in the top fifty in size in 1980. In 1990, Royal was the highest-ranked of the Canadian banks at Number 54. The Canadian banks had begun consciously to think of themselves as North American, but they had no claim to global status. "We're frankly kidding ourselves if we think in our own right we can be truly global competitors," admits TD's Macdonald. If TD had tried to be competitive in every major market globally, he adds, "we would have gotten ourselves in big trouble."

Unfortunately, some of the other Canadian banks made just that mistake in the 1980s. And they were starting from a very modest base. The Bank of Montreal, the worst organized in those days, had no internal accounting procedures whatsoever when Bill Mulholland arrived in 1974. It also had no set personnel system, no control over its investment portfolio, and no method to match its deposits and loans. Executive vice-president Don Munford recalls, "Profit was whatever was left in the till at the end of the year."

During the 1982 recession, the Canadians learned some hard lessons.

---

20 Switzerland-based Bank for International Settlements announced in 1988 a set ratio of bank capital to bank assets of 8 percent. Banks must conform by March 1992, but most are already using the measurement to determine their strategies.

They had serious problems at home, with real estate and oil and gas loans — including the famous international bailout of Calgary-based Dome Petroleum.[21] They also had a pile of bad debt to the Third World.

Still, when planning their post-recession expansion, including their investment banking thrust, some banks believed at first they could become global players. Commerce's Paul Cantor says his bank made that mistake in 1986. "When we first brought the investment bank elements together, our vision was to become one of the ten or fifteen greatest investment banks in the world," he recalls. "That's a formidable challenge. We've come to realize that that's a very ambitious goal for a company which is dependent on as narrow a base for its livelihood as the Canadian dollar." In other words, Commerce and all the rest were forced to pull back when these ambitious plans collided with the fierce reality of international competition.

Luckily for its own health, TD had been too small and too regionally based in Ontario to make a major push into international loans during the 1970s. For the same reasons, TD recognized early that it couldn't hope to be a truly global business force.

The others took a little longer to come to the same conclusion, but they all did eventually. CIBC closed stockbroker Grenfell & Colgrave Ltd. in London in November 1989, two months after selling a $456-million British commercial loan portfolio and announcing a general withdrawal as an active lender in Europe. At the same time, it placed its British residential mortgage operation up for sale and abandoned its Australian mergers business.

Royal still considers itself a bank with a global strategy. But it is definitely picking its targets carefully. It closed its own Eurobond broker and investment bank Orion in November 1987, moved out of the British bond and Eurobond markets, and sold British brokerage subsidiary Kitcat and Aitken in 1990. It also withdrew from Tokyo. At that time, Royal's senior executive vice-president for corporate banking, Bruce Galloway, told a reporter that "we're very conscious of the fact that the world thinks Canadian banks are all retreating."

But that conclusion was wrong, Galloway added. Canadians had simply realized that they should compete only where they could be effective. "We recognized there were certain countries and markets where we just didn't

---

21 Some analysts believe the Dome workout, which involved dozens of banks from around the world, could be the last big international bailout. These days, they say, there are too many differing aims and a more cutthroat attitude among bankers.

belong. We weren't making a reasonable return and there was no prospect." Canadians had realized that for them, going global meant concentrating on their main market—the United States.

Bill Mulholland, the Bank of Montreal's American transplant, always said that his 1985 purchase of Chicago-based Harris Bank was the best thing he ever did for the bank. At the time, the other banks were aghast. "Many of us scorned it at the time," says one competitor. "It was prescient." In early 1991, CIBC was talking of following in Mulholland's footsteps. The reasoning behind such a move is simple, as CIBC's Cantor had said many months before the bank's public announcement of a potential United States purchase: there is "a need for us to recognize that we're part of something: a North American economic system. I can't see how Canada can escape its geographical destiny."

At CIBC, he added, "we think that Canada will become increasingly one of the regional markets in the North American market. The strategy for any company which is one of the dominant participants in a regional market has to be to consolidate its position and redesign the 'home' market to encompass the broader geographic framework." For CIBC, with a quarter of the Canadian market, an American bank was the next logical step. However, despite the talk, nobody bought. This disappointed banking analyst Terry Shaughnessy. He thinks they missed a real opportunity by not bidding for, say, a Citibank or a Chase Manhattan. The Canadian banks can only be marginal players, he says, until they take that plunge. But TD's Thomson disagrees. And so far, the others think it's too big a risk to move ahead with a large United States purchase. This time, they are building rather than buying.

Free trade looks attractive to the Canadian banks when they're the ones doing the trading. They haven't been so happy, however, about the arrival of a few Americans on their own home turf. During the 1980s, while moving ahead aggressively in corporate and investment banking, they had lost ground as retail bankers to the trust companies, insurers, and other money lenders and savers.

But that they could handle. They didn't know how to handle the specter of American Express opening a bank in Canada. Amex applied for a bank license in August 1986. Around that time, Amex chairman James Robinson

III emerged in the United States as one of the most prominent proponents of free trade with Canada. Amex also added a few Ottawa lobbyists and board members with influence in Canada to its payroll. A special Schedule II license was granted by cabinet order in council on November 21, 1988 — the day that a federal election confirmed Prime Minister Brian Mulroney's free trade policy.

The bankers were upset both by the fact of Amex Bank and by what it symbolized. They believed it was the thin edge of the wedge. General Motors has a financial services subsidiary that is also a giant mortgage lender; Ford owns an American S&L. At the time, neither could get a United States banking license — but if the Amex case set a new policy, they could obviously get one in Canada. The smaller Canadian financial companies faced the possibility of being squeezed out of the market. The squeezing power of Amex alone is immense. It owns brokerage Shearson Lehman Hutton in the United States.[22] It was itself the largest money "overseer"[23] in the United States in 1989, with U.S. $274 billion money under management and U.S. $91.5 billion managed on its own account. It sells insurance, travel packages, and retail goods. With only $500 million in assets in Canada, Amex's real asset was its client base of 1.5 million Canadian cardholders.

And while it appeared that any American could come into Canada — whether or not it qualified as a bank in the United States — access to the United States by Canadian financial institutions was still somewhat limited. Somehow, total two-way access hadn't been included in Mulroney and Robinson's free trade deal. TD's Dick Thomson got himself into trouble after the 1989 annual meeting, when he made a few off-the-cuff remarks about a story that was circulating concerning an alleged secret deal between Mulroney and Robinson. A couple of hours later, he retracted his statements. But Thomson had said publicly only what the entire banking community believed privately.

The bankers had one small satisfaction; they effectively shut out Amex Bank from their system of automated teller machines. They raised the admission fee for their linked network of machines, called Interac, from $100,000 to $12 million. Amex refused to pay and joined a smaller proprietary system owned by the Bank of Montreal.

---

22 Shearson owned a control position in Canadian broker McLeod before it was sold to Scotiabank. Shearson turned into a disaster for Amex in 1989 and 1990.

23 More money passes through this company's hands than any other single company in the country, on a transactional basis.

Meanwhile, the question of United States-Canada free trade in financial services settled down after Washington made a few more concessions. There are still some limitations, but by 1991, with their artificial barriers breaking down, the United States is letting the Canadian banks do almost every type of investment banking function.[24]

In an era of bank mega-mergers and shakeups all over the world, the Canadian banking scene seems relatively placid. Not so. In fact, the waters are not all that calm on the home front these days. New broom Matthew Barrett is sweeping out the Bank of Montreal, trying to recoup lost business in retail banking. In fact, retail banking became the prime concern of the banks during 1989 and 1990; they began regrouping and spending money to regain market share from trust companies in areas such as RRSP accounts and personal loans. CIBC has been the scene of a major management shakeup, with the head of its retail bank, Warren Moysey, moving to a trust company after a policy dispute. CIBC chairman Donald Fullerton is determined at any cost to move his bank from the Number Two slot to Number One before he retires in 1992 or 1993.

As Scotiabank ponders a successor for Ritchie, it is faced with more problem loans, including bad United States real estate and leveraged buyout loans, just like the American banks. A couple of years ago there was a rumor that TD would do a reverse takeover of Scotiabank. The only problem was, it wouldn't do any good for TD to take on the larger but more troubled bank. In that regard, a comment Thomson made on potential foreign mergers hit close to home. "There will always be mergers," he opined. "But I'm not convinced that bigger is better. Banking is a business that has to be closely monitored and managed."

In Canada, however, he admits that there is certainly some merger potential. "Banking in Canada is very competitive. I don't know of another industry that has as many large competitors as banking does," says Thomson. "And whenever you have a very competitive situation like that, inevitably there is potential for mergers, because of accidents, or the desire to cut costs. So I guess you'd have to assume . . . there's been a history of mergers over the life of Canadian banking."

Despite their opportunities in the United States, Canadian banks are not exciting to investors these days. After all, the paper decade is over. There

24 The Glass-Steagall Act is still in effect in the United States, but Canadian banks can apply for exemptions in order to do some stock underwriting. Glass-Steagall, however, is currently under Congressional review.

were higher loan losses all over Canadian banking in 1991. For TD, poor economic conditions in its Ontario home market were hurting profits, proving once again that it had been smart to build business in the United States.

When Dick Thomson faced the crowd of small shareholders, analysts, investment advisers, board members, and members of the media at TD's annual meeting in late January 1991, he knew he was on safe ground. For successful companies like TD, annual meetings are rather like traditional family get-togethers: in good times there's a lot of hand shaking and back patting, in recession years like this one there's a more subdued tone, but still a sense of pride in the bank's accomplishments. Thompson faced a bit of sharp questioning on the rather rich level of board directors' fees, but that was a matter that could have been raised any year.[25] In typical Canadian fashion, however, everyone was too polite to ask the crucial question: what had prompted the threatened downgrading of the bank's debt rating by Moody's, the New York bond rating service?

The Moody's matter hung over Thomson like a cloud throughout the annual meeting week, as managers from all over Canada, the United States, and a few other outposts met to discuss TD's strategies and performance. The bond rating service had first announced in early December that it was considering a temporary downgrading of TD's long-term debt rating from Triple A (Aaa) down a notch to Double A (Aa1) because of United States real estate and commercial loans and Canadian consumer loans—but mainly because of its Ontario loan portfolio. Since it had been awarded the rating in 1979, TD had bragged regularly about being the only North American bank and one of a dozen worldwide with Triple A rating for long-term debt. At Aa1, it would still be the highest-rated Canadian bank. Still, if Moody's confirmed the downgrading after looking more closely at the bank's loan portfolio, that would mean TD would have to pay more for its long-term borrowings. Even more significantly, it was a black mark against TD, drawing the world's attention to a previously unsuspected weakness in its management and stability during a time of panic about the soundness of financial institutions.[26]

---

25 Thomson's answer was revealing, however. TD had one of the highest-paid boards in Canada at $29,000 each annually, he admitted, but in U.S. terms the payment was modest – and that was the comparison shareholders should be making.

26 Moody's had already downgraded two of the world's top Japanese banks from Triple A to Double A-1 in August 1990, and as of October had four more on its watch list; it downgraded them as well. It had also further downgraded the Bank of Nova Scotia's much lower rating the previous year, because of its United States LBO and real estate loans.

The Moody's people had already spent one week at the bank by the time of the annual meeting. They returned at the beginning of February for another week, closely scrutinizing the bank's operations and listening to senior management's explanation of its loans and investments. But Thomson, Korthals, and the other senior managers couldn't explain away the bad loans in the rapidly deteriorating Ontario economy. In fact, it became clear during those weeks that the final quarter of 1990 had been worse for the bank's loan portfolio than anyone had previously believed it could be.[27] At year end, non-performing loans totalled $928 million—double the total at the beginning of that year. During the first quarter of 1991, that rose again to $1.3 billion. In early February, Moody's announced that the downgrading was confirmed. In early March, one of Moody's Canadian counterparts, Dominion Bond Rating Service, followed suit, lowering TD's long-term debt rating to Double A (high) from Triple A. The Canadian agency said it expected that TD's results would continue to get worse right through 1991.

TD took it on the chin. The bank did most of its borrowing in the short-term money market, Thomson and Korthals kept saying, so a downgrading of their long-term debt rating wasn't that serious. True. And senior managers received a memo saying that the bank's lending policies wouldn't be dictated by Moody's. That meant both type of loan and location. "Customers will not be denied loans because they are based in Ontario." Still, it was a twisted irony that Moody's lack of confidence in TD's loan portfolio stemmed from its concentration of loans in Ontario. Thomson was quick to tell reporters after the annual meeting that although 70 percent of corporate loans had been in Canada during the last recession, half were in the United States now. Of course, much of TD's lending is still consumer and mortgage loans in Canada; in total, three-quarters of TD's loans were in Canada.

TD was hardly on its last legs. Of all the banks in North America, only four had a market value of more than $5 billion—the cut-off point for the top 1 percent of stocks followed by the American Value Line stock index. Two were Canadian—Royal and TD. And TD was the most profitable foreign bank in Japan in 1990. This was a question of profitability and performance, rather than one of stability. The very fact that this could be so upsetting to TD shows what good shape it's in. Some major American banks would like to have such a problem.

*

---

27 The bank's year officially ends on October 31; the first quarter results, for November 1990 to February 1991, were worse than analysts had predicted.

28 Value Line now includes CIBC as well.

The Canadian banks' movement into investment banking and into the United States has been good for the banks — despite the costs to those who bought brokerage firms. It's more questionable whether the bank-broker marriages have been good for Canada. Even the bankers point that out. "We really wish that one or two of the large brokers had been able to stay independent," says TD's Baillie. "Then, with a variety of approaches, we could see what's best for Canada." But once events were set in motion, it was impossible to hope for that type of diversity in such a small capital market.

It's not good for Bay Street that more and more money is raised by Canadian companies outside the country; that a higher and higher percentage of Canadian stock is traded outside the country; that our banks are encouraging these moves in order to keep some control over their Canadian clientele. In fact, every move the banks have made has enervated Bay Street. But it didn't happen because the banks made it happen; it happened because the banks were responding to outside forces — historian Bliss's "invisible strings."

Bank analyst Terry Shaughnessy has a cynical view of the Canadian banking industry's position. "It doesn't mean Canadians are conquering abroad," he scoffs. "It means Canadians are at worst conquered and at best too marginal to worry about." Shaughnessy's perspective, however, is that of a stock analyst faced with an uninspiring outlook for his product. A more balanced view can only be that the bankers were right back in Montebello. Canada was going to lose its independent brokerage community in any case, and the bankers needed to protect their backsides. Moving into the brokerage business secured their position as rulers of a diminished but still strategically important Canadian capital market. They had the luck of happy timing in 1990: the American banks fell apart and they were there to scoop up business. But they could make that move only because they knew they were safe at home base. The best defense is a good offense.

CHAPTER TWO

A Wing and a Prayer

C lick. Smile for the camera. The photographers and television camera operators assigned to the Parliamentary Press Gallery in Ottawa recorded the minister of transport and the heads of Canada's two national airlines side by side, shaking hands, exchanging pleasantries, and of course smiling—just the way they'd all agreed to do. The photo opportunity on March 21, 1991, in fact, was staged to transmit the message that both Claude Taylor, chairman and pro tem chief executive officer of Air Canada, and Rhys Eyton, chairman and chief executive officer of Canadian Airlines International, were onside about Doug Lewis's impending kick-off of the Canada-United States bilateral discussions on air transport—better known in the newspapers as the Open Skies talks. There had been too much press speculation in recent weeks about policy rifts and outright fighting among the trio over the future of the Canadian airline industry. Lewis needed this show of support before launching the talks in Ottawa in early April. So the two airline chieftains each hopped one of their own flights to Ottawa— Taylor west from Montreal, Eyton east from Calgary.[1]

The pix were great, but the meeting didn't, of course, quell the speculation about the future of Canada's airline industry. After all, there were some basic differences in opinion among the trio—differences that translated into quite different futures for Canada's airlines. They all agreed that the seventeen-year-old treaty needed to be renegotiated to give Canadians more access to the United States. On that level, both Eyton and Taylor supported Open Skies.

Taylor took an even more adventurous position: he was interested in the government exploring the potential not just for a new agreement on cross-

---

1 This chapter is based in part on the author's work on Air Canada's privatization while at *Maclean's* and the *Financial Times* of Canada.

border traffic, but for airlines to be able to travel freely within each other's country—a concept called cabotage. But he wanted to move only one step forward: to be able to set up flights within the United States using Canadian-United States flights as the jumping-off point. He didn't want the United States to have the same deal within Canada. Eyton was adamantly opposed to the idea of cabotage. In fact, Eyton feared that the renegotiation would give American airline companies too much access to Canada, threatening the Canadian companies. He counseled extreme caution at the negotiating table. As for Lewis, besides balancing the two airline executives' demands, his negotiators had to please communities eager to benefit from free trade–related travel, and consumers who wanted cheaper flights. Ottawa had to keep the industry competitive, while ensuring the continued existence of a Canadian industry. The airlines were balancing the risks and the opportunities of open competition. Like so many of the issues facing Canadian government and business during 1990, the future of Canada's airlines had reached a crisis point.

The strain was most noticeable at Air Canada, Canada's premier airline and for decades a symbol of national unity. Taylor, who had been chief executive between 1975 and 1984, was piloting the airline again as a result of a major disagreement over the airline's strategy between the board of directors and former chief executive Pierre Jeanniot the previous August, which had resulted in Jeanniot's resignation. Now, in late April, five weeks after the Ottawa handshake routine and two weeks after the Open Skies talks had been launched, Taylor was in Vancouver preparing to chair the company's annual meeting.[2] In the meantime, the Open Skies talks had been officially launched, and minister Lewis had just been shuffled out of the transport job, to be replaced by the innocuous Jean Corbeil, whose main qualification for the job seemed to be that he satisfied the cabinet's need for another senior minister from Quebec. Taylor hadn't yet had a chance to chat with the new minister, but he knew the government's agenda would remain the same.

Sitting in a pleasant but definitely not luxurious hotel suite at the Vancouver Delta Place hotel the day before the annual meeting, Taylor begins soft-pedaling on Open Skies. After all, the meetings aren't going to

---

2 Air Canada has chosen to show itself a national airline by shifting its annual meeting from city to city.

produce anything for months and months. In fact, Taylor has a $5 bet with one of his executives that the talks won't be finished by the end of 1991. It's a way of coping with stress: by gently joking about the inevitable delays surrounding the talks, they don't seem so fearsome, so all-important any more. Taylor is downplaying his lack of control over his company's future. But how does an early 1992 resolution of Canada's place in the North American skies fit with his own time-lines? He laughs and tosses off a quick response: "I'm not sure I've got any." Then, more meditatively, "There'll be lots of things happen after I've come and gone."

True. But there is also much happening in the meantime. Air Canada laid off thousands of employees during 1990 and 1991. And as Taylor re-organized the structure of the airline, he became increasingly aware that the company he would be handing over to a successor some time in the next several months was troubled. Air Canada lacked a clear direction. The employees weren't productive enough. The company needed money. In fact, in many ways Air Canada serves as a metaphor for the Canadian economy. Taylor's choices mirror those being faced by all Canadians.

For its first fifty years, Air Canada didn't worry about money. As a crown corporation, it had plenty—or at least the federal government did. The airline was inefficient and bureaucratic—but it flew to every airport that needed service across the country. Then it realized it had better shape up and become more of a business. The money in Ottawa ran out, and Air Canada was on its own. But the Canadian market isn't big enough for it to make money, and the airline isn't good enough right now to compete effectively with foreign competition. It's still too soft, too difficult to manage, too unprofitable. And it also suffers from higher taxes and service charges at government-owned airports; it's as if Ottawa is deliberately handicapping the Canadian industry. Meanwhile, the competition in the real world is a lot tougher than it used to be.

Now Air Canada, like Canada itself, is caught. Committed to competition, the airline is struggling to adapt to a more demanding and less forgiving marketplace. But if its skies become too open, too quickly, the company might not survive the transition. In the spring of 1991, the task of making the basic changes needed to ensure the airline's future lay with Taylor. He knew that if he succeeded in making Air Canada competitive with foreign airlines, it had a good chance at survival in the wide-open skies.

If Taylor failed, the airline and potentially the entire Canadian airline industry would go down with him.

Air Canada has long wrapped itself in the maple leaf. In the early days, after its 1937 formation as Trans-Canada Airlines, the airline epitomized the Canadian federation: it linked disparate parts of the country, joining communities as an agent of national unity. Former CEO Jeanniot remembers when people thought of the airline as "the railroad of the sky." As a flag carrier,[3] the airline existed to perform an essential service for Canadians. "We had such a large land mass and so few people, we almost had to have aviation," explains Taylor. And airlines, in flying to the North, developed technical expertise that made the Canadian carrier a leader in the industry. "That's nation building," declares Taylor. "I'm just not about to give that away."

But Canadians long since made the decision that the airline needed to redefine its role in the nation's life. They demanded more than merely essential service from an airline. Like consumers everywhere, during the 1970s they made it clear that they wanted to have access to flights to vacation spots, a choice of destinations, and a variety of levels of service and prices. Especially prices. Those in the industry look on this as the democratization of travel. But as the citizens' demands changed, so did the nature of the airlines. Air Canada stopped thinking about how it could service every small community and began to think about how to capture market share. It became commercialized and stopped acting like a public utility. It faced competition within the country. And the government became less willing to provide it with money to expand. "It was no longer the essential link to our frontier, and the link between our communities," recalls Jeanniot.

Since the airline industry is no longer an agent of nation building, the question arises: Do we need a national airline? Let alone two? I think we do. There are still arguments that support the need for Canadian airlines. They provide sophisticated jobs, particularly in airline maintenance, that further our computer-related skills. They provide spin-off jobs in the tourist industry, which is the largest single industry in the world and employs one in twelve of Canada's labor force. Jobs at airports and elsewhere in the tourist business, says Canadian Airlines' chairman Eyton, add up to five times as many jobs as those in the airlines themselves.

Eyton argues that foreign carriers wouldn't be as keen to bring tourists to

---

3 A flag carrier is an appropriate description for a government-owned airline; in Air Canada's case it was doubly appropriate since the airline boasts the maple leaf on its tail fin.

Canadian locations. "Do we want to put our tourism promotion in the hands of foreigners?" asks Eyton in classic nationalist-alarmist style. "It's one of our largest industries. I'm not sure if in the hands of Americans, Vail or Salt Lake City might not become a preference to Whistler." This is an interesting argument from a man whose business is also to fly tourists to exotic Asian and European destinations, as well as points south. Eyton's rhetoric is challenged by the chief financial officer of American Airlines, Don Carty, a Canadian and former head of CP Air. Carty insists that he could fly planeloads of travelers into Whistler if he only had the chance. Tourism, Carty counters, would be improved by open skies, whether or not there was a Canadian airline. "You could lose them and still be econom-ically ahead." But Ottawa believes that Canadian carriers are still more committed to an east-west flow of traffic than foreign-controlled airlines would be. In that sense, they are still promoting Canadian unity.

Flying is a business in which Canadians believe we can and should be competitive. We have been in the past, although we're struggling at the moment. But to survive in the future, Canadian airlines must be competitive outside the country. The market here isn't big enough to keep the com-panies going. Almost half of Air Canada's business is international now. To survive, it needs to increase that proportion. Taylor realizes, however, that the companies won't necessarily survive the competition outside Canada. But he sees no alternative, for the airline or for the country. "How do we in Canada with 26 million people become a major player in North America, Asia, and Europe? . . . Some of us are crazy enough to believe that we ought to try. Otherwise, where is Canadian industry going? If we don't do that, then is Canada simply going to become a branch plant for everything?"

It's difficult, however, to argue for any kind of protective nationalism in an industry that has become international in nature. Together with the communications revolution, Taylor says, "Air transportation is the thing that has created Marshall McLuhan's global village. I think there's a certain pride in Canada's role in that, because Canada has always played a very strong role in aviation. And I don't think we ought to give it away. I think we ought to take a run at becoming a player, because the thing that's going to drive this world of ours is going to be transportation. The globe is turning into one market. The thing that's going to keep it going is information and the movement of people. . . . I just don't think we ought to walk away from that."

Whether it's crucial to the Canadian economy or not, Air Canada remains a strong symbol for the nation. The problem is that Canadians' idea about the airline no longer matches reality. Air Canada is now a private business, dedicated to profits first. And it was Claude Taylor who made it that way.

Claude Taylor is a great communicator. When you meet him, you like him. And you want him to like you. It's a charm that he must have used to great effect behind the reservations counter in Moncton, New Brunswick, when he joined Trans-Canada Airlines in 1949 at the age of twenty-four. A child of the Depression era, Taylor had only a high-school education but a well-spring of ambition. The airline that Taylor joined valued diplomacy, perhaps above all other skills. It was, after all, a crown corporation, dependent on Ottawa for its continued existence. He fit well in the expanding horizon of the government-owned airline as he climbed the ladder of corporate diplomacy. Taylor guided the airline's course in the corridors of Parliament during the early 1970s as vice-president for government affairs, before returning to head office in Montreal as president and chief executive officer in 1976.

It was in those corridors and the small committee rooms on Parliament Hill that Taylor met Donald Mazankowski, then an opposition MP representing Vegreville, Alberta, and sitting on the Commons transport committee. The smooth eastern lobbyist and the expansive Alberta Tory found common ground in their passion for baseball and the business of transportation. "Maz" had a native interest in transport: he had a car dealership and had dispatched trucks during a stint in Chicago. Maz and Taylor, the airline's hired gun, used to wrestle with the future of transportation policy in Maz's tiny office on Parliament Hill well into the night. Back then, Taylor believed implicitly that his company could compete—and should be set free to do so by the government.

This was, however, inflammatory talk back in the 1970s, the era of regional development and social engineering. Then the wheel turned. In 1976 Taylor became Air Canada president; that same year, Air Canada was separated by an act of Parliament from its parent, Canadian National Railways. From then on, Air Canada had a mandate to make a profit. It finally did three years later—and Joe Clark's Conservatives squeaked into office. With Maz as transport minister, the minister and the company head began to discuss when—not if—the government would sell the company.

The dream had to be placed on hold when Clark lost his grip on power and Maz was again banished to the opposition benches. There were no baseball buddies or receptive ears among the Liberal ministers. However, even the Liberals were awakened to the need to ensure that Air Canada remained competitive after they began seeing the effects of deregulation on the United States airline industry. And with a mounting federal debt, Ottawa began to recognize that it wouldn't be able to supply enough money to keep Air Canada up to speed with foreign competition. Super-mandarin Edmund Clark[4] headed a special internal study of the airline's future. Selling shares to the public was a big topic of conversation by the bureaucrats and lobbyists at the table.

Taylor, however, wasn't a Liberal favorite; before the September 1984 federal election, he was bumped upstairs from the chief executive officer's slot to chairman. The CEO job went to a bilingual Air Canada veteran, Pierre Jeanniot. Still, Taylor had some consolation: after the Tories won the election, the prospects for privatization looked better than ever. And without daily responsibility for the corporation, Taylor planned to use his time working on the airline sale—a matter about which he and Jeanniot were in accord.

But Taylor wasn't able to capitalize on the Conservative honeymoon. On a clear, crisp morning in December 1984, he stepped off the curb at Dorchester and Peel streets on his way to the office from a downtown meeting in Montreal. A bus blocked his vision, and he didn't see a car approaching; it hit him and he flew through the windshield. Taylor landed in the Montreal Neurological Hospital. He was in a coma for several days and remained in critical condition for weeks. With both shoulders and his collar-bone broken, he wasn't back on his feet for six months.

Meanwhile, Maz was back as transport minister, picking a slate of loyal Conservatives for the Air Canada board and ruminating again on selling the airline.[5] The minister also kept in close touch with his old friend while Taylor was in the hospital and recuperating at home. In mid-1985, Taylor, still sporting a back brace at times, faced Maz across a table in Maz's fancy new office in the East Block and once again talked it all out. The government had the mandate, the minister had the urge.

The sale of Air Canada was the largest privatization deal Ottawa had in mind, but it certainly wasn't the only one. During the 1970s, Ottawa under

---

4   Known as "Red Ed" in the oil patch because of his involvement in the National Energy Program, he later became a Bay Street corporate workout specialist.

5   Since the airline's inception a board seat had been a patronage plum – among other things, it brings with it a no-holds-barred airline pass.

the Liberals had nurtured the concept of crown corporations. By 1984, there were dozens of them and almost all of them were losing money. Air Canada for years didn't try to make a profit, for example, because it knew Ottawa would simply take the money away. But for the most part, the government-controlled companies' failures were all based on the fallacy of trying to marry money making and social engineering. "In Canada, we don't know how to live with hybrids," comments former Air Canada president Jeanniot.

In the airline industry, for example, European countries own part of such international airlines as SAS, KLM, Swissair, and Lufthansa. Government and private interests co-exist peacefully. But in Canada, adds Jeanniot, "we can't resist trying to interfere." Both civil servants and politicians "could not come to grips or make peace with the idea that the government should be a silent investor."

The Conservative government also couldn't justify to private business why they were providing so much support for failing companies in selected industries. They came into office in 1984 prepared to sell. Under trade minister Sinclair Stevens, they introduced a policy that would see the eventual selloff of ten of its holdings, including its shareholding in Canada Development Corp.,[6] communications company Teleglobe, and aircraft manufacturer de Havilland.[7] But they still had to make decisions about their largest holdings—Petro-Canada, Air Canada, and CN Rail. Would the public accept the sale of these three national symbols? One of them would have to be a guinea pig.

In July 1986, after Stevens had been pushed out of cabinet by a scandal over his personal finances, Toronto MP Barbara McDougall was moved into a brand-new ministry devoted to privatization. Maz left the transport ministry during the same shuffle, but his influence in cabinet by this time was great: he was officially Mulroney's deputy minister, but was known as his right hand and tagged "minister of everything." By February 1987, cabinet had approved a short list of candidates for privatization. One of the

---

6 CDC was sold in three share issues: August 1986, June 1987, and October 1987. See also Chapter Three.

7 There was a storm of controversy when de Havilland was sold to aircraft giant Boeing Co. of Seattle, Washington, in 1986 for $90 million; people thought it a sweet deal. As it turned out, however, de Havilland remained a loser, and as part of the sale agreement, Ottawa ended up paying Boeing $161 million to keep it going. Finally, Boeing arranged to sell the company in 1991 for $150 million to European consortium Aerospatiale S.A. of France and Elenia S.p.A. of Italy, de Havilland's major competitors. The consortium asked the federal and provincial governments for up to $1 billion in aid, spread over ten years. At the time of writing, the request and the deal were up in the air.

names was Air Canada. The next month, brokers were hired by Ottawa; Air Canada already had its own advisers. A few Air Canada employees were seconded to the ministry; others traveled the Montreal-Ottawa Rapidair route almost daily. Brokerage RBC Dominion Securities showed Ottawa that Air Canada was in rough shape; it needed more money for new planes, or the value of the company would sink and the government would lose its valuable investment. It became clear to the bureaucrats that it was better for the government to bail out and let the company raise its money through the stock market in future.

By summer 1987 the government was ready to introduce draft legislation proclaiming the airline's sale. Then, in July, word began to spread that the deal was off—nixed by Mulroney at an early July cabinet meeting in Edmonton. The prime minister was nervous about going back on his word: two years earlier, Mulroney had made the rash declaration that Canada would always have a national airline. Since there had been no public announcement, however, there was no need for Ottawa to say officially whether the sale was off—or had ever been on. That made it a little easier for the bureaucrats to simply keep working on the fine print while those in favor of a deal continued to press Mulroney.

Then, on October 19, 1987, the free market took a sharp turn for the worse. The stock market crash was global, and it was the worst crash ever. Billions were lost in the market in minutes. By the end of the week, it was clear that the bull market was over. Experts, in fact, feared an immediate slide into recession in North America and Europe. One of the most high-profile victims was the British government's multi-billion-dollar privatization of British Petroleum.[8] But for the back-room politicking that delayed the Tories' decision, Air Canada could have been in the same situation. "We got blown out of the water in October," Taylor recalls with a definite wince. "It looked like we'd lost it. . . . Suddenly everyone became very wise and said, 'That's why we didn't go ahead, we knew the market was going to fall.' "

When an initiative is sidelined for political reasons, it's usually as good as

---

8 The company's stock issue had been marketed internationally, with brokers agreeing to a set price for the petroleum company's shares. With the crash, they would be stuck with stock that they couldn't possibly sell at those prices. Finally, British Prime Minister Margaret Thatcher relented and set a floor price below which the British government would buy back the shares. In Canada, the BP victim was Wood Gundy. The firm stood to lose as much as $60 million on the deal. Gundy lost $20 million and was shaken by the deal, and was sold a few months later to Canadian Imperial Bank of Commerce at a much lower price than stockbrokers had been sold for before the crash (see Chapter One).

dead. If, by coincidence, the decision is subsequently made to seem a wise one by unrelated events, the final nail is driven in the coffin. But that wasn't the case with Air Canada. Instead, the company's incessant need for money made it clear to the politicians that if they held on to the airline much longer, it could become a political liability. Air Canada's budget estimates in January 1988 demonstrated that it would need $3 billion during the next decade to buy new planes. One thing Ottawa didn't need was a cash drain.

By that time, the cabinet deck had been reshuffled—and the new minister of privatization was Taylor's close friend, Don Mazankowski. Maz had simply added this task to his other duties, including his role as deputy prime minister. With this sort of champion, the Air Canada selloff sailed through cabinet. In April 1988, it was officially announced that Air Canada would be sold through a two-step share issue: the company would sell shares to the public and receive the money while diluting the government's ownership position; then, down the line, the government would sell off its remaining piece of the airline and pocket the cash.

Maz introduced the legislative bill in May. From this point on, Taylor was the point man; he made sure the idea didn't have much trouble with the Commons committees. At the Commons hearings, he received a hearty welcome from chairman Jack Ellis; before the Senate hearings began, he dined in Montreal with committee head and former CP Ltd. chief Ian Sinclair to review the agenda.

The schmoozing paid off. On September 15, 1988, 43 percent of Air Canada was sold to the public through a 31-million share issue at $8 per share; the company raised $233.8 million, after paying its brokerage fees. The largest stock issue in Canadian history by a company that had never before sold shares, it made Air Canada one of the most widely held companies in the country. Many of the company's 20,000 employees bought shares; so did retail clients, including people who had never before bought stock—what Taylor described at the time as "the base of the great unwashed that the government wants to tap." Actually, the country was split on whether the government should let Air Canada go.[9] Once the government went ahead with the sale, however, they bought, according to Maz, because they had "a great sense of attachment to Air Canada."

---

9   A Gallup poll showed 42 percent of Canadians surveyed wanted the airline sold; 42 percent were against the sale; 16 percent had no comment.

But attachment doesn't pay dividends. The only ones who didn't buy into the hype being pumped out by Ottawa and the airline were the country's large institutions. These seasoned shareholders didn't buy stock because they knew the company was a big risk. It had an unthinkable debt. And its earnings would be subject to the vagaries of the market.

Taylor knew that his company would have to adapt to make it in what he always used to call "the real world." There, he said at the time of the sale, "the value that is placed upon you is what you read in the financial pages every morning. That's the real world that our people are going to have to live in. That's not a world that we're used to." He didn't realize at the time, however, just how much of a wonderland he and his company had been in.

At first the share price sagged, as Air Canada fought a price war for travel dollars with Canadian Airlines and Calgary-based Wardair. Max Ward, an entrepreneur who had built an impressive charter service, had recently pushed head-to-head into scheduled flights. That move, however, inevitably proved to be his undoing. In January 1989, a cash-strapped Wardair sold out to Canadian Airlines. With the price war over, Air Canada stock bounced to $12 — just in time for Ottawa to enter the market that July and sell its remaining stake in the company. At $12 per share, it raised $473.8 million, after paying brokerage fees — and all of that money went straight to Ottawa.

At this point, the buyers were the same institutions that had scoffed at the company a year and a half earlier. The earlier purchases of two of their number that had bucked the trend and bought — Boston-based mutual-fund giant Fidelity Investments Ltd., and Toronto's savvy investment counsellors Gluskin Sheff & Associates — had resulted in well-publicized big gains. There was talk of the stock rising to $18.

But the euphoria didn't last for long. The airline's losses were higher than management had forecast; the investors realized that its earnings were coming mainly from sale of aircraft leases rather than operating an airline; they thought costs should be slashed more quickly than they were. And questions began to be raised about Air Canada's strategic vision, both from the investment community and within the airline. And as air traffic fell off in 1990, the institutions began to think that they had been right to stay away in the first place. By that time, Fidelity and Gluskin Sheff had long since taken their profits and left.

It seemed that the world was too much with Air Canada after the government sold out entirely in 1989. Now there was no more safety from the sheltering arm of government. There was just the cold hard reality of profit and loss, live or die. "People have said to me, 'Why did you fight so hard for privatization when you did—why didn't you wait another ten years?' " Taylor ruminates in 1991, looking back on the sale. "My answer to that is that the parent had decided they couldn't afford us any longer, and I wasn't about to see the Canadian airline become another Via Rail."

Air Canada being a publicly owned company, Taylor adds, he could change the airline. Necessary changes, but tough. Layoffs. Route cancellations. Closing maintenance centers. "Things that as a crown corporation we would have had terrible difficulty doing. If we'd ever had an NDP government we'd have never done any of them. So we couldn't have bought airplanes. Pretty soon we'd have had a bunch of very old airplanes that nobody wanted to fly in. Instead of having 42 percent of our business international, we would have ended up with nothing.

"I believe, and I wake up at night dreaming about it, that we would have gone out of existence as a crown corporation. Because we had no God-given right to anything." It's no wonder Taylor is having nightmares about Air Canada these days. After the privatization was complete, Air Canada would find out that it was not in the fighting shape it needed to be in order to do battle—both with competitor Canadian Airlines and with foreign competitors. Taylor realized soon enough what can happen when someone is granted his fondest desire.

Rhys Eyton and a gaggle of directors walked through the construction-phase entrance and into the white-on-white waiting room of the Canadian Embassy in Tokyo on a sunny morning in March 1990 with an air of quiet confidence. The guard behind the glass barrier immediately dialed upstairs and Eyton and Co. were whisked away to the ambassador's corner office for an unofficial chat. The tête-à-tête was occasioned by Canadian Airlines International flying over its directors for their first-ever Tokyo directors' meeting. But this is familiar territory for Eyton. Canadian Airlines and its predecessor, CP Air, have been flying the Canada-Japan route for forty-one years. Says Eyton of the route: "It's our equivalent of Air Canada's Heathrow [route] in London."

London has been Air Canada's and Tokyo the western carrier's ever since 1950, when the world was carved in half by Ottawa for the purposes of Canadian air travel. That should soon change, however. Air Canada is arguing that since Canadian Airlines acquired former charter airline Wardair and took over its routes to Britain and elsewhere in Europe in 1989, Air

Canada deserves access to Tokyo. And it thinks it can do a better job. The Tokyo route, in fact, is a bit of a dogfight.[10] Eyton insists Japan would balk at two Canadian carriers flying into crowded Narita airport, and would require the two carriers to share the number of slots now allocated to Canadian Airlines flights. It would be "extremely damaging," he adds, for Air Canada to be given a chance at the market. "Air Canada is determined to move in there because it's not successful elsewhere in the Pacific," Eyton charges. "It requested Korea and didn't start up."

Of course, Eyton feels very differently about Air Canada's complaints that Canadian Airlines has already arrived in London. The United Kingdom, he declares, ranks with the United States as the two markets where Canadian airlines should overlap. As for Canadian Airlines' back-door entry into the market via its purchase of Wardair, that was fair play. "I was extremely shocked when we took on a failing carrier and restructured the industry at enormous cost, that the bellyaching began in Montreal. All of a sudden this carrier that had always gotten what it wanted from the government was crying . . . that it wanted to even the world. Well, they've had the world all to themselves for so long and all the prime facilities. I'm not about to listen to that argument."

Eyton knows a lot about competition in Canada. He has painstakingly built an airline, starting with Calgary-based PWA in 1976 and executing crucial mergers to build a national airline. In the process, however, he has borrowed far too much money. Canadian Airlines is a more entrepreneurial company than Air Canada. Its costs, although they are 15 percent above American airlines' — in good measure because of the pernicious taxes — are still 15 percent below Air Canada's. But on balance, analysts are betting on Air Canada. Even Eyton admits that "our pockets aren't as deep." And he'll need a pile of money to survive this year's markets and any hint of North American competition.

But Eyton is a tough operator; he's used to coming out on top. For instance, soon after PWA merged with a much larger company, Vancouver-based CP Air, it was clear that the reverse-takeover meant the boys at PWA would dominate. Among the CP executives who bowed out was Don Carty, who headed back south to a former employer, American Airlines. "It

---

10 A spokesperson at the Ministry of Transport says that the Tokyo route question is "still being assessed."

was his choice to go back to American," says Eyton. "I don't think there's any bad blood." Apparently not; at any rate, Carty's brother Doug is still Canadian Airlines' treasurer.

There is one subject on which Canadian Airlines and Air Canada are in agreement: the costs of running an airline in Canada are too high. Like their fellow travelers the long-distance truckers, the airline magnates are up in arms over taxes on fuel and other government service charges. There have been jokes that the politicians who were upset by the truckers blockading Parliament Hill in spring 1991 haven't seen anything yet; wait until the airlines arrive. They have a good argument: in 1990, for example, Canadian Airlines spent $500 million on fuel, and lost $113 million on the actual business of being an airline.[11] When the company's number-crunchers ran a computer program that replaced Canadian fuel costs with American prices—one-third less—Eyton says they found that Canadian Airlines could have earned $74 million in that period. This, he says, is part of a government policy that is unstructured and unfocused in terms of the survival of Canadian business. "In our search for money to fund our deficit and our ongoing operations at both the federal and provincial levels, we've put taxes on things without realizing the full impact they can have."[12]

In fact, Ottawa was reviewing the issues of charges and taxes and hoped to be able to tell the airlines some good news by autumn. That would be none too soon: at the same time that Air Canada was adapting to life as a Canadian airline outside the protective wing of mother government, the Canadian airline industry was being buffeted by forces beyond its borders.

The shakeout began south of the border more than a decade ago, when the United States deregulated its marketplace in 1979. By the late 1980s, the United States airline industry was beginning to fall apart. Some companies couldn't stand the cutthroat competition and price slashing. By 1991, five of the top fifteen companies in the world couldn't meet their bank payments. The companies that were making money were facing the prospect of mergers or alliances in order to provide worldwide connections for their customers. With once-mighty TWA in trouble, Eastern in receivership, and others long since gone, the market is settling into an oligopoly of the fittest.

---

11 Before taxes and gains on sales of aircraft.

12 Air Canada has estimated that it pays 38 percent more for its fuel than the American carriers. That adds up to at least $80 million a year for domestic flights alone. There are also hefty landing fees at major Canadian airports: La Guardia charges Cdn. $900 to land a 747; Toronto charges $1,100. Los Angeles charges $200; Regina charges $600.

Elsewhere in the world, however, the shakeout is only beginning. In Europe, national barriers are giving way to a pan-European system although there is still opposition to large American carriers gaining slots at airports such as Heathrow. Asian airways have always been fairly laissez-faire (with the exception of Japan's airport access problem), and now the rest of the world is following suit. And the airlines in more protected markets, such as Canada, realize that once their national barriers to entry are loosened or dropped, they'll be fighting for market share with anyone and everyone—especially the battle-hardened United States giants such as American. The Canadian airlines aren't the only ones losing millions. Certainly, Canadians were shocked when Air Canada laid off or retired 3,400 employees between spring 1990 and spring 1991. Cuts were made in all areas; there was a 22 percent reduction in management, for example. Canadian Airlines had already laid off 1,900 workers in 1989, but that was in good part due to its merger with Wardair.[13] But that's not unusual these days. In Australia, Qantas laid off 25 percent of its employees. British Airways laid off 5,000 people. Even American Airlines, the industry darling, wasn't making money. "We lost a quarter of a billion dollars in the fourth quarter of 1990," says American's Don Carty. "And we're the most successful airline in the world."

In a funny kind of way, the airline business isn't about making money. Most airlines don't make a cent from running their airlines. Oh, certain Asian airlines such as Cathay Pacific and Singapore Airlines make money—but their wages are one-third the Canadian level. As for the rest, some pay their cabin crew and the cost of food on board their flight out of the proceeds from their in-flight duty-free shops. A few make profits by operating airports. But they all make their real money by buying and reselling aircraft—they're really in the used airplane business.

Airplanes have long been like a real estate market that never falls. Part of the reason is that the airlines must write down the value of their planes on the company's books. So after ten years, an airplane has no value to the company—but is still worth 40 percent of its original price. When the company sells the plane, it reaps a big capital gain. That's important, since 85 percent of an airline's capital is tied up in its airplanes.

The money they make on their airplane sales doesn't, however, become a cushion to ensure the airline's profitability. Instead, it's calculated in advance and the money they expect to make is used to ensure that ticket

---

13 Canadian Airlines has laid off a total of 5,000 employees, mostly because of mergers, since 1986.

prices are as low as possible. During the past decade, airplanes have risen in price by 300 percent, just like automobiles. Airline tickets have risen by only 100 to 140 percent in the same period. And the airlines have been borrowing money to buy new planes. This puts a lot of pressure on the companies to be efficient—and to find the money to pay their debts.

The airline business is always flying on a wing and a prayer. "It's one of the most difficult businesses there is," remarks Jeanniot. "We're seasonal, cyclical, capital-intensive, labor-intensive, and fuel-intensive.... It's a high-risk business. And at the same time it still has this glamorous dimension. It's magical to fly." But the magic dust has faded for investors, such as those ordinary Canadians who bought Air Canada stock. Investors who buy airline stocks don't expect cash dividends, but they do expect performance and growth at the company. That causes the stock price to rise, and they can sell at a profit should they choose. In recent times, however, returns have been at best reasonable and usually meager. At that rate, says Jeanniot, "when you hit a recession then you're really in trouble."

We hit the recession. And we certainly faced a lot of trouble. Part of the problem was that we can't hope to compete outside our borders from a standing start. Canada is now contemplating trying to play catch-up to the United States and compete in the American airlines' home market. But deregulation south of the border has left the Canadian carriers far behind. The United States airlines have developed a hub-and-spoke system with one airline dominating a certain number of airports; for instance, Dallas acts as a hub for American Airlines, with other airports feeding passengers into the Dallas-Fort Worth airport, to be flown to a network of other destinations. There is very little room left for newcomers at any of the best hubs. "All the key airports in the U.S. are tied up like drums," says Canadian Airlines' Eyton. "They're like fortresses."

The Canadian industry is suffering now because of past policy mistakes in Canada. American's Carty thinks it's too bad that Canadians didn't deregulate in tandem with the United States. A decade ago, he says, the Canadian airlines "would have made it or not made it based on an even playing field. None of us was better suited to take on the North American marketplace than the Canadian carriers. We had no hubs, we had all the same problems Canadian carriers have today."

One answer to the cold winds of the free market is for airlines to wrap themselves in the protective cloak of international alliances. Jeanniot is voicing a common wisdom when he suggests that as a result of an open skies policy, "what could well emerge is associations of major airlines in each of the three economic blocs which may not merge but would form a very strong partnership." Partnerships may involve more traditional business relationships—for example, booking seats on one another's flights. Or they can include owning stock in other airlines—although Canadian law now limits foreign ownership to 25 percent. Stock trades, however, may be the only way to assure the consumer that an airline's reach is global, that it can get the customer from Point A to Point D via points B and C with the same type of service all along the route. This supra-national approach has already been adopted by American airline Delta, Swissair, and Singapore Airlines: the three companies have swapped about 5 percent of their stock and set up a twelve-year business association for international flights. "There's no merger," notes Jeanniot, "but there's a very close association which has been sealed with the exchange of rings."

But which European or Asian airline would choose a link with a smaller Canadian company rather than an established American giant if both had full access to the North American marketplace? At the moment, it would seem, very few. Right now, everyone's playing a wait-and-see game until the Open Skies talks are completed. For the Canadian carriers, however, the choice is stark. Jeanniot sums it up bluntly: "Let's face it, there are only a couple of alternatives. Either you decide that you're going to be a major player or you're going to be satisfied to be an affiliate."

Unfortunately, if they become little more than franchisees of a United States-based international alliance, the Canadian airlines would be eliminating all the reasons in their own argument for the need for separate Canadian airlines. The technical jobs would surely move south, with the Canadian carrier performing the same distribution function as a regional distributor or a branch-plant subsidiary.

Another solution often suggested is to merge Air Canada and Canadian Airlines. Those arguing for this are betting that a merger would give a Canadian carrier the international clout and the stable domestic base to build an internationally competitive company. Claude Taylor likes the idea. But one of its most virulent opponents is Canadian Airlines CEO Rhys Eyton. Instead, Eyton has tried to speak to almost every American carrier about a potential alliance—including a stock trade.[14] So far, no response.

---

14 Canadian Airlines has a 4 percent limit on individual positions in the holding company, but no limit on the airline itself. That limit, however, is now under provincial legislative review.

Eyton says he doesn't blame the Americans for sitting in the bush until the Open Skies talks are completed. "The U.S. carriers are going to see what they can come in and take on their own. I'd take the same position if I were in their place. Why negotiate until the rules are clear?"

Eyton doesn't have to worry much about a Canadian merger at the moment. Ottawa is against it, and with good reason. There's no reason to think that merging the airlines would make them more efficient. Besides, Ottawa is being pressured by consumers and nationalists to prevent any move to a merger.

If there was ever a time to argue for one Canadian airline, it has now passed with the approach of more open competition with United States airlines. It doesn't make as much sense in a North American marketplace. After all, much of the traffic flow is north-south. And although the airlines' survival depends on domestic business, it is also predicated on increasing international routes. The only remaining question is whether a Canadian carrier needs control of the entire domestic market to have the clout to push into the United States. Instead, with an integrated airline system in North America, Jeanniot points out, "one Canadian airline might want to become the satellite of a United States airline; the other Canadian airline might want to buy or get a satellite in the States."

But should Canadian Airlines become a junior partner of a United States airline, it's likely that it will eventually cease to be a truly "Canadian" airline, providing home-grown high-tech jobs—unless the competition watchdogs and Investment Canada crack down on any alliance and demand job guarantees. For the most part, the future of a Canadian airline industry then rests on the shoulders of Air Canada, the larger and better capitalized of the two airlines, and the one that says it's prepared to go toe-to-toe with American competition down the road. Before Air Canada can do that, however, it must first finally put its own house in order.

Pierre Jeanniot's sudden resignation from Air Canada in August 1990 was a shock to the business community. It evoked some frenzied gossip over the reason he would choose to step down after thirty-four years with the airline and six years in the top job. Those close to the company, however, had known a storm was brewing. Jeanniot wasn't seeing eye to eye with Air Canada's board on strategy—including layoffs—or on succession.

Jeanniot believed Air Canada should continue on its long-time course: competing internationally by selling service and letting the costs take care of themselves. By building the best airline he could, Jeanniot believed he could build a reputation that would attract business travelers from all parts of the world—the industry's lifeblood.

Like many former CEOs, Jeanniot is now a consultant. The chairman of the Council for Canadian Unity, Jeanniot is on the boards of the Bank of Nova Scotia and McGraw-Hill Ryerson publishers. He has also become a board member of the newly formed Edmonton Regional Airport Authority and of Memotec Data Inc.[15] Says Taylor hopefully of his former colleague: "He's building a life beyond Air Canada." In the spring of 1991, however, the ties between the former CEO and the company were still close: Jeanniot was running his business from a small office in a secondary Air Canada building in downtown Montreal. And when he talks about the future of Air Canada, he still says "we."

Jeanniot is the champion of the Canadian airlines. They're competing abroad quite well today in a number of markets, he says. "The question really is, can we get access to more markets?" He is gung-ho about Open Skies and cabotage. Some of his arguments are the same as those used by free trade proponents a few years ago: the market is right on our doorstep, we have to move into it. If the Canadian airlines could penetrate even 4 to 5 percent of the American market, they could double in size.

They need to develop niches, of course, so that their higher cost base won't matter as much. For example, the trans-Atlantic business class that Air Canada developed a few years ago immediately gained 17 percent of the route's market share with its improved level of service. On certain United States routes, Jeanniot brags, Air Canada is already doing very well, thank you. "Our Canadian brand of business class could sell very well in United States markets, for the same reason that these guys buy expensive foreign cars."

This sounds like one of those great globalization strategies that economists and corporate gurus are always espousing. It fits the mold of all those one-line management slogans: create a great company; play from strength; build to win.

But the board didn't buy into Jeanniot's search for excellence. Instead,

---

15 Jeanniot's May 1991 appointment to the Memotec board was part of a compromise between management and major shareholders, following a campaign by Gordon Capital Corp. to unseat management of the Montreal-based data-processing and telecommunications company. Memotec also changed its name to Teleglobe Inc.

key members of the Canadian business establishment (such as Raymond Cyr, CEO of Bell Canada Enterprises; Rowland Frazee, retired chairman of the Royal Bank of Canada; and Bill James, former CEO of Falconbridge Ltd. and, more recently, hired gun at Denison Mines) believed that if Air Canada stayed the course, it would crash and burn. And they didn't agree with Jeanniot's choice as successor and chief operating officer, executive Leo Desrochers. They wanted a new strategy—and a new CEO.

Exit an embittered Jeanniot. Followed, involuntarily, by a few thousand employees during the next several months. When asked about his differences with the board, Jeanniot balks. "I'm not sure I really want to talk about that." Finally, he pins it to the question of cost. "It depends whether you believe that the cost disadvantage that you're facing as an industry can be mostly changed by reducing your size and attempting to achieve that by maintaining a cost structure which is closer to our United States competitors." In other words, cutbacks. "Or whether you believe that your cost disadvantage can be largely reduced by aggressive expansion and increasing your volumes, which also lower your operating costs. They're two slightly different approaches to the problem. Now, there is nothing totally black or white. I think it's a question of degree. I tend to be an expansionist."

In 1990, Jeanniot thought the company was ready for expansion. He had improved its debt levels; bought new planes and rebuilt old ones; reduced the number of technical centers from twelve to three. Some of this groundwork was done while Air Canada was still a crown corporation, so he had to work carefully. "We couldn't do it overnight because it would start all kinds of political flak," he recalls.

Essentially, Jeanniot saw his as a Canadian approach to getting the job done. "You are doing a lot of things to improve the situation, but you have to do it in a way that's acceptable and tolerable. Canada is a nation which doesn't like abrupt changes. We're a nation of compromises. We're not the Americans. We don't like these shoot-outs at the OK Corral at five o'clock in the afternoon. That's how we did our deregulation in this country; not all at once but over seven or eight years. And that's how we were doing our improvements." He takes a shot at present management's methods: "In my tenure as president the management ranks were cut by about 30 percent. But I never tried to make headlines out of it because making headlines scares people. My policy is to make those painful changes as invisible and as easy to take as possible."

Like the Canadian bankers, Jeanniot very much believes that the best defense is a good offense. He favors mottoes such as "to live is to risk."

Jeanniot continues, "Quite frankly, I would rather have tried and failed than not have tried and wondered."

That approach didn't cut it with the board. Air Canada was in the red and didn't have the money to try and fail. The directors didn't like the fact that Jeanniot and his executive suite spent a lot more money running Air Canada than their counterparts at other airlines. Two years after it was privatized by the government, there was still something of the feel of a government organization to the airline. Employees figured their jobs were safe no matter what, and the company had too many layers of management.

The board, of course, was chosen by Taylor and the Prime Minister's Office at the time of Air Canada's privatization. And it was to Taylor that they turned when their differences with Jeanniot became irreconcilable. Taylor had been looking forward to retirement, but he agreed to take on the job of CEO—on an interim basis. He and the board agreed to have a replacement chosen by the end of 1990.

Under Taylor, the approach to expansion is much more cautious, with an underlying realization that Air Canada isn't quite ready for the real world yet. "Before the car can race in the Indy, you've got to get the car ready," says Taylor. "What we're trying to do now is to get Air Canada ready for that global competitiveness." Asked to explain why the car wasn't yet ready two years after privatization, he admits he's not sure. "We had a very proud history. I guess somehow we got all caught up in that and felt that that would propel us into the future without us having to get ready for the future."

There's a certain irony in all this for Taylor. He hadn't wanted to give up the CEO job in 1984 when the Liberal government appointed francophone Jeanniot in his stead. Jeanniot resents the suggestion that he was given the job because he's a French Canadian. He had been the chief operating officer, with twenty-eight years of service and experience in thirteen other jobs at the company. The relationship with Taylor afterward, however, was not close.

Then, just when Taylor was ready to step down as chairman, he was pushed back into the CEO job. He had to use Jeanniot's executive team, including Leo Desrochers, the executive vice-president Jeanniot had been grooming for the top job. The entire executive, in fact, contemplated leaving after Jeanniot was fired. But they stayed, even though it became clear that Desrochers was not in line for the CEO job.

Many others didn't have the choice. To cut costs, Taylor cut jobs. The biggest shock came in October 1990 when 2,900 employees—from pilots to ticket handlers to mechanics—lost their jobs. Another 100 were let go a few weeks later. Many had never thought this could happen; after all, they had been government employees for most of their working lives. There were also criticisms that not enough managers were laid off. That changed, however, when 400 managers lost their jobs in spring 1991. Management was cut by 22 percent; union ranks by 13 percent.

Those employees who still had jobs were upset about the company's rapid change of direction. They didn't understand the rationale behind the decisions about which routes were to be cut back or canceled and which were to be promoted. They didn't feel they were getting enough information. And they didn't like what they were reading in the press.

Most of all, they didn't like being compared to cockroaches on a wall. Who would? But that's what Taylor said to *Report on Business* magazine writer John Stackhouse as part of a feature on the changes at the airline. "Somebody drew me a tombstone the other day," chuckles Taylor ruefully a few months after the story's publication, "and it had that [reference to cockroaches] on it." At the time, however, he wasn't as calm. And as he recalls the incident, his dander rises again. "I'll tell you exactly what I mean. Culture. I wasn't talking about people. John Stackhouse said, 'What is it that is stopping you from doing some of these things?' I said, 'Well, we've got so many cockroaches on the wall. It's the culture of the company. It's the bureaucracy.' I probably should have said, 'John, the problem is we're just too damned bureaucratic.' I have no idea why I said cockroaches, but I said it and I don't deny it."

Then he goes and says it again: "I've got to clean out this bureaucracy. I've got to get rid of it. I've got to fumigate the bloody thing. That's what I was driving at. The company has to be cleansed, for lack of a better word." Taylor is becoming heated at this point. "It has to be cleansed of its bureaucracy and cleansed of its processes which are complex, protective, and not action-driven."

In response, Jeanniot wrote a letter to the *Globe* criticizing the story and particularly the cockroaches comment. "I wrote the letter," he says, "because I felt that employees of Air Canada deserved a better portrayal." Yet Jeanniot agrees that there had to be changes at the airline, especially with the Gulf War's effect on air travel. "Don't believe for one minute that if I was in charge of the airline, I would not have taken some drastic actions."

And after the story appeared, Privatization Minister John McDermid

suggested to Taylor that the Air Canada chief was saying Ottawa shouldn't
have gone ahead and privatized the airline. "McDermid said, 'You mean,
Claude, that you're telling me I really shouldn't have privatized it?' I said,
'That's not the message at all.' It had to be privatized. We did it at the right
time. All I'm saying is that internally we weren't as well prepared to manage
a private company as I thought."

Of course, there are still operational problems to iron out. Air Canada
has cut both European and Asian routes. Critics charge that it isn't being
aggressive enough in building these foreign routes—that it has given up too
soon. There is also the question of ticket prices. Air Canada is keeping them
relatively high; if it lowers them, it will sell more seats and gain market
share, but it will actually lose more money. Air Canada recently spent $125
million on its Terminal Two in Toronto, largely in order to compete with
Canadian Airlines' Terminal Three. But this is merely to hold on to business
that it already has. It doesn't solve the question of how it can make money.

Speaking of product design, Taylor says Air Canada is ready now. But not
in its organization or attitude. "You go to a meeting in Ottawa and you
think you're going to have lunch with the deputy and you end up with
about twelve people. Well, it got to be that way at Air Canada; if we went to
Ottawa we had to have twelve people, too. We had to defend ourselves. So
we developed our own internal bureaucracy. We would analyze and research things to death. Accountability is very difficult to find in
government."

In mid-April, Taylor announced a new management structure, one that he
hopes solves the accountability problem. Among those reassigned was Leo
Desrochers, who became chief operating officer after all. But there was still
no sign of a new chief executive officer to lead Air Canada into the future.
In fact, it seemed for the present that Taylor would stay at the helm for
quite a while. Some observers say that despite his protestations about
wanting to retire, Taylor is enjoying the job these days. "What's he going to
do, go back to Moncton?" asks one board member. "He's never been
happier." Others speculate there will be an announcement by the end of
summer 1991.

But almost everyone believes that Air Canada is stuck for a new CEO
because they couldn't get the man they wanted: Don Carty from American
Airlines. Carty knows the industry; he's the former president of Canadian
Airlines and also once worked at Air Canada. He knows the way the United

States airlines play and has done a good job at American. And best of all, Carty is a Canadian. He grew up in eastern Ontario, and his family still summers in Renfrew, Ontario. In mid-1990, Taylor asked Carty to come home.

Carty won't admit that he was courted. But he does say that theoretically at least, there's an attraction to working again in Canada. "How you spend your time every day is part of how you get your kicks, obviously. Managing something that's broken and needs to be fixed, as we did at American in the early 1980s, is a tremendously exciting time. Managing Canadian Pacific for a couple of years when there was a question of whether there would be two [airlines] or one airline in Canada was a tremendously exciting time. Not to say American today isn't exciting. We're on the verge today of becoming a global industry and American is nicely positioned to take advantage of that—but there's a lot of challenge in front of it. But Air Canada and the Canadian airlines are, as you say, under some serious duress. They're at a crossroads."

And if Mr. Globalist, Mr. Free-Air, Mr. Let's-Play-Bourassa-off-Against-Ottawa-for-More-U.S.-Montreal-Routes were running a Canadian airline? "If I was running a Canadian airline, it would not be a dramatically different view from the one I have. . . . Ideally I'd turn back the clock to 1978 and I'd get a clean start with American and Eastern and others. And if I could I'd have a hub, oh, who knows, say St. Louis, Toronto, Vancouver, three or four strategic places so that I could be a player. But I can't turn back the clock, so what can I do to get that eight years back? One of the things I guess you'd do is to somehow get access so that you can try to catch up while at the same time not allowing the Americans to gain more than they've already got.

"So I think that's where you get into these discussions of how do you phase in such an agreement. If I was a Canadian carrier I wouldn't have foreign ownership off the table. I'd have it right on the table. Not because I wanted somebody to buy me but because I want to buy someone." Of course, that's hard to do without the dough, Carty admits. "Clearly, Air Canada's got to deliver some profitability." Then, he believes, it could get the money from the international investment community to fund such a purchase.

"If they move the stock back up to $12 to $15 and they have some idea as to how they want to spend the money, they can go sell another couple of hundred thousand shares and raise $200 to 300 million, on which they can borrow another $700 million. And suddenly you can buy who knows what." Of course, that means a large dilution of the company's stock. So coupled with that there must be a management able to convince the investment world that they have a workable vision of the future.

These are all interesting and well thought-out ideas, combining the boldness of Jeanniot with the realism of Taylor. Unfortunately, by spring 1991 it appeared that Carty would not be implementing them. Air Canada simply was not willing to pay the price for this particular American executive. Taylor would not admit that the board had turned down a proposed compensation package for Carty. "Where'd you hear that?" he asked. "You won't find me confirming that."[16]

When asked about his taking on the top job at Air Canada, Carty will only say, "I wouldn't bet on it." Then he laughs. "Besides, my brother's the treasurer at Canadian. I wouldn't want to compete with my brother." But he does offer that he's shocked at the cost of being Canadian. He understands that it lies in a higher per-capita cost to run the country, but it's staggering nonetheless. At American, Carty earns a base salary of U.S. $300,000, with bonuses of more than $300,000 in profitable years and stock options that have been worth about U.S. $130,000 a year in recent years. In 1989, his total compensation package came to U.S. $797,287. In Canadian dollars, an equivalent base salary would be about $345,000. Add onto that a bonus for being the top gun, and try an estimated minimum of $1.5 million (plus stock options, a housing allowance or interest-free mortgage, and compensation for a higher tax rate and higher cost of living) for Don Carty to take on the Air Canada job.[17]

"Most Canadians just don't recognize how expensive it is to be a Canadian. If your average worker really understood the after-tax difference economically to him, he'd be shocked. He might not give up being a Canadian, but he'd be shocked. He just has no idea how big that difference is."

So until he finds his own successor, Taylor soldiers on. Neither Carty nor Eyton thinks Air Canada yet has a clear vision of its future. But it seems to be leaning toward head-on global competition—once it finishes cleaning

---

16 Both Taylor and Carty denied a news report that Carty's appointment was scheduled to be announced at a February industry meeting in Florida, but that Carty backed out at the last minute.
17 The Air Canada estimates are based on a human resources expert's calculations using industry data.

house. Taylor is selling the head office and the Enroute credit card business. He wants to concentrate on the business of running an airline. But he's still in a tough spot, stuck with no money and facing a set of potentially explosive decisions.

In early 1991, he was negotiating with United States carrier Delta to sell airplanes. There were rumors that the talks included discussions about alliances. "Right now," says Taylor, "I'm talking to about six different people to find out what it would take for people to be interested in an alliance with us." So he's finding out very clearly what obstacles the airline faces.

Still, Taylor believes that he can make the airline attractive to others, so that he will have some control over the alliances Air Canada does eventually make. And they're more likely to be foreign alliances than a merger with Canadian Airlines in the end. "I like to be courted because I think I bring something to the table—or the bedroom, or wherever people get courted. And I think we can bring something to the table so people will court us. They don't want to court a dying flower."

Taylor's moves during early 1991 were crucial; time was running out. Although Taylor can joke about the Open Skies talks taking months, that's not a long time in which to overhaul an airline. And even then, as a well-structured, productive airline, Air Canada's future will still depend on the deal Ottawa cuts at the Open Skies negotiations.

Everyone wants the old Canada-United States airline agreement updated. Right now, it's so old and worn-out that it just doesn't reflect reality. It was signed before the United States airlines developed hubs, so Canadian carriers feel they're at a real disadvantage in arranging their United States connections. It allows United States customs to pre-clear Canadian passengers at Canadian airports, with no method of Canadian customs instituting its own quid pro quo. Canadian airlines want better access to United States airports. The existing rules won't give them that.

For the United States, the transportation talks are an important symbol: they reinforce the notion that the United States wants free trade on all possible fronts. And if successful, they could serve as a model for new flight agreements with Europe and with various Asian countries. But for Canada, Open Skies is much more than a concept. It is the only way in which Canadian airlines are going to become internationally competitive. But it is a risk; open competition could mean the end of the Canadian airlines.

By re-opening the 1978 bilateral air transportation agreement with the United States in the Open Skies talks, Canada was pursuing a number of goals—and it didn't just have the airlines in mind. The decisions are not simple for Ottawa's negotiating team, led by External Affairs trade bureaucrat Jim Harris on lines dictated by cabinet rather than the Transport ministry. Consumers want better service. The federal government is anxious to keep its Free Trade Agreement operational by providing easier access to cross-border transport. And as always, there are provincial pressures on Ottawa. The provinces are interested in more routes to their regional centers, of course. Carty and American are a big part of that; Carty is always flying north to tantalize local politicians with the thought of more flights, more tourists. "How long do you think it will be," he asks boldly, "before Bourassa says, 'If you guys can't get your shit together here, we'll handle aviation because we need flights into Montreal'?"

The talks are dealing with cross-border flight access: for example, getting Canadian flights into overcrowded United States airports. That's what Open Skies actually refers to. Updated regulations for cross-border cargo services, regional services, charter flights, and specialty services such as aerial surveying and firefighting are also being discussed. Everyone involved agrees that revising rules in these areas can only be for the good.

But that's not the case with one part of the negotiations, which takes the idea of Open Skies one step further. The negotiators are exploring the concept of freer access to each other's markets for travel within the country, not just across the border, a type of access known by the marine term cabotage. The United States isn't pushing hard for the idea, but it's interested. The Canadian contingent is clearly divided.

Ottawa agreed to explore the issue. The negotiating team is proceeding on the basic assumption that the country needs domestic airlines. Canadian carriers, they believe, have more of a commitment to east-west transportation routes than foreign carriers would. They want to ensure that Canadian communities are linked, not abandoned. At the same time, they recognize that the Canadian airlines need greater access to the United States. At the moment, Canada-United States flights provide the two carriers with 16 percent of their revenue; with better access, that number could increase dramatically. No other international market has as much promise. Carty says Ottawa understands the dilemma of risk and opportunity for Canadian carriers that cabotage represents. "By opening the border you do two things for Canadian carriers. You increase their peril but you also dramatically increase their opportunity. It's going to be a far higher risk-reward scenario for them than it has ever been before."

If the government opts for free trade in the air, it might choose to subsidize unprofitable routes that it feels are crucial for Canadian unity, thus satisfying both the nationalists and the price-conscious consumers. Ottawa understands that there is a risk if they choose to implement a more open skies approach—let alone some form of cabotage. But they can't ignore the issue. Without a new agreement with the United States, Taylor emphasizes, the airlines can't survive anyway. "Nothing comes for free," says Jeanniot. "We have the inventiveness in this country. Hopefully, we also have the guts."

The cabinet reflects all of these views. Besides Corbeil, there are four former transport ministers sitting at the table: Benoît Bouchard, John Crosbie, the unhappily unseated Doug Lewis, and Donald Mazankowski. As always, Maz is most important. And as always, Maz is for letting the free market work. He's been for open skies for a long time. He believes in the Canadian airlines and thinks they will be able to find a way to survive and prosper in a North American marketplace.

But Maz is also an Alberta MP, as is Joe Clark. Canadian Airlines has the advantage on that score, Carty points out. "Canadian Airlines' wishes and Canadian Airlines' interests are always going to be protected in this government by some very strong cabinet representation from Alberta. You have both Mazankowski and Clark. I know they're going to listen to their Alberta constituents. They'd be irresponsible if they didn't."

The political haze swirling around the issue of cabotage is so thick it's hard to see the issues clearly. While the decision on whether to proceed with Open Skies talks was before Parliament, the airlines and the unions were lobbying for their own positions with every available MP. The Lewis-Taylor-Eyton handshake scene led to rumors of an impending merger of the two airlines' international routes—denied—and reports that Lewis had said he would kill the idea of cabotage—also denied. Meanwhile, Eyton also met with members of the United States congress to try to turn them against cabotage.

The funniest thing about all this toing and froing is that it was originally the Canadians who put cabotage on the negotiating table. Actually, the United States has never been particularly interested in open skies. For one thing, it would have to change its own transportation legislation, a long, tedious process that could open the entire transportation industry to congressional scrutiny. It would also set a precedent for cabotage between United States and European and Asian markets, something the Americans haven't yet decided they want.

Back in 1984, however, Canadian airline executives were eager for the opportunity to compete head-on with the United States. At that point, the Americans were still struggling with deregulation. Carty, as head of CP Air, was pushing the idea. So were Jeanniot and Taylor at government-owned Air Canada. Maz was at Transport and eager for the chance to see the airlines compete head-on. The United States simply never responded to the Canadian request to open the issue. Canada offered cabotage again during the free trade discussions, and again the United States backed away. "The U.S. blinked and Canada got up and walked away from the table," recalls Carty. "Now the Americans are back with exactly the same offer and what do you hear about cabotage in this country? 'Oh, my God.'"

There are reasons for that dramatic shift in position. The United States is looking at Canada these days as a place to increase what Carty describes as its "home" market share by, say, 10 percent. The arithmetic is simple, he adds. "As we approach the true globalization of this industry, which ultimately means a single world market, the faster your market can grow, the better." And with fewer airlines, the American politicians wouldn't mind seeing a little competition from the Canadians. Then, when they decide to look at opening to other foreign competition, they'll have done their test run.

But while Canada is just one option for growth by the American carriers, the United States is really the only choice for the Canadian airlines. And the Canadians should pay special attention when the Americans talk about other eventual agreements. Using the Free Trade Agreement as a model, once they sign an agreement with the United States, they'll be forced to take part in any other American initiatives, whether they want to or not. The present Mexican free trade negotiations provide the best example of this: Canada had to agree to negotiate with Mexico in order to protect its Free Trade Agreement with the United States.

The Open Skies negotiations, once begun, limped along through the spring and summer of 1991 as these talks usually do. A meeting in April. A meeting in June. July. September. The preliminary talks were to be completed by October. The key to the talks' success, from the Canadian perspective, would be the type of improved access the Canadian airlines would gain—and the adjustment time the Canadians would be granted before having to compete with the United States airlines on equal terms. The Canadians say that the United States will just have to realize that Canada needs some concessions. But it's a difficult bargaining position to justify. And if they get the concessions, the Canadian airlines had better be ready to take advantage of them.

On many levels, Air Canada is a metaphor for all Canadians. It desperately wanted its independence, but it wasn't prepared for the responsibility that freedom brings. It had too much debt and too grandiose a view of itself. It used to believe that its job was to link Canadians, that it was part of the grand Canadian vision. Then it realized that Canadians couldn't afford that vision—and didn't want it enough to pay the high price it cost. So it became very calculating and self-serving; just another business. But by doing so, it forfeited its claim to loyalty from the Canadian public. Lately, the company's executives have realized that it must be both a profitable company and a Canadian company—and that means having loyalty to Canada in terms of jobs and service.

No one is more anxious about this uneasy compromise than those running the planes. In April 1991, a group of two dozen anxious employees flew out to Air Canada's annual meeting in Vancouver on their employee passes, staying at their own expense at Aeroplan hotel the Sheraton Landmark.[18] At the meeting, they peppered Taylor with detailed questions about operations. And on the plane back to Toronto, they sent a message from hospitality class to Taylor's head of communications, Doug Port, up in first class. The letter told him that they had made the trek because they cared about their airline's future—and asked him to make sure they were kept informed of any major decisions.

Claude Taylor traveled on the next plane, the red-eye to Toronto. At 7:30 a.m., he switched to a Rapidair flight to Montreal. From the airport, he went straight to the office. He hadn't yet heard about the employee message—both a boost and a form of pressure tactic. But he didn't need to. Taylor already knew that as he charted the future of his company and his industry in Canada, he had supporters and dependents on all sides. But he was flying on his own.

---

18 Taylor and other Air Canada executives and directors stayed at Delta Place, a slightly upscale but hardly luxurious hotel that is not an Aeroplan choice.

CHAPTER THREE

Under the Microscope

There is a shrine of sorts in the entrance of the Banting and Best
Diabetes Research Institute on College Street in Toronto. Charles
Best's doctoral robes are displayed in a glass case, along with a letter from
Frederick Banting and one of the original instruments the pair used in their
historic discovery of insulin in a University of Toronto lab in the summer of
1921. Insulin's discovery ranks as one of the high-water marks in medical
history. In more romantic terms, it represents a step forward for civilization, the triumph of knowledge over disease. Indeed, it seems on a muggy
summer afternoon seventy years after the discovery that there is a particularly peaceful, almost reverential atmosphere in this hushed, dim academic corridor. I have to suppress a sudden urge to bless myself.[1]

Banting and Best are worthy of a shrine. But their discovery has left
subsequent generations of Canadians worshiping a false god. Looking for a
concrete symbol of the insulin miracle, Canadians transferred their loyalties
to the company that manufactured the product for Canadians, Connaught
Laboratories. The connection, however, was always suspect, as is most of
the Canadian myth that has grown up around Connaught.

Given the importance of Connaught to Canadians, both as a company
and as a symbol of Canadian skill in scientific research, it's amazing how
few people have any real understanding of Connaught's history and *raison
d'être*. Few people realize that if French competitor Institut Mérieux hadn't
made a successful $942-million takeover bid for Connaught in November

---

1 A carefully worded Historical Board plaque outside the university's medical building
   reflects the controversy over who should share credit for the discovery; Banting and
   University of Toronto professor J.J.R. Macleod received the Nobel Prize for the
   discovery in 1923. Banting shared his prize money with Best; Macleod with biochemist
   James Collip, who purified the substance so that it could be used on humans.

1989, the Canadian company would have had to make another foreign alliance. That if Connaught had continued as a purely Canadian company, it would surely have been a victim, not a victor, on the battleground of international competition.

Its original purpose was not to set the world on fire with its research capabilities, but to be a workhorse lab copying others' formulae for Canadian consumption. The laboratory was founded in 1914 by Dr. J.G. Fitzgerald at the University of Toronto to find a low-cost vaccine to fight diphtheria. In 1916 it was named Connaught Laboratories, and its mandate was to produce low-cost drugs for Canadians. It spent the years of the Great War producing 250,000 vials of tetanus vaccine, mainly for Canadian soldiers.

Connaught coasted for decades on the insulin coup. Despite the legitimacy that the discovery conferred on it, the company was never more than a factory churning out products. The image of two men huddled over a microscope was not only outdated, it was inaccurate. The rest of the Canadian-owned pharmaceutical industry had sold out to foreign buyers in the 1950s. Connaught soldiered on under the wing of the University of Toronto, until even the academics couldn't justify supporting the money-losing lab. Ottawa stepped in and Canada Development Corp. carried the company for a dozen years—longer than it really should have.

Mérieux executive Michel Dubois says that the sale by CDC of its Connaught shares in the mid-1980s doomed Connaught. Because it didn't have a controlling shareholder, it couldn't make the expensive, long-term commitments to research and development that it needed to make in order to survive and prosper. It was undercut by the short-term demands of the public marketplace. In other words, Dubois argues that Canadians lost Connaught because neither the government nor investors were willing to make a long-term commitment to a research and development company.

He has a point. But it's questionable whether Connaught's research capabilities would have made it a winner even with investor support. It was doing the best it could in research terms—and it had a few successes. But it was no world competitor; it didn't have enough money, and the industry was expanding much more rapidly than this small Canadian company could cope with. After the takeover, Jacques Martin, the general manager of Mérieux who spearheaded the takeover team, said bluntly that "it is certain Connaught had no future alone."

People don't really want to hear that. All they hear is that Canada lost control of Connaught to a French company. But Canadians didn't deserve to control Connaught Biosciences, even if it had been the gem they wished it to be. The story of Connaught is proof that Canada has never had a scientific research policy that promotes the development of internationally competitive research companies; that it won't fund comparable laboratory research; and that our deep pools of private capital refuse even to consider supporting research on any sizable scale.

"For any country, the takeover of an important company by foreigners is felt as a sort of failure. That is true for us, too," admitted Martin. "But one must make the effort to get past the emotions and say what is the reality of the situation." Yet whenever foreign takeovers are discussed these days, Connaught is inevitably mentioned. It has become the emblem for the nationalist argument that Canada is losing its best companies to foreigners, the talisman of those who decry our research policies. Look at Connaught, they say with a knowing nod. All right. Let's look at Connaught.

Connaught Labs was one of about 150 different proposals that came across the desk of Anthony (Tony) Hampson, chairman of the newly minted Canada Development Corp., back in 1972. The CDC had only recently been established by Pierre Trudeau's Liberal government, and Hampson was still trying to sort out its mandate. The idea of having a publicly listed company with Ottawa as its controlling shareholder was to combine business's initiative with government's long-term strategy. CDC was formed to invest in Canadian companies—social engineering with a profit motive. Hampson, a former vice-president at Paul Desmarais's Montreal-based Power Corp. of Canada, created CDC for the government. An economist by training, he had served on Walter Gordon's 1955-57 Royal Commission on the Economy, and on the Porter Commission on Banking and Finance in the mid-1960s. He envisioned CDC as an instrument of economic nationalism. Hampson believed that CDC should focus on half a dozen companies in various industries. They should all, naturally, have the potential for rapid growth and profitability, as well as a strong Canadian flavor.

Connaught certainly had the latter, what with Banting and Best and all that good Canadian mythology behind it. And health care sounded like both a potentially profitable and a socially uplifting field. Connaught, the CDC board and Hampson decided, would be the centerpiece of a string of health-care investments for the new CDC portfolio. Unfortunately, nobody at CDC understood enough about the health-care area to know that there was a very big difference between a pharmaceuticals company and a biologicals company. Connaught did not make pills and potions for over-the-counter sale; it sold vaccines and purified blood for the Red Cross, much more of a public service slant than Hampson had in mind.

Still, Connaught cost enough to qualify as a CDC purchase. Hampson didn't plan to spend less than $50 million on any particular purchase; after all, he didn't want to scatter Ottawa's investment all over the map.

CDC wasn't necessarily the ideal purchaser from Connaught's point of view. But Connaught didn't have much choice. After sixty-two years of nurturing Connaught as a separate little fiefdom within the university that had its own operations on the outskirts of Toronto, the University of Toronto's advisory board was anxious to sell. Connaught was losing money. The lab had lost $1 million the previous year on $11 million in sales. The board, says Hampson, "really didn't know what the hell was going on." Connaught, he adds, "had sort of insulated itself even from the university." But the university fathers certainly didn't like the look of things. And they could use the money from the sale. This was the beginning of the period of university cutbacks. There was some protest in the university and research communities, but the board soothed spirits by using the money to set up a Connaught endowment fund for scientific research.

The University of Toronto made no full-scale marketing effort. When they heard about the sale, the federal and provincial governments simply said they didn't want the lab sold to a foreigner. (Life was obviously much simpler in those days.) The university looked around a bit and talked to a few people. But there was no other serious bidder.

Once he was inside, Hampson soon found out why. "It was clearly very badly run. I mean, it was a disaster." Hampson compares it to a Communist country. "Connaught had spent fifty years in the backwaters. Every once in a while a bright scientist would come along and do something. But it had developed a culture of sloth."

Connaught had long since shifted from innovation to simply trying to produce a pure source of insulin and a few other products. "It was sort of like an Ivory Snow company," says Hampson, "that decided to make soap 99.45 percent pure instead of 99.44 percent pure. I mean, maybe an interesting challenge, but really sort of irrelevant."

Connaught's place as a supplier of polio vaccine illustrates its most basic problem during the 1970s. Connaught, contrary to what many Canadians think, didn't discover the vaccine for polio the way Banting and Best had discovered insulin. The discovery was actually made in the United States.

But Connaught soon established itself as the world's largest supplier of the Salk polio vaccine. That meant it was not acting as a pure research lab, but as a business, a mass supplier of needed medical vaccines. The Salk vaccine was an oral vaccine. A few years later, however, two American researchers developed an injected virus; this Sabin virus soon became the vaccine of choice. It was cheaper to make and easier to store and handle, particularly important in the Third World. And Connaught was left out in the cold. Rather than working on developing this type of vaccine, it had spent its time on purifying and refining the Salk vaccine.

With the company losing money, there were few resources for CDC to use as building blocks. The first thing CDC set its eyes on, however, was the valuable land surrounding the lab. Selling it was a way to finance a turn-around. Before making that decision, however, it had to deal with the basic step of making Connaught into a corporate entity. Connaught had never had a president or a real management team. The idea of an executive staff and an outside board of directors horrified the scientists.

Given the man picked by CDC to head the new Connaught, it was no wonder that the scientists fretted. Hampson chose Don McCaskill to head the company. McCaskill was a marketing man from Warner-Lambert. He knew how to sell pharmaceutical products. But with McCaskill's back-ground and nature, there was bound to be a culture clash. "His personality approach was at the other end of the spectrum from the traditional Connaught one," admits Hampson. "That put a fair amount of tension there." The tension didn't take long to move from the lab to the pages of the newspapers. The *Globe and Mail* ran a series of articles about the changes at Connaught under CDC management—and they were sym-pathetic to the old guard. It was clear that the reporters thought science and profit shouldn't mix. According to Hampson, the source for some of the stories was Dr. Andrew Moriarty, who had been research director when CDC bought Connaught. He was very unhappy with McCaskill's approach to R&D and with company management to boot. According to Hampson, Moriarty was "discontented" and "very ambitious." "He wanted to be president. But I didn't think he was suited to be president, and I told him so. I think that was what really set him off." Moriarty left the company. After the Red Cross was approached with allegations about Connaught's blood purification program, the Canadian Medical Association launched an in-vestigation of the company. It found the stories about product problems had been incorrect or overblown, but that morale was low and the public was losing faith in the company. And "scientific performance was less than one would have predicted twenty years ago," the CMA report noted.

After the public airing of Connaught's problems, McCaskill was fired. "He did a lot of good in some ways," Hampson insists. "But I suppose he wasn't the right person. It was hard to know who the right person was, because Connaught was really a unique one-off kind of animal." McCaskill was succeeded by Rod McGuinness, also a marketing man, brought in from Kellogg Canada. "He accomplished some more things, but again, we never really felt it had got up and running." When McGuinness left a couple of years later to joint Carling O'Keefe, the CDC didn't replace him immediately. Instead it left chief operating officer Alun Davies in charge while it figured out what to do next.

It almost bailed out. By the late 1970s, CDC board members were beginning to question why the crown corporation even owned Connaught. The company was still losing money, and it quite clearly needed about $15 million pumped into it over the next few years in order to expand its research program. But Hampson was determined to give the great experiment another try. Dome Petroleum's Jack Gallagher, a CDC director and back then still a man whose opinions were listened to, suggested his great friend Bill Cochrane as the next Connaught president.

Cochrane was just the sort of man Hampson was looking for. He had had it with marketing types; what Connaught needed, he now decided, was someone who understood business, science, and how to run a government-oriented organization with a public service slant. A former president of the University of Calgary, Cochrane was a physician, an academic, an entrepreneur, and a proven manager. He would be able to understand and organize Connaught's scientific ventures and restructure the company. Hampson talked about the matter to U of T president George Connell, former president John Evans, and others, and they agreed with this approach. Hampson felt that Cochrane's people skills, connections in government, self-confidence, and ability to understand complicated scientific questions and deal with the researchers at Connaught were what was needed. And most of all, Hampson liked Cochrane.

By the time Cochrane came on board, however, CDC had decided on a new corporate agenda for Connaught. The grand plan this time was to make Connaught the center of a health-industry research and development and production juggernaut for Canada. CDC had created a holding company called ConnLab, which besides Connaught held a ragtag assortment of scientific research companies. They needed someone to pull the whole mess together.

The man brought in to execute this new strategy, as Bill Cochrane's boss and the CDC point man at a variety of assorted other holdings, was Australian expatriate Brian King. A chemical engineer and pharmaceuticals expert, King had arrived in Britain from Australia in 1960 and spent a decade there with Fisons. He landed in Toronto in 1970 to begin Fisons's North American operation. The plan was to start with Canada and expand into the United States. Finally, in 1978 he was ready to relocate again, this time to Boston. But a disagreement with headquarters over strategy led to King leaving after seventeen years at the company. He decided to stay in Toronto and work for CDC as the resident health-care expert. But make no mistake; this was no public-sector, big-government, Canada-first type.

King arrived to find the CDC's grand scheme for a health-care sector research juggernaut had never gelled. Aside from Connaught, ConnLab Holdings controlled four other companies in five different health-care fields—and there was no connection between any of them. "It was a rather weird collection of companies," King recalls. Raylo Chemicals in Edmonton made "exotic chemicals" for specialized research purposes. Bio-Research Laboratories, bought in 1976, was a tiny testing lab for agricultural and pharmaceutical products, with its research facility still being constructed in Senneville, Quebec. Nordic Laboratories in Laval, Quebec, was a 70-30 joint venture with the provincial pension fund Caisse de dépôt et placement du Québec; Hampson says CDC went into Nordic as a favor to the Caisse.[2]

ConnLab's 75 percent holding in the Danish generic drug company Dumex (for Danish United Export) was questionable as an innovative investment. It was ConnLab's only financial success, selling mainly to Asian and African countries—but it used bootleg ingredients from eastern Europe to duplicate other western companies' patented drugs and had what King describes as "a somewhat questionable reputation in health-care circles."

The theory behind this odd assortment was that each brought some advantage that should somehow meld well with the others. Connaught

---

2 Nordic is a pharmaceutical company specializing in cardiovascular and gastrointestinal drugs. It has one main product, which it developed, and makes three others under license for an American firm. This business developed after Connaught became a partner with the Caisse in Nordic; later an American partner was brought in.

offered research and production facilities in Canada; Raylo's exotic chemicals could be turned into new drug products; Bio-Research's testing facilities would be used for any new products developed; Nordic would be the domestic marketing arm; and Dumex the international exporter and international marketer. "It was a crazy idea," says King. "It was never going to work."

King began sorting through the companies, one by one, to see if they were worthwhile holdings individually. He sold Raylo in 1980. He found a joint-venture partner for Nordic in Lyons-based Institut Mérieux, which was developing a couple of the same drugs that Nordic had licensed. The deal was drawn up in July 1981 and approved by the Foreign Investment Review Agency early the next year. As part of the Nordic partnership, the Caisse de dépôt ended up with 14.4 percent, ConnLab 35.6 percent, and Mérieux 50 percent and the management role. King would someday regret that he had ever made this particular introduction.

Bio-Research was refocused solely on the pharmaceutical market for its tests. King replaced the scientifically oriented president with Mike Ancroft, a CDC employee with a drug industry background, in his place. "He was a commercial guy," King says. "He knew how to make a buck, which is what it was all about." A top manager at Dumex was also replaced, and a hand-chosen successor made the company even more profitable. King sold Dumex in 1983—enabling ConnLab to pay off almost all the $45 million it owed directly to CDC.

There were organizational changes at both the holding company and Connaught itself as well, including a lot of staff departures. King is especially derisive about some of the consultants whom he found at ConnLab. "It was a classic case of people recognizing a good thing when it was going on, ex-academics, ex-government people who had latched onto the company and were drawing nice consultancy fees and contributing absolutely zip. So I got rid of them."

When King and Cochrane arrived, there were some very basic things to do at Connaught Labs: setting up a management structure; arranging for timely and believable financial reports. And there was the little question of strategic direction. Connaught was still a Canadian biologics business supplying insulin vaccine to all provinces but Quebec. But to survive, it would have to become a North American company. Its competitors were the big foreign drug companies such as Merck, Parke-Davis (part of giant Warner-Lambert), Bristol-Myers Squibb, Eli Lilly, Pfizer, and Sandoz. Apart from the government-sponsored companies, Connaught was a small player, which left it at a distinct disadvantage. "Connaught had an image of being a much bigger company than it really was," says King. "It dominated the Canadian market, which gave it the big image." Exports to Third World countries also gave the firm a profile in health circles. And certainly it had grown: from $16 million sales, $1 million research when CDC stepped in six years earlier, to sales of about $40 million and research of almost $4 million. The research money, however, was still mainly from government grants.

With the new management, Hampson says, by the early 1980s, "I was convinced we were going to make it, and make it in a quite significant way." Connaught reversed its traditionally sorry record in the United States by buying a pediatrics specialist, Smith Richardson, in 1978 and building a strong American pediatrics marketing force. Influenza vaccine was the main product. At one point, mounting liability insurance costs for the DPT whooping-cough vaccine forced Connaught to withdraw from the market. Unable to justify operating with the higher costs, it decided to set up a self-funding self-insurance system and raised prices substantially to cover it. That gamble paid off when the competition followed its lead.

Cochrane and King brought discipline to the research effort. Researchers began to work with marketers, to define products that could be developed and properly marketed. Cochrane and King were more selective about which products would actually be developed, so that money could be funneled as productively as possible. They always faced the tradeoff: they needed to develop a number of projects simultaneously so that at least one would pay off; but they also needed to channel money into a number of areas.

In 1983, that led to the end of insulin production. Although it would still be identified as the insulin company in the public mind, Connaught effectively left the insulin business and became a distributor for Novo, a Danish insulin producer. In doing so, it took advantage of the only strength it had in this product area: market domination. Connaught was simply uncompetitive in insulin manufacture by the early 1980s. Eli Lilly and Novo had surged ahead quickly and Connaught hadn't invested enough money in research during the 1970s. As a result, it hadn't kept pace. Novo produced a much purer form of insulin than Connaught, and Lilly was working on a genetically engineered form.

This quickening pace in research—and the switch to genetically engineered vaccines—demanded more and more money. The University of Toronto had recognized this when it made the decision to sell Connaught in the early 1970s. CDC and Connaught management initially didn't understand the urgent need to step up research, to Connaught's great cost. King's most damning observation about Connaught's research weakness when he arrived in 1978 was about the scientists' backward attitudes. "I can remember some people at Connaught telling me that all this genetic stuff was a waste of time, it wouldn't be worth it."

In the vaccine business, however, there was a better research program and more chance at competitiveness in the marketplace. "It was our clear decision to throw all of the financial resources and scientific resources we had at maintaining and building our vaccine technology," says King. Cochrane also took a very personal interest in the quality of scientists at Connaught. A new research director and a number of new scientists were brought in. Cochrane replaced the old-style vaccine scientists with microbiologists and geneticists.

Focusing their research efforts had a cost, of course. Cochrane recalls some work on a new technique of administering insulin that he hated to see scrapped. "But we didn't have the resources and had to close it out. We couldn't afford the trials." A few companies in the United States later picked up the concept. "We had to concentrate on the vaccine business," he adds. "That's where we were generating our dollars."

This led, in the mid-1980s, to the development of the ProHIBiT influenza vaccine. ProHIBiT was the first vaccine of its type that could be used to immunize children as young as eighteen months against *haemophilius influenzae* b (HIB), which causes meningitis and other diseases. Here, and with a few other products, Connaught was finally on the cutting edge of vaccine research again.

By 1984, Connaught was making money and had a clear sense of direction. Cochrane ran the company, but CDC and King were actively involved in strategy. CDC was never a passive holding company; it worked on business plans and financial plans and marketing plans and research plans and budgets. Connaught, by this point, wasn't about to run out of money. It had raised a healthy $89.8 million through a public debenture issue in 1983. But by 1984, when ConnLab became CDC Life Sciences, Hampson was anxious to sell shares in the pharmaceutical holding company[3] to the public. He planned one day to sell out CDC's interest entirely. He saw the crown corporation's role as taking companies that had needed long-term, higher-risk money but had potential for an eventual return and developing them. He saw this as a venture-capital business; holdings were like children,

---

3 It later changed its name again, to Connaught Biosciences, after CDC sold out entirely a
   few years later. Connaught Laboratories remained the main subsidiary.

to be nurtured and then sent off on their own. Or, in business terms, once they were profitable, he thought the holding should be sold and the money channeled into new ventures.

He didn't see the CDC as a pension fund for the federal government. "Holding companies that become merely holding companies lose their dynamism and their *raison d'être* when they get more interested in who they're going to have lunch with that day, or which bank is in the underwriting group or which business reception they should go to that night than they are in actually building companies," he says. "I didn't think CDC had any justification if it was going to become more conservative and have us stay in the office and collect dividends."

Hampson insists CDC's decision to sell part of its holding in Connaught wasn't tied to the 1984 federal election of the Progressive Conservatives. He had tried to keep CDC free of any government influence, he insists, including during the Trudeau era, when the prime minister "tried to pitchfork Maurice Strong in."[4]

But the Conservatives planned to privatize as much as possible, especially the holdings in CDC and its parent, Canada Development Investment Corporation.[5] And there was good reason for the Tories to be dissatisfied with CDC—and for Hampson to be anxious to sell a major asset. CDC had bought Aquitaine Co. of Canada in 1981, piling up a mountain of debt. Then, only a few months later, it purchased Kidd Creek Mines from Texasgulf for $3.8 billion. Then came high interest rates. CDC needed cash. By mid-1984, selling shares in the now-profitable CDC Life Sciences seemed the answer.

That first public share sale, for one-third of Connaught's shares at $12.50 per share, finally took place in November 1984.[6] King and Hampson had

---

4   Hampson is quite proud of that moment in history. "We fought that off and said, 'Look, we've got minority shareholders here, you've made a commitment to them that you won't interfere,' " he recalls. " 'You can't run CDC for government aims. If you do, we'll all quit.' So they backed off."

5   With Sinclair Stevens and later Barbara McDougall, Don Mazankowski, and John McDermid as minister responsible, the Tories privatized ten companies by mid-1990. That total includes CDC, but not the companies that CDC itself sold, such as Kidd Creek and Connaught. The government's CDC shares were sold in three stages, in August 1986, June 1987, and October 1987.

6   There was one share split in Connaught's five years as a public company. Original shareholders bought in for the equivalent of $6.25, while the stock sold five years later for $37—a 600 percent return over five years.

done a big sales job on the investment community, but there was real skepticism about investing in a company when the CDC was a major shareholder. Particularly this type of company. "It wasn't an easy sell," says King. And the day Connaught went public, the *Globe and Mail*'s lead business story accused the firm of withholding pertinent information from potential shareholders about problems with its blood treatment operation. If true, this would have been a violation of securities regulations.[7] Still, the issue sold well, especially to individuals. Over the next couple of years, as is usually the case once a firm has a track record, the stock moved more into the hands of institutions. The Caisse de dépôt was one of those. Still, despite the lack of a "golden-share" provision limiting individual share-holdings in the company, there was no single large shareholder except CDC.

Two years later, all that changed. By this time, CDC was ready to get out of Connaught entirely. King recognized CDC had been a "benevolent shareholder"—patient and long-suffering. Although a poor investment philosophy proved once again that government industrial policy and the profit motive don't mix well, CDC at least kept Connaught alive—if not for CDC, Connaught would have died in 1972. But now Connaught would have to survive without it. Before CDC's stock sale, Hampson visited Canada's large private pools of capital—mostly family money—to try to convince them to buy the CDC stake. He was looking for a long-term investor. Fat chance. "I can't remember all the people I talked to," says Hampson, "but there were people like Imasco, the Reichmanns, Bell, and a number of others." King says there was always polite interest, but then would come the inevitable excuses. It was a different kind of business. They were uncomfortable with high-tech research. They wouldn't know how to run it.

King and Cochrane had resuscitated the company and started a new research program. But it became clear that the company wouldn't be able to gain adequate funding in Canada. That's no surprise, given Canada's record for research funding by private enterprise. In Canada, 54 percent of R&D is done by industry; that compares to 73 percent in Sweden and Germany and 70 percent in the United States. Canada scores lowest among eight countries in the amount of R&D performed as a percentage of our gross domestic product—both in total and in the amount of money spent by

---

7 Connaught won an out-of-court settlement; a retraction was printed several months later.

industry.[8] The low level of domestic research is partly explained by the structure of the Canadian economy: we're still harvesting resources rather than investing in new technologies. Neither our large family groups nor our pension funds will support research-intensive businesses; they don't understand them and they don't want to understand them.

And even in businesses in which R&D can benefit companies, less is done in Canada than in other countries. Canadian companies just don't identify with the idea of spending money on long-term research. In the pharmaceutical area, Canadian spending on research in 1987 was one-tenth of the average spent in OECD countries.[9] Connaught wanted to change that figure, but it simply wasn't going to find the backers at home.

Finally, King and Hampson gave up. CDC knew it would get the most money if it sold its stock in stages. In November 1986, it dropped from a 66.6 percent to a 25 percent block. The Caisse de dépôt had obviously been waiting for this; it picked up just under 20 percent of Connaught. King wasn't a happy man. Having the Caisse as a partner in a small Quebec company like Nordic was one thing; having the Caisse as the largest single shareholder next to CDC in Connaught was another.

The Caisse is unique in Canadian business circles. It is the only pool of capital with a social mandate: to act in Quebec's best interest while making the best possible profit. The rest of the business community doesn't trust it for just this reason. At times that distrust has been justified, because the Caisse has acted in concert with Quebec government policy, and at the expense of other shareholders or of companies' managements.

At this point, the Caisse saw Connaught as a long-term holding, in the three-to-five-year category. King and others met with austere Caisse president and ardent Quebec nationalist Jean Campeau to suss out his position. Campeau made it clear that Caisse wanted board representation. As holders of more than 10 percent of Connaught, management and CDC agreed they were entitled to nominate board members. They didn't agree with Campeau that he was entitled to choose his own people and have them rubber stamped. Eventually, the two groups agreed on two choices. Hampson, however, was not happy with the turn of events. "The Caisse always had a parochial attitude," he complains. "And you're never completely sure, you know, what sort of side deals they might have had with other people." That

---

8   The other countries were the United States, Germany, France, Sweden, the United Kingdom, the Netherlands, and Japan.
9   The twenty-five member countries of the Organization for Economic Cooperation and Development.

remark, however, may be prompted by hindsight over what came next. Within a year, the Caisse would become the fifth business in Connaught's life.

Hampson left CDC in late 1986. The leave-taking was not a happy one; in his sixteen years as CDC's chief visionary, he had engineered the purchase of $7 billion in assets—and piled up $4 billion in debts. The companies ranged from petroleum and sulfur producers to Connaught to industrial automation to a photocopier distributor. Many were in rough shape. Canterra Energy had a questionable value at best; CDC had written down its interest in photocopier company Savin Corp. Hampson became a consultant, leaving himself plenty of time to remain involved in Connaught's affairs as a member of the board of directors.

Hampson was replaced by Bernard Isautier, a French import who had arrived at CDC when it purchased Aquitaine. He was less the freewheeling visionary and more the analytical professional manager.[10] Hampson, however, stayed on the Connaught board. That gave him a front-row seat for the fun still to come. He had an idea how some of it would unfold. He knew, for instance, that in April 1986, Brian King had received a telephone call from Jacques Martin at France's Institut Mérieux.

Mérieux had been for most of its life a family-owned company, founded as a serum producer in 1897 by Marcel Mérieux, a student of Louis Pasteur. His son Charles moved the company into veterinary medicine and expanded abroad, and Charles's son Alain oversaw the sale of the company to Rhône-Poulenc, which was in turn nationalized by the French government. But the family still owns 20 percent of the company and Alain Mérieux remains a very active chairman, as well as being an important voice on the board of Rhône-Poulenc.

Mérieux's vaccine sales were concentrated in France, where regulations allowed it to dominate its domestic market, and in the developing world. It had virtually no presence in North America. And since sales sponsored by UNICEF and the World Health Organization in Africa, South America, and Asia don't allow for much in the way of profits, Mérieux knew that it had to

---

10 Isautier eventually sold many of CDC's holdings and the government sold off its entire holding in CDC. Renamed Polysar Energy and Chemicals Ltd., it was taken over by Nova Corp. in a bloody 1988 battle.

gain that foothold in the United States market. As well, its protected status in France was about to disappear because of European integration. Connaught looked like a likely answer to Mérieux's problems.

King had certainly heard of Martin, but the two had never met.[11] Martin said he was coming to North America and wanted to meet with King in Toronto to discuss the way the industry was heading. At first, the pair did just that. "It was quite clear to both of us that the research stakes in this business were escalating rapidly," says King. "You had to have a global orientation and could not research and develop products on the basis of small, domestic markets. And we agreed that both of us were faced with competitors many times larger than ourselves, who have significant resources to draw on from their parent companies."

Now they were getting closer to the bone. They did talk about the potential for collaboration. King insists, however, that the conversation didn't amount to much. Not then. But Mérieux's interest was clear. The link was a natural one in Mérieux's mind, if not so clear to King.

Still, like Mérieux, Connaught began doing its own thinking about strategic alliances. It had to. Around the world, companies were taking their first steps toward alliances — or outright mergers. This would result, in the next few years, in mega-mergers such as the one between Beecham Group PLC of Great Britain and SmithKline Beckman Inc. of the United States in 1989 or the merger of E.I. Du Pont de Nemours and Company's pharmaceutical and radiopharmaceutical businesses into a joint venture with Merck and Company, one of the world's largest pharmaceutical companies. Research costs were driving the mergers: the new Du Pont-Merck company had a 1990 research budget of $230 million.

Ever since the tragedy of the thalidomide babies, born between 1959 and 1962, product testing standards had been steadily raised. Testing costs, however, were only part of the research cost spiral. They combined with the cost of biotechnology and the difficulty in finding unique new products to ensure that fewer innovations survived the development stage to become marketable products.

Connaught, then, was facing rapidly increasing costs, a move to fewer, bigger competitors, and increased competition for fewer products — as its major shareholder was pulling away. And it couldn't expect the type of patient support that CDC had provided from small shareholders. Connaught needed another backer with deep pockets and lots of patience if it

---

11 Martin is a Rhône-Poulenc career executive who was parachuted into Mérieux in 1976.

was to survive as an independent company. But all the major Canadian pools of capital had already turned it down flat.

And even with such a backer, Connaught needed a partner with whom to share some of the costs of product development. In February 1987, the board pushed King for an intensive strategic overview. Part of that was a profile of what Connaught would want from any potential partner, including a wish list of names. "We sent the management out to start talking with some of them about whether there was anything we might do together," says Hampson. "But we were not soliciting a takeover. Rather the reverse. We were trying to avoid a situation where at some point we would be so close to running out of funds—and, more importantly, product—that we would kind of have to lie down by the roadside looking seductive and say to the first passer-by, take me, take me."

The list included about eight smaller companies. The big ones, adds Hampson, "we knew would have an NIH syndrome—Not Invented Here—and not want to link up with us." Smaller companies, however, would be interested in Connaught's money and its marketing abilities, which it had now spent more than a decade developing. A few of the names on the list already had links with larger companies, but King and Cochrane thought there was still some room for another hookup. Although it was just as big as Connaught, Mérieux had already expressed interest, so it was naturally on the list as well. King and Cochrane talked to Martin again. But nothing gelled; the personalities and the corporate culture were too different, and there wasn't a particularly good product fit. "We didn't see a major link-up with Mérieux as being what we needed," says Hampson. "We were really looking for the more inventive, smaller companies."

One of those companies was California-based Chiron Corp., an innovative research lab with a specialty in genetic engineering. Chiron already had a link with Swiss firm Ciba-Geigy. But it said it might be interested in a project-based link with Connaught as well.

In the meantime, Connaught was preparing for CDC's final stock sale. On June 29, 1987, it concluded a private placement of stock with institutions, through American broker Goldman Sachs, of the remaining 25 percent of Connaught. The Caisse and Mérieux split the shares. Added to its earlier purchase, this gave the Caisse 19.3 percent of the company. Mérieux held 12.6 percent. Together, they had a controlling block of almost one-third of Connaught's stock (31.9 percent). "We did not want to be perceived as starting a takeover," says Mérieux's Michel Dubois. "That was absolutely not in the spirit of the investment. We just wanted to open the door for a constructive discussion. And this is why we looked for a Canadian partner." They even talked the strategy over with the head of Investment Canada, who actually suggested the Caisse.

But they couldn't have made a worse choice if they were really trying to make management and other investors feel secure. Recalls King: "So in the middle of 1987, we were sitting there with three quite successful businesses [Connaught, Bio-Research, and Nordic], and as shareholders we had the Caisse and we had Mérieux, one of our erstwhile competitors. And no CDC."[12]

In July, King and Cochrane spent time talking with Mérieux's Jacques Martin and others at Mérieux. This was very different from their earlier set of meetings; Mérieux clearly had the upper hand now. Still, King said that while in principle he thought any investor with more than 10 percent of the company should have a board seat, he didn't want Mérieux on the board because of confidentiality problems. The Mérieux group readily agreed. They were trying hard to be friendly. After the French holidays in August, the two sides began another series of getting-to-know-you meetings on both sides of the Atlantic. "To their credit," says King, "they did not push to exercise their rights." Of course, he adds, "time was on their side."

As a result of the 1987 strategic review, Connaught's board agreed that although the firm's R&D spending had jumped 50 percent during the past two years to 17 percent of sales—much higher than the industry average—it still needed to increase R&D levels to survive. "The level of competition that was occurring in vaccine research was escalating dramatically," recalls King. "That was stimulated by changes occurring in molecular biology. And all the surveys showed very clearly that vaccine research projects had come from virtually nowhere over the previous five years to being the fourth or fifth largest area of research [by pharmaceutical companies]." All

---

12 He may not have had Big Daddy any more, but King still had a personal safety net to protect him: with the sale of the CDC's final 25 percent, the board arranged a termination agreement—the so-called "golden handshake"—for King. He says it would have been difficult to run the company if he had been worrying about his own future. The same obviously applied to his senior employees: in July 1987 and February 1988, similar agreements were made for a number of King's colleagues at the holding company and senior management at the other companies.

When King and other executives finally left in March 1990, the plans kicked in: King was to be paid his annual salary of $468,750 for three years and would also receive health and life-insurance benefits during that time. The estimated total: more than $2 million. It was a fortunate thing for him that he made the arrangements, as he was still unemployed in mid-1991 and had minor surgery earlier that year.

this research competition, of course, would mean commercial competition down the road, even if Connaught managed to do everything right. Because of its size and limited number of research projects, it would still be left in the dust by larger competition. An alliance was essential.

At the end of 1987, Connaught raised $100 million in the Eurobond market. Now it had the money to spend on an alliance or acquisition of a smaller biotechnology company. But it had to be a friendly investment, since it wanted the talent. Research is people, after all. The company they were most interested in was California-based Chiron. "They had got into bed with Ciba-Geigy in a joint venture," recalls King, "but we still thought in terms of their technology base and the quality of their science. It was in our interest to try and pursue that. And there was substantial interest on their side as well."

King was interested in Ciba-Geigy as well. Ciba and Chiron had no vaccine manufacturing operations and would have been a good fit with Connaught's product and marketing operations. Ciba, headquartered in Switzerland, already had Canadian operations, including 1,600 employees, in unrelated businesses. But they also saw the potential. And being Swiss, they were used to all manner of international alliances and operations. "We were well into [the talks]," recalls King wistfully, "at the time Mérieux and the Caisse made their bid for the company." Suddenly, Connaught was a takeover target. It would never again be completely in control of its future.

Brian King is still particularly incensed about the way that he heard Institut Mérieux was making a bid for control of his company. He had taken an early-morning flight to Montreal for a regular meeting with Bio-Research officials on the morning of April 28, 1988. "I got a phone call from an analyst whom I knew in New York," he recalls. "He said, 'Brian, what's the matter with your stock? It's stopped trading.' I said, 'What the hell?' It was 9:35, five minutes after the market opened. So I said, 'David, I don't know, but I'll find out.' And we immediately tried to get in touch with the TSE. It took us about twenty minutes to get hold of someone there and find out what was going on. It turned out that they had put the stop-trade on the stock because of a forthcoming announcement. I said, 'Thanks for calling me.' " The TSE lamely said they had tried the Toronto office, but King thought that a curious explanation, since the analyst had been patched right through to Montreal. "They told me eventually that Mérieux was making the announcement, and within minutes I found out that it was a partial bid in conjunction with the Caisse."

Mérieux was offering $32 a share for the 20 percent of Connaught stock it needed, together with the Caisse holding, to gain a 52.5 percent majority position. If the Caisse tendered its 19 percent holding to Mérieux, however, it would receive a special premium for its stock. A sweet deal all round — except for Connaught's minority shareholders. King had expected, of course, that there might be a further overture by Mérieux ever since their stock purchase the previous summer. But no one had expected this. King was still in the interminable discussions with Mérieux about what, if anything, they could do together. Now he had to deal with the Caisse-Mérieux alliance.

Dubois insists the partial offer wasn't meant to be a hostile bid. It was merely Mérieux's reaction to Connaught's plans. "You have to understand," he adds, "they started to look very aggressively for another partner." But it was hard to read it as anything other than a predatory move on Mérieux's part. Certainly, Connaught responded with the standard maneuvers of the takeover target. Hampson was outraged. "I think the Caisse's ethics weren't all that good," he says. Hampson emphasizes, however, that he doesn't feel that way about the two Caisse representatives on the Connaught board. "They acted, as far as I could tell, always as board members of Connaught, and not as emissaries of the Caisse. I think in some instances they were as surprised as the rest of us at some of the things the Caisse had done. Including this famous deal they did with Mérieux."

Hampson and others at CDC and Connaught suspected that the Caisse had made a secret side deal with Mérieux that would allow the Caisse to buy Connaught's two Quebec subsidiaries, Nordic and Bio-Research, once a Mérieux control position was established. A Caisse officer testified at a set of securities hearings into the offer that this wasn't true.

After a marathon ten-hour board meeting, the board naturally came down against the bid. The decision was unanimous—including the two Caisse representatives. The board felt that the Caisse had an advantage over other shareholders. The American shareholders were excluded from the offer altogether. And the board felt it wasn't enough money to pay for a controlling position in Connaught.

A lawyer for Connaught approached the Ontario Securities Commission and its Quebec counterpart claiming the bid was unfair because it didn't treat all shareholders equally. The two regulators held a three-day joint hearing into the bid in Montreal. After hearing both sides, they ruled against the Mérieux bid, agreeing that the Caisse was receiving preferential treatment.

Connaught couldn't go back to business as usual, however. As soon as the bid was thwarted, the Street began to rumble about a proxy fight at Connaught's annual meeting. By combining their votes and soliciting the stock proxies held by other institutions, Mérieux and the Caisse could have the board and management replaced with their choice of candidates. King and crew spent much of their time lining up the support of institutional shareholders such as the Ontario Municipal Employees Retirement fund, the Ontario Hospital pension fund, other pension funds, and large American investors such as Boston mutual fund Fidelity Investments and Fiduciary Trust of New York. By the day of the meeting, May 6, 1988, King was holding the proxies of twenty American and two dozen Canadian institutions. "We went into the meeting with a dominant number of proxies in support of the existing board and management."

Of course, all this wasn't helping Connaught with its problems of research and development and its need for competitive alliances. "From then on, the Street was wondering who was going to make a bid. And it was impossible to talk to anybody else about cooperative things," says Hampson. "Nobody wants to talk strategic alliances or cooperative research ventures with somebody when they don't know who is going to be the controlling shareholder. We went and saw a number of companies. But people would just simply say, 'Look, if SmithKline winds up as your controlling shareholder, I don't want to be involved because they're our competitors in some product lines.' The Mérieux thing distracted Brian's and the board's attention from thinking about those longer-term issues."

Although the smaller companies were too nervous to talk, the larger ones joined the list of potential acquisitors. "We received an absolute deluge of so-called white knights . . . which is a terrible misnomer, because most of them are crocodiles," says King. Connaught management met with seventy-two companies or groups interested in seeing what was in this tasty little takeover situation for them. Some King sought out; others simply showed up. "A huge number of them were lunatic, particularly the Canadian-originated ones," says King. "I had an absolute deluge of people who wanted to come and buy the company, and frankly they couldn't raise $5 million, let alone pay $800 to $900 million for the company." Nevertheless, King spoke to everyone who showed up at the door, although he was picky about who received financial information.

One last time, he went to talk to the big Canadian business names, looking for someone to make a hands-off investment in a large chunk of stock. But while Connaught was a much more successful company than it had been back in 1984, it was also much larger. "Frankly," King says, "we just couldn't get them comfortable with the business."

To handle all this activity, Connaught struck a special takeover review board committee, headed by ex-CDC head Hampson. The entire board was also briefed regularly about the various meetings. King, Hampson, and their coterie spent much of 1988 meeting and rejecting—or being rejected by—other companies. And they also began talking to Mérieux again.

Mérieux still wanted Connaught. Badly. Thwarted in the deal with the Caisse, Mérieux decided to come at Connaught another way. That summer, Jacques Martin approached Tony Hampson as head of the takeover committee. "He was claiming that he had been received in a hostile way by Brian King. And I told him quite frankly what the problems were." They included the rigid French governmental mindset that King and the others at Connaught believed they saw at Mérieux. Especially a lack of concern for minority shareholder rights. "I told him that we weren't going to go around behind Brian's back, that there was absolutely no reason to do so, and that if he wanted to talk to him to start things going again, that was fine with us, but it had to involve all the shareholders, it had to be fair to everybody. And that we preferred to keep our independence. But if they wanted to make a bid, we'd have to consider it seriously."

There had definitely been trouble between Martin and King. King attributes some of it to simple differences in corporate culture. "We were typically North American, we were driven by issues of shareholder value, our remuneration scheme was heavily oriented toward incentives for performance." Mérieux, in contrast, didn't have to worry about pushy shareholders or quarterly results. It had in Rhône-Poulenc a controlling shareholder and the legacy of beginning as a family business. "Mérieux derives a lot of its characteristics, its culture, from the legacy of the Mérieux family, obviously," says King. This gave them a good reputation and belief in their public health responsibilities. But it also meant they didn't have a professional management mentality.[13]

---

13 Although Martin was front and center in the bid for Connaught, CEO and 20 percent shareholder Alain Mérieux is at the heart of Mérieux—and on the board of Rhône-Poulenc as a government representative. "He's still the driving force, and the company takes a lot of its cultural and philosophical leadership from him," says King.

King had no choice but to be more willing to talk this time around. He hadn't found a Canadian source of capital, and he couldn't negotiate another alliance with the Caisse-Mérieux stockholding hanging over his head. Funnily enough, after being thought of as the enemy by Mérieux, he would work so closely with Martin and others at Mérieux during the next several months that he would eventually be condemned by analysts and competitors as being too closely aligned with the Mérieux forces. And King would say when all was signed and done: "On a personality basis, we were relatively compatible, even though I'm a wild colonial from Australia and he's from France."[14] He quickly adds a cautious note, however: "Don't get the impression it was a love-in or anything like that. We got along well together but we had some pretty heavy negotiations."

While King was negotiating with Mérieux, it looked at one point as though there might finally be an alternative buyer. The month after Martin's visit to Hampson's office, Hampson was told to expect another caller. This was one that Brian King would have welcomed with much more open arms. Ciba-Geigy of Basel, Switzerland, was about to bid $32 per share for Connaught. It was the Friday before the August long weekend in Ontario. But Ciba's executives and investment bankers never showed up. For some reason, they backed off at the crucial moment. It could have been that the executive in charge, who was near retirement, didn't want to recommend such a risky idea. Connaught never really knew why Ciba changed its mind.

All the others backed away as well. "Slowly but steadily," recalls King, "the lead candidates eliminated themselves for one reason or another." Then, in autumn 1988, Connaught gave Mérieux a wish list. King proposed that the two firms merge their vaccine operations. This idea was fundamentally different from Mérieux's original proposal, and Martin hadn't even wanted to discuss it at first. But by the end of the year he finally came back with a yes. The two firms would propose to shareholders that they merge the human health-care operations.[15]

The product overlap that had made the prospect of a Mérieux takeover particularly objectionable to King only a year earlier suddenly seemed a point in Mérieux's favor. King insists that the difference lay not in his desperation for a solution, but in the different opportunities offered by a straight merger of operations. Together, they could rationalize operations. And the overlap was mainly in Third World markets. Besides, he was proud of the negotiating job that he had done. "We drove an extremely hard

14 The control-driven, understated King is hardly anyone's idea of a wild colonial.
15 Mérieux also has veterinary vaccine operations; Connaught doesn't.

bargain on value," claims King. "Mérieux was a company of human health products with sales of $350 million, and ours were about $200 million, and we negotiated essentially equal value." They still had most of the details to work through when they announced the merger idea in March 1989. They went public because they believed that any extensive negotiations would soon become common knowledge. As King says, "Things leak."

He also labeled the eventual proposal "one of the most innovative share structures that has ever been created." Everyone else called it impossible to decipher. At 338 pages, it was too long and too repetitive. It involved a new parent company based in Holland, and tax laws in all three countries.[16]

There was also, finally, a dissenting voice on the Connaught board. Jim Gillies, former Conservative cabinet minister and professor of business administration at York University, refused to agree to the plan. "We were extremely surprised when Jim Gillies voted against the merger at the board," says King. "After a long, long board meeting, in fact two meetings, we finally put it to the vote, and his was the sole dissenting vote." Gillies even insisted that his opinion be included in the merger document. His was a nationalist position, but he also didn't believe that Mérieux was the best fit for Connaught, or that shareholders had enough financial information to make a decision. His stand gained a lot of attention in the press.

The anti-merger forces were against a high-technology company being sold in any way to a foreign group. They didn't want the company of Banting and Best to cease to be Canadian. But they didn't have a live Canadian bid. There was, however, one group that decided to try to take advantage of all this nationalist sentiment. And it had sympathetic ears in Ottawa.

Bob Church breaks into his busy day at the University of Calgary medical center to explain a bit of background about Connaught.[17] But first, a bit of background about Bob Church. He's the former president of the Calgary Stampede. A scientist. A doctor. A teacher. A venture capitalist and small business consultant. A horse man and a rancher. An old friend of Bill Cochrane's. And a former director of Connaught.

---

16 Chris Montague from McCarthy Tétrault was responsible for this wonder document.
17 ConnLab became CDC Life Sciences, then finally Connaught Biosciences when the company went public. Connaught Laboratories, the company Cochrane ran as chief executive officer, remained one of three Biosciences subsidiaries, together with Bio-Research and Nordic.

Church's story is complicated, like all conspiracy theories, but it boils down to this: he was the spokesman for a Calgary-based Canadian bid for Connaught. He lobbied for Alberta government money and he had support in Ottawa. His group planned to move much of Connaught's research and development facilities out to Calgary and sell off Connaught's valuable Toronto real estate to help finance the bid. And he had a few other backers.

But underneath all this neat planning, Church had a sub-agenda. He knew Connaught couldn't stay Canadian without an alliance. And he had good friends at Ciba-Geigy and Chiron, too. In fact, he planned all along to bring them in, about a year or so down the road. He mentioned that to his Alberta and federal government backers. "They knew about the alliance [idea]," says Church. "But it was never put on the table formally, because that makes it a foreign bid." Hampson, told of Church's "I-would've-brought-Ciba-in-all-along" story, smiles. "That to me just reflects his naïveté." Perhaps John Godfrey of the *Financial Post* said it best: "Big hat, no cattle." The Connaught board would have preferred a Canadian bid—but not if it meant breaking up the company. King and Hampson didn't meet with Church, but with others in his group. It was reportedly a curious mixture. "They were all shooters and developers and quick-buck artists and financial engineers," says Hampson. That comment, however, is rather too dismissive. Well-established business people both in Toronto and in Alberta were involved in the bid. Gerry Kendall of Calgary-based venture capital company VenTech Healthcare Ltd., was one of the bid's main supporters. (Bill Cochrane, who had stepped down as president in 1988, but who remained chairman of the board of Connaught Laboratories, was connected to VenTech. But he was not involved in the bid.) Peter Snucins of Toronto's Roy-L Merchant Group was quite public about negotiating with the group to provide financing. There was also talk of a Southeast Asian trading company. Toronto developer Rudy Bratty was called about the land, but that idea never really went anywhere. Besides, Hampson says, that would have raised only about $50 million in a $900-million bid.

Even the idea of moving Connaught raised complications. The facilities for a vaccine company must be kept running for two or three years until the product from the new facility is proven to be pure. Connaught looked at a move in the early 1980s and estimated it would cost about $250 million back then.

"He was always about to make a bid," says Hampson of Church, "and quite frequently we'd be told by management, 'He's called, he's going to come in at three in the afternoon, or two the next day,' " says Hampson.

"And then he'd cancel the meeting." Hampson does acknowledge, however, that Alberta took the group seriously. It considered participating, backed off, then contacted Hampson again. "The second time they sent around Preston Manning, who was then a management consultant, and one of his associates. And I said to him, 'Look, don't start this up again if you're going to come to another negative conclusion.'" They again assured Hampson they were serious. Again, nothing happened.

The board bent over backward for the Canadian group, King says, waiving financial capacity tests. "We put them in the category of the serious group, and while we couldn't get a clear view as to their financial capability, we thought, 'Well, they're Canadian, we'll give them legal time like everybody else,' and we went through a number of sessions with them . . . We disclosed an incredible amount of information on the activities of the company to them, as we did to all the others. They had complete and equal access." But King insists he never saw any evidence that the group had the money to buy Connaught. "I kept saying, 'Show me some evidence of financial credibility.' And it was always, 'Oh, we're going to do this . . .' It was all hot air. I wanted to see some tangible evidence."

Needless to say, the Alberta group didn't like Brian King. They claimed they had support from former Connaught executives. King's reaction to that idea is swift: "Absolute eyewash." He had similar problems with the only other potential bidder ever mentioned, Quebec-based IAF BioChem, a company in which the Caisse held an interest. "They never did come and talk to us," says King. "They conducted their bid and their interest to the newspapers but not to us."

The Ontario government under David Peterson didn't like losing Connaught, but didn't see what it could do about it. It did, however, delay research funding from the Premier's Council until the matter was all sorted out. Connaught officials did what they could to ease relations; they met with Industry, Trade and Technology Minister Monte Kwinter and his deputy Peter Barnes. But David Peterson, who publicly agonized over the sale, didn't want to meet with King and Connaught forces. They met with a couple of his aides, who asked lots of questions but gave nothing away. "Clearly," says King, "[the company] was a subject of intense assessment and intense debate and, I think, differing points of view within government." Still, he was surprised by the fierceness of Peterson's viewpoint. Hampson didn't take it seriously; in his opinion, Peterson was merely "playing politics." For a time, Peterson talked of setting up a pool of capital like Quebec's Caisse, but that idea faded. There were also stories that he was meeting with the Canadian bidders. "If there had been a Canadian buyer, he might have come up with the last $25 million to make it fly," shrugs Hampson. "Who knows?"

Meanwhile, federal bureaucrats were watching the merger negotiations with Mérieux closely. It's the job of the director appointed under the Canada Business Corporations Act to ensure that shareholders are treated properly. But it's usually only a formality. This was not the case with Connaught. "The director of the CBCA got involved in this one heavily, heavily, to the point where frankly I thought it was almost politically motivated," says King. He quickly adds that he's not talking politicians but small-p politics, the interpersonal and interdepartmental squabbles that riddle the bureaucracy. "It seemed almost as if there were various people in the bureaucracy who said, 'Gee, we don't like this transaction, we're going to make it difficult.' "

A few western politicians had their own problems. They were being pressured by the Church group. Harvie Andre was in a particularly difficult situation. As minister of Industry, Science and Technology, he heard from the research community. As minister responsible for Investment Canada, he was in charge of the review of the proposed merger with Mérieux. And as a politician from Calgary, he had personal ties to consider.

"Fundamentally, he's an economic nationalist on this issue," says King. "I met Harvie probably three or four times. He listened to my assessment of the situation, he asked questions, he kept his counsel." He was skeptical, King recalls, but trying hard to be impartial.

Luckily for Andre, in the end no Canadian group ever made a bid. As for Church's idea about an alliance with Ciba-Geigy, he did end up joining Ciba's Canadian board of directors. But he was finessed out of any bid he may have been contemplating. Because on September 15, 1989, Ciba made a $30-a-share all-cash bid for Connaught. It was late on a Friday afternoon, after the markets closed. King was in his office with his managers, preparing to meet investors the following week on his final road show for the proposed Mérieux merger. When they heard the news, there was "a collective sigh of resignation." King says he had to ask himself in wonder, "Why did they go away in 1988? But the world changes for everybody."

That was the end of the Mérieux-Connaught human vaccine merger. Mérieux went off on its own to nurse its wounds and reflect. A week later,

Mérieux was back. King encouraged it to make a higher bid. It knocked everyone for a loop, however, by offering $37 per share cash on September 27. King's discussions with Ciba weren't as successful. They didn't raise their bid, although King suspects there was a real split in opinion at Ciba on how high it should bid.[18]

Ciba knew it couldn't win on price, so it tried to convince Investment Canada that it had a far superior bid for nationalistic reasons. Ciba's proposal to Investment Canada promised that Connaught would become the worldwide head of vaccine research. It was everything Connaught had wanted and needed. "That's what we saw when we were talking to Chiron way back in late '87 and early '88," King says. It was commonly agreed to be a better fit, but Connaught remained neutral. It told Investment Canada that both transactions would be of significant industrial benefit to Canada and would mean growth of research. That being the case, it added, the government should let the shareholders benefit. "There is no doubt in my mind that the fundamental science of Ciba-Geigy and Chiron is stronger," King said later. "But equally, there lies an opportunity for Connaught and Mérieux to merge and between them, they will be able to, by eliminating duplication, put money into fundamental science. And I think quite a lot of that will happen in Canada."

King had a feeling at times that the officials at Investment Canada were in over their heads with this one. "They asked for the same information two or three times in different ways. And we didn't actually feel that they knew exactly how to deal with what they got. Well, let's face it. They're called upon to assess business situations in so many different industries, they can't be experts in all of them."

Besides, Investment Canada had its own pressures. Both big- and small-p political. They knew about Andre's situation; they were hearing hostile noises from the Ontario government about any foreign takeover; Mérieux had Quebec support; and the University of Toronto weighed in for Ciba-Geigy.[19] There were even divisions within the government depart-

18 In the middle of all this, an ironic aside: Bill Ryder of Chiron had already been invited as a special guest speaker at a Connaught two-day scientific symposium to celebrate its seventy-fifth birthday. "We like Bill and have had great respect for him as an individual and a scientist," says King. "There's no reason you can't have that sort of thing and at the same time be involved in the commercial bid."
19 The University of Toronto launched a lawsuit against Connaught during the merger negotiations, claiming it held guarantees that Connaught would remain Canadian. It eventually backed away, after Mérieux guaranteed $15 million would be spent over ten years on research projects at Canadian universities—$9 million of that at U of T.

ments involved.

"I think there were two quite disparate factions up there [in Ottawa]," reflects King. "There was a lot of smoke up there and I presume where there's smoke there's fire. They [the bureaucrats] were very active in the Connaught thing, very." He points to a study by Boston Consulting Group on the potential sale of Connaught as proof that various bureaucrats were trying to influence Connaught's future course. The study, he says, "came out of the Ministry of Industry, Science and Technology—Andre's ministry. It wasn't Investment Canada. It wasn't a joint thing, it was driven by the ministry."

The consultants' report actually favored the Mérieux offer.[20] One objection in Ottawa, however, concerned Mérieux's government ownership. "Especially a government like France," says Hampson, "which has got a whisper in the ears of the directors any time there's a crucial decision to be made." Such as where to do research.

There are all sorts of rumors surrounding Investment Canada's final decision. "One can speculate as to how close the government did come to turning down Mérieux. If you believe some of the stories, they came very close," admits Hampson. "To me, it isn't fully credible, but you never know." François Mitterand is rumored to have talked to Brian Mulroney about the sale on a few occasions, including the 1989 Houston summit. "One heard these stories," recalls Hampson, "of three-to-three votes [at Investment Canada], and finally the Prime Minister's Office having to settle it."

On December 14, 1989, at 8:20 a.m., Brian King received the call from Investment Canada. It was none too soon; within twenty-four hours, both bids were due to expire. The government had decided both bids were good for Canada. It would come down to price and shareholders' choice. "I had a couple of my senior colleagues sitting with me, Norma Michael and Gerry Wood, as we had done every morning at that time for the past nineteen months. We kind of looked at one another, and I said, 'Thank God.' " Within two days, they would know. "We had been sitting on this knife edge for nineteen months." In the end, Ciba backed away. Hampson thought the Ciba bid was badly managed—it came in below the Mérieux partial bid, then Ciba was unwilling to raise its offer. "I think they botched it." In his

20 King is still bitter about getting the report from the press. It was delivered to news organizations in a plain brown wrapper, and he says he still doesn't know who leaked it. But Church always thought the Mérieux forces leaked the report, to damage his group's credibility.

opinion, it's because the man managing the bid for Ciba was retired at this point. "He had no motive to really win the deal. It wasn't going to augment his pension, and taking risks was perhaps something he didn't want to do. I mean, he was sixty-five and retiring. So they didn't top the bid."

For King, there was finally release. After the Christmas holidays came the transition. Mérieux closed Connaught's head office. King and his executives received their formal notice the third week in February 1990, although he continued to work on Nordic until July and is still a director of Bio-Research.

As for Ciba, Hampson estimates it could cost that company $250 million to build a vaccine marketing force and production facility from scratch — or another $40 a share. But it can also be argued that Mérieux paid too high a price for Connaught. Finally, Hampson weighs in with an ironic comparison of the two foreign and the putative Canadian bid: "It could be said for both Mérieux and Ciba that they were clearly in it for the long term. They weren't going to pay this kind of money just to break it up and sell the land and trade the scientists to the Montreal Canadiens, or whatever the scientific equivalent is."

The executives at Mérieux's corporate headquarters, a cluster of modern peach-colored brick buildings outside Lyons, France, were exhausted after the takeover. The merger had obsessed Mérieux executives and dominated the company's agenda for months on end. Jacques Martin told a reporter shortly after the battle ended that he wouldn't want to do it again. "From a personal perspective, if I had to start again it was too long. There was a total contradiction between the interest for the company and human limits. I found it all passionately interesting but very hard, too."

Six months later, the executive team had not yet recovered. Martin's right-hand man during the takeover, Michel Dubois, sat in an office still lined with the English documents detailing Mérieux's five-year pursuit of Connaught and admitted that he and his boss were finding it hard to look beyond the deal. In his mind, Connaught was a night-time pursuit; night flights across the Atlantic, nights spent in front of those files sorting through the legalities and the politics and the money. "Five years," he sighs. "To achieve an objective which was shared by the management of the two companies from the beginning. Five years which cost a lot in legal fees, money which could have been invested in research and development. And five years during which the two companies wasted a lot of attention on side issues, instead of on really strategic issues."

This is worrisome. Mérieux can't afford an exhausted executive suite. They must be ready to make crucial decisions on research and development. There is an opportunity for expansion to North America; but there is also a challenge from other companies eager to capitalize on European integration. That's why Mérieux's 51-percent owner, Rhône-Poulenc, has recently bought Rorer in the United States. While Mérieux was pursuing Connaught, Rhône was designing an international corporate strategy that included pharmaceutical and biologicals.

Martin and Alain Mérieux are both worried about increasing their research efforts. Even as he was buying Connaught, Martin admitted, "I'm not convinced that this merger will be enough." In December 1989, as the merger closed, Alain Mérieux concurred in an interview with *Le Monde*. R&D spending at Mérieux rose to 18 percent of sales in the first half of 1989, he said; R&D would remain a problem. "That's a very high figure, and one we can only just support."

The increased research will be done in good part in Canada. As part of its commitment to spend $160 million on research and development in Canada by 1994, Mérieux has made Connaught's Willowdale headquarters the North American center for testing and production of the experimental anti-AIDS drug HIV Immunogen. Human testing will begin in 1992. Connaught is spending $2 million to convert its old blood plasma plant to test the drug. Immunogen, like the polio vaccine that was once one of Connaught's major products, was developed by American biologist and inventor Dr. Jonas Salk; Mérieux bought the development rights.

There are other links to Connaught's past as well: joining Mérieux executive and new Connaught Laboratories chairman Georges Hibon on the board[21] of the Canadian subsidiary are a couple of familiar faces: Bill Cochrane and former University of Toronto president John Evans, the man who sold Connaught to the CDC.

Yet Mérieux is viewed in Canada as a heartless predator, the company that stole a national treasure. Martin now realizes this was partly Mérieux's fault—its initially hostile offer for part of the company only set it up as the bad guy. "I think the one error we made was to consider Canada like the United States, that business is business, whereas the truth is that, in your country, business is first politics," added Martin. "It is a smaller world,

---

21 Connaught is now the Canadian subsidiary of the renamed Pasteur-Mérieux.

where everybody knows one another and where influence is sometimes unofficial."

Mérieux isn't, however, making that mistake any more. As part of the $29 million that it committed to spend on vaccine research—including the AIDS drug—it has gained government support and funding. And it is trying hard to fit into the Canadian community.

It could have been a company picnic. Staff lounged around the grass in shorts or sun dresses, happily enjoying the hot 10 a.m. sun and lining up for coffee and doughnuts being served under a blue-and-white-striped marquee. A podium was set up to distribute prizes, and there were about sixty white plastic chairs ranged around the suburban North York grounds of Connaught Biosciences. But on second glance, it was clear there were too many suited dignitaries gathered for this to be a simple corporate fun day. Visitors' tags were prominently displayed and there were a lot of cameras and notebooks hanging out. The staff had been invited along, but this was a media event: press conference, tour, and luncheon for municipal officials, university types, and Ontario government reps.

There was a different type of three-legged race on the program as well. Government, academia, and the business of scientific research were invited to step up to the podium. The matter drawing them together this June day in 1990 was some pre-election, pat-on-the-back money. Monte Kwinter, Ontario minister of Industry, Trade and Technology, handed over $13.9 million from the Premier's Council research fund for university-linked projects by Connaught. This was money Connaught had been waiting for while its fate was being decided. Not a huge amount, but happily received by two newly appointed university presidents, Rob Prichard of the University of Toronto and Geraldine Kenney-Wallace of McMaster. Connaught executives Peter Martin (one of the few from King's team still in place) and Georges Hibon (in for the occasion from Lyons to represent Mérieux), were ready to join in the mutual back-slapping as well. No one mentioned the recent discord among government, Connaught, and U of T.[22] Instead, everyone talked about the benefits of cooperation; the long research record of both Connaught and Mérieux. And everyone was careful to mention the Pasteur-Mérieux "family of companies."

Later, Hibon and Kwinter were chatting amicably while posing for a

---

22 In fact, the university and Mérieux were still negotiating the legal wording of their $15-million research agreement. By July 1991, the agreement had not yet been signed.

camera shot. Hibon casually mentioned the check. Kwinter just as casually answered, "It's in the mail." It's a good thing. Connaught, even as part of Mérieux, needs to spend as much money as possible on research. Hampson notes, "We were spending something like $30 million on research the last year at Connaught. Almost three times the total sales when we bought it. You've got to allow for inflation, but it was still a sizable percentage of sales. . . . When we started, the conventional wisdom was to take five years and $25 million to bring a product to market. It went through seven years and $50 million, then $75 million, then ten years and $100 million, now I've seen numbers like $150 million-plus."

He thinks Connaught now needs to double its research spending, just for starters. "At a hundred million a pop, looking over ten years, if you were spending $30 million a year you could, in theory, have only three major projects going. Which isn't enough." Dubois is blunt (and of course self-serving) in his assessment of Connaught's prospects on its own: "It did not have the size to keep up. And it didn't have the money." Still, the trouble with Connaught was not simply size or capital. It was also whether it had the ability to come up with the innovations. It was not a fundamental research firm; at its best, it did good applied research. In its last days as a U of T lab, as Hampson points out, "what they were doing wasn't even really that."

Connaught overcame many obstacles in the intervening years. It became a profitable organization and successfully expanded into the United States market. But it needed that link to an innovative group of scientists. That doesn't mean it needed a takeover. Ideally, it would have been better for the firm to arrange for R&D projects with a company like Chiron.

So much for rewriting history. Now, with more money and an increased size, Mérieux is pursuing both European and North American markets and pushing for international patents on its products—Connaught's in Europe, Mérieux's in North America. There could also be another twist: some sort of alliance between the biologicals company and pharmaceutical company Rorer, as a result of Rhône-Poulenc's 1990 purchase of the American pharmaceutical giant. There are certain interesting fits between the two firms. Rorer owns a company called Armour, which does a big blood fractionization business. This would take Connaught right back to the old days of supplying blood for the Red Cross. But combining Rorer's operation with Mérieux's blood-protein business would create a worldwide competitor in this one area. Just the sort of strategy a global company like Rhône-Poulenc should be following.

We shouldn't lose sight, however, of the fact that Rhône-Poulenc is controlled by the French government. Connaught had no control over the Rorer purchase; its future is in Rhône's hands. And Connaught could never have bought Mérieux; the French government wouldn't have allowed it. Ciba-Geigy is also protected by government restrictions on its takeover. As Canadians, we need to ask ourselves whether we need similar rules about certain types of industries, the same kind of protection we have for cultural industries. Not a FIRA-style lock on the nation's assets, but stricter rules about foreign ownership.

If we make these rules, however, we have to be ready to support those companies. Without the money to do research and especially to test new products, Connaught couldn't have survived as a Canadian company. "I was disappointed as a Canadian," says Cochrane in retrospect. "I would have loved to have Connaught stay in Canadian hands." But that is, as Jacques Martin would say, the emotional side. Looking beyond that to the facts, Cochrane is blunt: "By God, if Canadians aren't willing themselves to put their bloody money in, then the only way enterprises are going to survive is by going somewhere else to find the dough." If restrictions of takeovers don't allow that, he adds, entrepreneurs will simply close up shop and move.

"For two years the nationalists grumbled that we can't lose this jewel. I'd turn to them and say, 'How many shares have you got?' They didn't have any. So I'd tell them, 'What you're after is a wonderful big building with a Canadian flag on top—but it will be totally empty.'"

Connaught followed a number of paths during its seventy-five-year history. A university research lab; a crown corporation; a publicly traded company; and now a multinational subsidiary. Each has reflected the mood of the times. But so far, each finally has had flaws. Dubois says it will now take "another century" to build the new company. Let's hope, for the sake of the research money that Mérieux is still funneling through Canada, that this time the result is worth the effort.

CHAPTER FOUR

Family Matters

The elevator doors whisked open to reveal an opulent penthouse salesroom that Olympia & York had outfitted in their Great George Street offices in the City of London. Michele Julian appeared, a Sloane Ranger or near facsimile. In fact, she looked so much like Princess Di that I did a double take. I came to think of her as Di as she toured me around her Lilliput version of the Reichmann's Canary Wharf development site.

We weren't actually at Canary Wharf. It was still under construction in the London Docklands area in May 1990, when Di and I did our private tour. To show prospective tenants and curious journalists what a wonder Canary Wharf would be once the first phase of the project was finished, O&Y used mock-ups. The scope was impressive: two dozen buildings on seventy-one acres, with parks, courtyards, plazas, and a half-mile-long waterside promenade. Ten million square feet of offices—7 percent of the total office space available in all of London. Restaurants. Shopping. A hotel. Research facilities. Parking for 6,500 cars. To start, eight buildings were rising even as we gazed at their tiny counterparts. They accounted for $3 billion of the estimated $7 billion being spent on the project. Phase One was to be completed by mid-1991; the second phase by mid-1993; the final phase of the project by the end of the century.

O&Y's miniature sales models had all the latest gizmos, including different colored lights for the different public transit routes. The British government is chipping in for those, to the tune of £3 million (close to $6 million Cdn.). A river bus is already in operation. A light rail transit system is being built to connect with a 1995 extension to the London Underground. There's also a new conventional rail tunnel and connection set for mid-1993 completion.

Of course, all these new transit lines were needed because Canary Wharf is way off the beaten path, three miles east of the Bank of England and the core financial district, known as the City. For early tenants who must ride the Underground to work before all the new rail lines are in place, that's a lot of traveling, even though a Peat Marwick study done in February 1990 claimed that it takes only about eleven minutes to travel to the docklands from Bank Station and twenty-seven minutes from Waterloo.

I remained skeptical, however, about the company's ability to attract these pioneer tenants, given the additional Tube time required for the ordinary office worker. Di wasn't particularly sympathetic; it turned out that she never took the Tube. My concern about the traveling time, however, was not unusual; it was the question everyone asked about the project. But it implied a larger question: do the Reichmanns know what they are doing in London? I had another question in mind as well: what did the Reichmanns' investment strategy at Canary Wharf and elsewhere mean for Canada?

The Reichmanns believe that they are the world's best landlords. Canary Wharf, then, is to be the best of the best. It must be; it is their biggest move yet. And this is real estate, their forte; they will have no excuses if it is not a resounding success. It's also arguably the most high-profile foreign investment of any Canadian group.[1] The entire Canary Wharf development, in fact, goes beyond a mere business decision. It is empire building. It even sounds a bit like one of those grand visions pharaohs and kings used to have. This time the empire builders were Margaret Thatcher and Paul Reichmann.

Soon after my visit to O&Y's London offices, Thatcher resigned, brought down by a party revolt against her rigid opposition to economic integration with the European Community. The question remains whether Reichmann can pull off this fantastically large and complicated urban renewal project, or whether he would join Place Ville-Marie's Bill Zeckendorf and so many other builders and dreamers as someone whose reach has exceeded his grasp.

Still, there are arguments in its favor. More than half the existing London office space is outdated. Canary Wharf is only eleven minutes from a commuter airport for managers who make frequent trips to Europe. O&Y

---

1 The competition for that title includes Bob Campeau's disastrous United States retail purchases, and McDonald's of Canada's Moscow restaurant.

can offer better conditions for less money, because of tax breaks. The Reichmanns acknowledge the risks involved, but feel they're more than equal to it. In fact, the Reichmanns can't understand the buzz against the project. The family has come to believe that there is a conspiracy among the traditional office landlords to mount a whisper campaign against them. The reasons are obvious, particularly since other buildings are also rising in London, during a time when most firms in the City have slashed staff. The rents at Canary Wharf are designed to be lower than those in the City. But the Reichmanns are cutting even those low rental fees, according to the competition. Canadians have to be concerned about whether Canary Wharf has been draining money from other Reichmann operations.

During 1990, the whispers about the Reichmanns grew louder, and they were no longer just about Canary Wharf. In the wake of the stock market crash and a real estate bust in the United States that became very public with the collapse of the savings and loan industry in the late 1980s, people began questioning the Reichmanns' other real estate holdings, including those in New York, the properties that had made their reputation.

Financial vultures even began speculating that it was New York that would be the Reichmanns' undoing. After all, the financial frenzy that had made the World Financial Center and all their other buildings hubs of activity was gone, gone, gone. This came home to O&Y when junk bond financier Drexel Burnham Lambert went belly-up and left them with an empty building. O&Y's entire office building strategy, which had been based on owning clusters of towers in financial centers, was questioned.

Toronto wasn't in great shape, either. And O&Y's practice of investing in other real estate companies had begun to backfire. In 1989, they twice walked away from a deal to buy Bell Canada's real estate subsidiary, BCED. They were right; BCED's portfolio in the United States was collapsing as values plummeted south of the border. But it made them look hesitant, unsure of themselves. During 1990, they also had trouble with Trizec's investment in developer Bramalea Ltd. Bramalea had made some unwise investments that involved big writeoffs, and the CEO was pushed aside. The public became aware that the Reichmanns weren't infallible after all.

The much bigger public relations problem, however, was Campeau Corp. Robert Campeau had cultivated Paul Reichmann during the 1980s, and O&Y held a small investment in his company. When Campeau bought Allied Stores and moved into United States retailing, he offered Reichmann half of his Toronto bank-tower-in-progress, Scotia Plaza. Reichmann bought and also bought more stock and debentures in Campeau Corp. Then Campeau bought Federated Department Stores as well, and Reichmann helped finance that purchase by buying debentures in Campeau Corp. He wasn't, however, told all the arrangements of other financings. That would later lead to trouble.

When Campeau's junk bond-financed empire began to unravel, Reichmann had to choose between stepping in to try to protect his investment, or walking away. He took another step forward. Wrong move. In 1989, Reichmann provided interim financing backed by Campeau's half of Scotia Plaza and other Canadian real estate assets. Reichmann also arranged for a new board, with Lionel Dodd (the chief operating officer at Olympia & York) as head of restructuring. In early 1990, O&Y decided Campeau should go into Chapter Eleven in the United States and fought with Campeau himself over the Canadian operation. Campeau was pushed out of the company completely by the fall of 1990. But the Reichmanns were caught in the middle, as both shareholders and debt holders. This damaged their credibility. And given the high-risk nature of the Canary Wharf development, they needed people to believe in their acuity at this particular time.

It all came back to Canary Wharf. If people believed the project was turning into a success, they would again lavish praise on the canny Reichmanns. The image would be intact. But if they thought the project was turning into a real boondoggle, the entire Reichmann empire would continue to be under attack from the gossip mongers.

And in London, the talk hadn't stopped by mid-1991, when the first tower was up and the first stage almost completed. Tenants included Morgan Stanley, the Reichmanns' investment banker; Crédit Suisse-First Boston, the firm that handled Campeau's Federated Stores purchase; Texaco; and Conrad Black's *Daily Telegraph* newspaper.[2] Paul Reichmann didn't understand why questions were being asked about the project's future. Sure, Merrill Lynch had backed out, and Morgan Stanley, Crédit Suisse-First Boston, and others had decided not to make an actual investment in the project, but to remain simply as tenants. And although the first tower was three-quarters leased, that was less than the 85 percent that Reichmann had been assuring people would be filled in the first tower by

2   The Reichmanns bought Black's *Daily Telegraph* building in the City as part of the deal; Black made an $18.6-million profit on the arrangement.

this time. But considering the global recession and London's post-stock-market-crash financial industry depression, they had done well. Now that all the expensive infrastructure elements—transportation routes, sidewalks, sewers, and the like—were in place, the rest of the development would be less risky to proceed with.

Reichmann cared, however, what people thought. Canary Wharf must be considered a success before more tenants would sign up. And the Reichmann reputation was at stake. While the Reichmanns had always cultivated a reputation for secrecy, they had successfully dealt with the press for years, picking their spots and their interviewers in order to set out their viewpoint on takeovers and property dealings.[3]

In mid-1991, that strategy led to an exclusive for *Financial Post* columnist Diane Francis, Peter C. Newman's competitor for the title of best-known Canadian business journalist. Francis had built on her reputation as the writer of "The Insiders" column in the *Toronto Star* and later the *Financial Post* (where she was named editor in mid-1991) and the *Toronto Sun*, with almost daily television or radio appearances and a best-selling book on Canadian family fortunes.[4] By 1991, Francis had shifted her focus to more issues-oriented pieces, but she is still always on the alert for the Big Interview. Francis had initiated the contact; she knew Paul Reichmann on a first-name basis and was tracking down the latest round of anti-Canary Wharf gossip.

Reichmann admitted to being steamed about the chatter and agreed to an interview. But he was off to London the next week. That was fine, said Francis; so was she. They met on Sunday, May 26, at the London Reichmann offices and continued their discussion over a two-and-a-half-hour lunch. Then Francis toured the site with Peter Marano, the project's leasing manager. She had arrived an ardent Reichmann fan; she came away impressed with the project and ready to take on the nay-sayers.

While she was there, Francis made sure that she asked all the right questions about the family's strategy for the future. The Reichmanns had just sold Consumers Gas in Canada, as well as their 10 percent holding in Britain's Allied Lyons food and beverage conglomerate. And Paul Reichmann told Francis the family was considering selling Home Oil and their stake in Interprovincial Pipeline—if the price was right. But they were

3 Peter Foster documents this press strategy in his book *The Master Builders: How the Reichmanns Reached for an Empire*, Key Porter, 1986.
4 *Controlling Interest: Who Owns Canada*, Macmillan, 1986.

hanging on to Gulf Canada and paper company Abitibi-Price. Reichmann told Francis that while O&Y is a multinational company, "we are a Canadian family. We're staying in Canada."

All this is important to the Reichmanns and their executives, not to mention their bankers, the other property developers who depend on their stability in setting prices for their individual markets, and their employees—nobody wants to see jobs lost. The average Canadian, however, is worried about recession and taxes and job security, and when he or she has time to look beyond that, is scared about the potential disintegration of our country. How will the decisions taken by the wealthy Reichmanns about their holdings and their heirs affect the life of the average Canadian? Why do the Reichmanns matter at all to the rest of us?

For one thing, it matters how they spend their billions, because if their money is spent in Canada, that helps all of us. But we can't assume that just because they're headquartered in Canada, they're automatically better owners than foreigners are. Or that their corporate goals jibe with the public policies that best serve Canada.

It would surely matter to all of us if the Reichmanns were ever to falter or fail; such a business catastrophe would mean lost jobs and the Canadian banks and insurance companies that had lent them money would suffer. And a Reichmann collapse could happen only if the North American economy was so bad that they couldn't find tenants to fill their buildings at a profitable rent—which would mean that our entire economy would be on the brink of collapse anyway.

But it also matters to us what the Reichmanns do with their money when they're doing well; how they invest it, how committed they are to continuing to invest in Canada, and what type of investment they do within the country. The traditional criticism of foreign investors in Canada has been that they merely want to grab our resources, not to build businesses that benefit the economy as a whole with research and development, training, and a climate of investment and innovation. They don't, in effect, invest in the development of a prosperous community.

Multinationals have had a sorry record in this regard. But Canadian-based businesses also have a lot to answer for. And a good proportion of the pools of capital in this country are controlled by family groups. In fact, a look at the Reichmanns says a lot about the structure and very nature of business in Canada, and about the link between Canadian ownership of businesses and a commitment to the economic success of the Canadian community.

*

The Reichmann mystique is Canadian at its heart. It has been called the country's most influential family, but that family is defined by what it is not: it is not part of the Toronto social establishment, nor the Canadian Jewish establishment. The Reichmanns would have trouble, with their immense holdings and huge influence in business spheres, leading such a detached existence in the United States. In that sense, their Canadian headquarters insulates them from the pressures of living in a city like New York or London. This is the ultimate Canadian immigrant family, refusing to be integrated into the melting pot, insisting on its place in the Canadian mosaic.

We usually hear of the three Reichmann brothers, Albert, Paul, and Ralph. But they are the three youngest of the late Samuel and Renée Reichmann's six children. Brother Louis lives in New York and brother Edward in Israel; neither is close to the Canadian contingent. Their late sister Eva was more involved with the younger trio, and her children are looked upon as potential inheritors. The family was in the egg business in Austria and Hungary in the 1920s and 1930s, emigrated to Morocco via France and Spain, and eventually moved to New York and Toronto in stages in the late 1950s. They were in the tile business by this time and started a tile company in Toronto—Ralph, who is fifty-eight, still runs the tile business.

Albert, sixty-two, and Paul, sixty-one, are O&Y Developments, the private O&Y real estate company and O&Y Enterprises, their investment holding company. Albert is known for his commonsense approach to business. Author Walter Stewart, loitering in the Reichmanns' lobby in 1979, heard a New York business acquaintance prepare an associate for a meeting: "This is a most unusual man you're going to meet," he said of Albert Reichmann. "I've been dealing with these people for four years, and he operates without contracts. He'll just shake hands, but he'll never double-cross you. And he'll never make a mistake about what was agreed. When these people built the Shell Centre in Calgary, it was three-quarters done before there was a contract. We did a $60-million deal in New York and never a difference of opinion. These are very efficient people."[5]

But it is Paul, the Talmudic scholar and former teacher, who has earned a special brand of reverence from the business community for his quick wit and sharp sense of judgment. O&Y's Lionel Dodd singles out Paul

---

5 From "Good and Rich" by Walter Stewart, *Weekend Magazine*, October 13, 1979.

Reichmann's strategic abilities. "The outside world, as highly as they think of him, underestimates the strengths." Paul took his brothers into the development business by building the tile company's warehouse. In 1965 they built their first highrise office; in 1969 they officially formed O&Y Developments; and in 1974 they began work on one of the tallest buildings in North America, the Bank of Montreal's First Canadian Place in Toronto.

Then they turned their attention to New York, with the legendary 1977 purchase of eight buildings in Manhattan for U.S. $320 million. At that point, the family needed a public face. Paul took on that role. His mid-European inflections accented the developing Reichmann aura of mysterious infallibility. Their orthodox approach to Judaism, for example, became a symbol of high morals and good faith in business dealings. It also set them apart as people who would do business their own way; business stories always mentioned the kosher dining room and the fact that they didn't work on any Jewish holidays—but did work on Sundays.

Their private life, while at first well shielded from the press, was occasionally revealed in tantalizing glimpses. They have built a private *schul,* or temple, for their daily worship; they are quiet benefactors of charities both in Canada and abroad (they built a U.S. $65-million civic center in Jerusalem through Ron Engineering International, and Albert Reichmann spearheaded a relief drive for earthquake victims in Armenia in December 1988; together with Campeau and Edward DeBartolo, the family donated $400,000). Paul has also been shown to possess a few very human pretensions. He rented a suburban Toronto Four Seasons hotel for the day when his daughter was married a few years back and flew in guests from around the world. The estimated price tag: $1 million. In recent years, he has also battled with neighbors on his North Toronto street over the inconvenience caused by construction delays on a major home expansion and the size of the granite curb at its entrance.

The Reichmanns have made it clear, however, that they will not tolerate incorrect information about their private lives. In the most high-profile and certainly the most expensive libel suit in Canadian history, the Reichmanns sued *Toronto Life* magazine for $102 million after a 1987 article speculated about their pre-Canadian family history. *Toronto Life* ran out of its million dollars in libel insurance in mid-1990, by which time the Reichmanns had spent at least $3 million in private investigators' fees alone. The magazine eventually ran a full-page apology and donated money to charities to settle the suit. The lawsuit introduced Canadians to the term "libel chill" and provoked heated discussions about the power of the wealthy to control what is written about them. This is a particular worry in Canada because its underdeveloped economy is dominated in many respects by a few powerful families.[6]

Still, aside from how rich or poor they actually are, there's very little controversy about the family. They do their business well; they avoid the party circuit; they give to charity and have a strong moral base. If they want to keep to themselves, that's fine. Besides, no matter how aloof they are, the Reichmanns can't escape the fact that their place in Canadian society links them to the other dominant business families. They are set apart from the Establishment and they are at its pinnacle at the same time. When they adopt a course of action, to the average observer they represent the power of family money in Canada.

Family control of much of Canadian business is evident when we look at our stock market. For example, forty-seven of the largest one hundred publicly traded companies in Canada are controlled by only twenty-four families. And that doesn't include Conrad Black's Hollinger, Molson's, and others. It's estimated that three-quarters of the stocks on the TSE 300 are closely controlled—that is, more than 20 percent of the stock is held by one individual or group. A recent *Canadian Business* magazine "power list" of Canadian company heads was dominated by family names; thirty-nine of the fifty listed were either entrepreneurs or chief executives of family-owned companies.

The Reichmanns, although many of their real estate holdings are private, control about 5 percent of the index through their diverse holdings. While working for the Reichmanns in September 1987, Marshall (Mickey) Cohen told the *Globe and Mail* that "this is still an economy with a few large public companies. There's not a middle class in corporate Canada."

The Reichmanns are like many of the other families in the types of

---

6 Elaine Dewar's 55,000-word article, "The Mysterious Reichmanns: The Untold Story," ran in *Toronto Life* magazine in November 1987. The full-page apology and retraction included this statement: "The Reichmann family has earned an enviable reputation over the years, not only since coming to Canada but also prior to that in Tangier, Vienna and Hungary, as a family of great integrity and charity and adhering to strict ethical principles in all of its activities." Donations were made to the Hospital for Sick Children, Mount Sinai Research Institute, Toronto Hospital, and John P. Robarts Research Institute. A book that Dewar had written on the Reichmanns for Random House was canceled.

investments they have chosen to make in Canada. Like many foreign investors, Canadian family groups prefer tangible resources: real estate, oil and gas, forest products. The Reichmanns aren't interested in research and development or high technology. They aren't helping the Canadian economy develop in these crucial areas for future generations of Canadians. They're building their holdings for future generations of Reichmanns.

The dominance of a few families over Canadian business has, like the Reichmanns' omnipotence in business dealings, taken on a mystique that no longer reflects the reality of the marketplace. Studies are finding that business tycoons are less powerful than we once thought. Taxes and inflation have reduced their wealth and world events are well beyond their control these days. Pension fund money is also growing, essentially placing more and more power in the hands of the ordinary individual.

It's still true, however, that in relative terms the smaller Canadian economy gives a few families much more individual sway than they would have in the more diverse American economy, for example. Unfortunately, that influence hasn't been toward capital investment in the companies they control, but toward large dividends and financial maneuvers. One of the most popular Bay Street maxims of the 1980s was that companies had to "maximize shareholders' value." Translated, that meant pump out as much money as possible, as quickly as possible.

One of the reasons investors were so anxious about companies concentrating on profits is that Canadian companies have traditionally awarded investors with very high returns on their money. We didn't have much competition in this country, and we didn't spend money on our companies to keep them competitive. Foreign competition has meant that we had to do more of that in the 1980s—although we still didn't do enough.

So while Canada's corporate research levels, for example, are much lower than other countries', we continued to do nicely in the area of profits. Canada's pools of capital ranked second only to Germany's in the amount of value they gained during the past decade, in a survey of twenty leading industrial countries. Canadian corporate profits averaged 10 percent of our gross domestic product during the past decade; in the United States the average was only 7 percent. This number is even more interesting when we remember that commodity prices fell steadily for much of the 1980s—which placed resource-based Canadian companies at a disadvantage in profits. The money that was passed on to shareholders didn't come, then, from increased profits on resource sales. It came from reduced spending by companies on the company operations.

At the same time, Canadian family groups were forced by the commodity price plunge and by the increasing size of their holdings to move their trade and investments abroad, in order to maintain any growth and balance in their portfolios. This means that Canada's moneyed families are less and less Canadian in their business dealings. That's great for the families. And if it results in them coming back from their experiences abroad with a different outlook on how they should be running their Canadian companies in order to make them more productive and competitive, that would benefit the country. So far, however, it has only made them more disdainful of Canada's economic policies and more pessimistic about the country's future.

This detachment of wealthy families from their home community is heightened when Canadian families must make succession plans. A few years ago, the Bronfmans of Montreal had to decide on the future of their Seagram liquor empire. Two of Samuel Bronfman's four children had moved to the United States, and many of the company's operations are now run from New York. The family decided to sell its Canadian real estate company and distribute the proceeds to the heirs; an American pension fund picked up the company. Canadian business is being restructured by this sort of sale, whether it's Michael DeGroote's 1988 sale of his waste disposal and transport firm Laidlaw International to Canadian Pacific, or the Maclean family heirs' 1990 sale of Canada Packers to a British food company.

At times, governments have stepped in when they thought family interests were at odds with public policy goals. The Steinbergs sold their Quebec grocery chain to a local group backed by the province in 1989, after the Quebec government blocked a sale to Ontario interests. The Quebec government didn't need to make quite such a fuss about control of the business leaving the province. But it was right to recognize that when the family had to deal with its personal interests, it was up to the government to rule on whether those dovetailed with the public interest.

The Reichmanns fit into many of these trends: they're involved with resource-based companies; they have moved abroad; and they are facing decisions about succession. Their pattern of investing and building businesses in Canada during the past decade provides a good perspective on the patterns of Canadian family-controlled businesses—and what that has meant to the country.

*

New York was the scene for the Reichmann triumph of the 1980s, Battery Park City—also known, in developers' grand style, as the World Financial Center. Their canny purchase of the eight office buildings throughout Manhattan in 1977 had already made them minor heroes in New York because of their obvious faith in the city. This second move to build multi-stage new development made them lions of Wall Street. The financial boom of the 1980s was to prove them right—at least until the end of the decade. And the Reichmanns' Battery Park development meant they were able to capitalize on that boom. They broke ground in 1980; at 8 million square feet it was the largest private commercial property development ever. It would become the home of many of the financial giants of the 1980s, including junk bond kings Drexel Burnham Lambert.

Battery Park represented one of the two roads the Reichmanns would take in the 1980s: giant real estate projects outside of Canada, and within Canada, diversification outside real estate, mainly through the purchase of control blocks in public companies. That second string in their bow showed the Reichmanns are fallible. In hindsight, some of their company purchases could be viewed as a wrong turn into a blind alley. Still, their diversification out of real estate into public industrial companies has also made them some sizable profits at times. Between 1980 and 1985, their companies were only on par with the TSE index in their stock performance, but in 1986, their eight public holdings earned them a return of 32.3 percent, compared to an average return on the TSE that year of 5.7 percent. Too bad they didn't sell then; the next year their companies didn't do as well as the index.

The Reichmanns for the most part have chosen to diversify by buying companies where they felt that their financial expertise could make a lot of difference to the bottom line. When there were exceptions to their emphasis on resource companies, they were real-estate related: in 1978, they bought Vancouver-based real estate broker Block Brothers. In 1979, they bought the largest single interest in English Property, the third-largest British property company. The company also had a large interest in Calgary-based Trizec, controlled by the Bronfmans through Edper Enterprises. This led to a close working relationship between two of the wealthiest and most powerful of Canadian family groups.

In 1980, the Reichmanns made one of their worst-ever buys, 50.1 percent of petroleum and mining company Brinco. The company consistently lost money—and dragged down the performance of their entire stock portfolio until they sold it five years later at an 83 percent loss. A more interesting deal was an initial 9 percent purchase of Royal Trust in 1980, when the Reichmanns cooperated with some other Establishment groups to buy stock in Royal Trust during a takeover bid by Robert Campeau. Royal Trust later fell into the Edper Bronfman orbit, a second link between the two families. And because Paul Reichmann had contacted Campeau to tell him about the family's decision to purchase Royal stock, a relationship grew between the two developers.

The three companies that would become the cornerstone of their industrial holdings were purchased during the next five years: Abitibi-Price in 1981, for $537 million; Gulf Canada in 1985, when they paid $2.8 billion for 60 percent of the company; and Hiram Walker Resources in 1986 for $3.3 billion. Each had its measure of controversy; paper company Abitibi, because it was the first major non-real estate move by the Reichmanns; Gulf, because it involved a billion-dollar tax break—which became a *cause célèbre* as an example of a tax system that favored rich families and corporations; and Hiram Walker, because it was a hostile bid. Hiram Walker was itself the result of a merger between Consumers Gas Ltd. and the liquor distillery Hiram Walker only a few years earlier. During the takeover bid, Hiram Walker sold its liquor business to Allied Lyons of Britain, and the Reichmanns tried to block the sale. Prime Minister Margaret Thatcher lobbied Brian Mulroney on behalf of Allied. In the end, Allied won the liquor business. Allied bought it by giving Hiram Walker stock in its own company; once the Reichmanns had Hiram Walker, they ended up substantial shareholders in their old antagonist, Allied.

The Reichmanns made the bid for Hiram Walker through Gulf. In fact, Paul Reichmann had a vision of the family owning its own version of CP Ltd. through Gulf, and he restructured the family holdings so that Abitibi became a subsidiary of Gulf. Industry experts had advised him against this grandiose idea, and they were right: the public investors who were minority shareholders in the companies never bought into the idea. By 1987, the Reichmanns began to untangle the complicated Gulf corporate structure. On July 1, Gulf shareholders traded that stock for shares in three new companies: oil and gas company Gulf Canada Resources; Atibiti-Price; and a new company called GW Utilities. GW owned the Allied Lyons stock, 83 percent of Consumers Gas, and 40 percent of Interhome Energy. Interhome, which is also 22.8 percent owned by Gulf, owned Home Oil and Interprovincial Pipeline. It would take until 1991, however, for the family to reorganize these holdings more to their liking—and in some cases, that meant selling out.

That same year, the Reichmanns were back in the United States, bidding for the Santa Fe Southern Pacific Corp., a railway company. Despite Santa Fe's name and history, the Reichmanns were interested in the company for its real estate and oil and gas holdings; the railway operations were beside the point. They ended up with 19 percent, a good bargaining position for any corporate restructuring. This was happening at the same time that they were negotiating for Canary Wharf in London. Needless to say, the corporate diversification was spreading management too thin. Lionel Dodd, Olympia & York's chief operating officer since 1989, insists on seeing O&Y's lean management style as an unmitigated plus: "O&Y did not make the mistakes of a lot of other holding companies and put in a large holding company staff," he says. "You know, a whole bureaucratic level. We try and work directly with the management, the CEO and the board of directors."

That meant time. A lot of time. On all the major acquisitions, Dodd says, "We spent the time from the date of the acquisition to the start of 1989 getting a good grasp of the companies that we had acquired. Getting to know the boards and the managements, the key success factors . . . just getting a better grasp as to which lever you should pull to create value in each one of the companies."

But such a lean management group can't excel at everything, as the decision to invest in Campeau and the stumbling around with Bell Canada over BCED in 1989 showed. Then there was the collapse of tenants such as brokerage Drexel Burnham Lambert in New York to worry about. And what had they built during this decade? A company that was, despite the Canadian diversification, more international in scope. In 1980, Paul Reichmann said that the family wanted to keep most of its assets in Canada. At that time, 55 percent of its holdings were inside the country; 25 percent were in the United States; and 20 percent in Europe. By the end of the decade, however, that balance was shifting, in particular because of the giant Canary Wharf project in London. But the decision to move on Canary Wharf had been taken on the heels of Battery Park; the Reichmanns had realized that they didn't have any more mountains to conquer in Canada.

By the end of the 1980s, the Reichmanns had decided that although they would maintain the holdings they had in Canada, they would also not hesitate to sell Canadian assets in future years. And they certainly wouldn't invest much more money in the companies in their portfolio. Not that their emphasis had ever been on developing research and development or even encouraging innovation on the operating side of the companies. Their skills are financial, and they did a lot of work on debt financings and tax treatments at the companies they owned. They left the managing to the managers—but they didn't encourage innovation or increased capital spending. And the companies in which they have investments have not proven to have a strong interest in research or innovation. At Gulf, for example, several research initiatives have been canceled in recent years. Abitibi certainly hasn't turned into a technological leader in the paper business. Consumers Gas had a shamefully low research commitment. And the Reichmanns turned away Brian King of Connaught Biosciences, choosing at that time instead to invest in Campeau Corp.'s high-risk high-debt vision of an American retail empire.

Despite opting for the certain route of capitalizing on Canada's resource wealth, the Reichmanns didn't end up with a stellar portfolio of companies after their decade of diversification. Not that they were on the ropes, whatever their competitors might say. But in early 1990, when a bond rating service took a close look at their operations and investments—as close as anyone except their bankers can, given that their holding company is private—it was clear that buying resource companies and waiting for the checks to come in was no longer a sure route to corporate success in Canada.

The team of investment analysts from Dominion Bond Rating Service (DBRS) arrived at Olympia & York in early 1990 because they were nervous about all the rumors already flying around about Canary Wharf. O&Y is not a public company, but DBRS and other rating services provide debt ratings on commercial paper issues for a number of O&Y properties and public companies such as Gulf. The issues were all based on the value of the individual property or company. But underlying the property financings in particular there was a guarantee from O&Y. It was time, DBRS decided, to make sure that O&Y had the wherewithal to make that pledge.

Since O&Y is a private company, a bond rating service could not give it the same kind of scrutiny that they would be able to give the Toronto-Dominion Bank, for example. DBRS could only ask questions and hope that the Reichmanns would provide the answers. It was to the Reichmanns' benefit, however, to cooperate, so the bond raters could find out much more than brokerage firm analysts and certainly more than reporters could about the state of O&Y's financial affairs.

The report, completed in March 1990, left no doubt that the Reichmanns were doing just fine, thank you. Although it questioned the results at Canary Wharf and the New York and Toronto real estate holdings, the first line said it all: "The real estate portfolio is one of the most attractive of any real estate company known to DBRS." Long-term leases with large, credit-worthy customers. Well-located, low-vacancy buildings. Good cash flow. And even in this day and age, the buildings were worth much more than the Reichmanns had valued them at on the company books.

Canary Wharf was still a problem. But O&Y's investment portfolio in companies such as Gulf, Trizec Corp., and Santa Fe was worth at least $6 or $7 billion, not counting the substantial premium that could be added because the family owned key control positions in a number of the companies. DBRS had to guess at some of its numbers, but guesstimated that there was about $2 billion of debt owed against the stockholding. A comfortable position to say the least.

The report also put some matters in perspective. Although the Campeau deal was causing O&Y a lot of negative press, O&Y's total holdings amounted to $610 million—of which $600 million was in the form of partially secured debt, which ranks ahead of stock when a company is broken up. In a worst-case scenario, the valuators estimated that O&Y could lose $150 million. By comparison, some of the group's other holdings were much more significant, such as its $1.1 billion in Trizec stock or its $2.4 billion in Gulf stock. Even its Abitibi-Price shareholding was higher, at $900 million. In fact, Abitibi was a trouble spot for the Reichmanns. What with newsprint prices, environmental issues, labor negotiations, the unstable Canadian dollar, DBRS flagged it as a weak company for some time to come.

It was Gulf, however, that DBRS called a danger point—not just because of the company's performance, but because $2.4 billion was too much money to have in one stock investment. Gulf has lots of debt and few prospects for new oil finds. So much for the Reichmanns helping their industrial companies with their much-noted financial skills. Gulf was much better off before their arrival. The Reichmanns had been only mediocre as empire builders; it was time to rethink that strategy.

The Reichmanns recognized in early 1989 that they needed to shake up their $8-billion real estate and resource empire.[7] In part, this was because

7 *Forbes* magazine estimated the Reichmanns' holdings at U.S. $9 billion in 1990; in 1991 the magazine was more vague about all its estimates and classified the Reichmanns in the U.S. $5 to $10 billion category.

they saw that they couldn't help some of the companies to achieve better results, so they might as well cash out. They also had to plan for the next generation. "Three individuals control Olympia & York at this moment," Paul Reichmann told *Time* magazine in October 1990. "I am sixty, Albert is sixty-one and a half, Ralph is fifty-seven. We are at the stage when you start to think about succession." In fact, although they have always been lauded as long-term thinkers, it was none too soon. O&Y majordomo Lionel Dodd defends the timing. "The portfolio had come together in a very short period of time." And, he adds, they didn't want to move until they knew just what they had and what they could do with their $6-billion investment portfolio. "In a way," muses Dodd, "it's remarkable we got to it as quickly as 1989."

The succession plan they eventually devised for their clan of fourteen children included an important shifting of the empire's holdings. For once the Reichmanns did take a close look at their investments, they didn't like what they saw. Much of the problem lay in that 1980s shift from developers to industrialists. Some assets were sound, but some were peripheral, and a few were simply more than they could handle. The group at O&Y began looking at what they had acquired in the past seven or so years, Dodd adds, in the context of the next ten. "We were getting in position, let's say, for the next decade, not knowing what opportunities would also surface in the next decade."

Every day during 1989 there was some discussion, although there weren't always formal meetings; O&Y is run much more on the fly than that. But during the year, "we sat down and said, okay, some of these things we've acquired deliberately, some things we've acquired as by-products of something else." The misfits were fairly obvious. The Santa Fe railroad. The Allied Lyons shares. And the regulated utility Consumers Gas, which didn't actually own any gas but merely distributed it—and had its profit level set by the government. The government handcuffs particularly bothered the Reichmanns about the Consumers holding.

Dodd agrees the decision making was done quickly, but denies it was too quick for comfort. "Each one of these was a good decision; the decisions resulted in good value. There's no appearance of hastiness or bad decisions. All of them were very thoroughly worked out. And often they were very complicated. And in all cases, we looked at other options—which makes it far more laborious than it appears on the surface. If you have five options or three options in each case, and only one is implemented—well, we had all those things going on simultaneously. Really behind the scenes there was much more thorough evaluation."

The Reichmanns began publicly hinting about a major restructuring in 1989. The most fascinating aspect of the restructuring was that they actually wanted to sell partial ownership of their American real estate portfolio. Eventually they planned to sell off part of the Canadian portfolio; they were already looking for partners for Canary Wharf. By the end of 1989, the strategy was in place. Says Dodd: "The pieces began to unfold in 1990."

The United States property selloff shocked North Americans and real estate people worldwide when it was publicly acknowledged in mid-1990. But it was actually much like the Montreal Bronfmans' decision to sell their Cadillac Fairview holdings a few years earlier. They needed cash for the next generation. And an institutional partner would involve a different type of management for these assets—one that would be better suited to the personalities of the inheritors. "Ultimately that would lead to a more institutional manner in running the American business, say through a board of directors," Dodd points out. "And with succession, family members could participate through a board of directors in running the American operations with other professional investors. That is a way of an investment becoming more public, but not in the full sense of a public company."

They were simply trying to tailor the holdings to the children. Albert's son Philip and Paul's son-in-law Frank Hauer are active at O&Y, and Philip is also involved with Toronto-based developer Counsel Corp. Ralph's son David is also in the company, and Albert's son Steven has an investment together with Bruce Bronfman in on-line financial information company Hav-Info Communications Inc. However, as Paul Reichmann told *Time* magazine in October 1990: "Some will want to stay in the family business; some won't. In a private company it becomes an issue how they can go their own way if they wish to."

But with rumors already flying about the Reichmanns' gamble at Canary Wharf, and with the New York and Toronto property markets in a swan dive, this move to reduce its property portfolio was widely misinterpreted. "When it became of public interest in the middle of last year, it was old news inside the company," Dodd said in spring 1991. "But it got a twist to it that gave it more prominence at the time that the facts came out. And the twist was that the real estate business was depressed in the United States and that O&Y was going to sell its holdings because business was depressed and it needed the cash." This, he underlines, was never "on anybody's mind within O&Y and certainly didn't in any way relate to the genesis of the idea."

It was time for some damage control. "It certainly took a while to turn the view around, but we tried to get it re-understood in the context of the original strategic decision," says Dodd. *Time* magazine was part of that public image turnaround, as was the Francis piece and a number of other interviews. And, it could even be argued, the settlement of the *Toronto Life* lawsuit. The DBRS report helped as well; one O&Y official took to discreetly handing out copies.

O&Y employees weren't, however, so forthcoming about the DBRS results of April 1991, when the bond rating service rechecked its calculations. An update was necessary: the recession and a poor stock market had substantially weakened the Reichmanns' position. The stock portfolio was now worth less than $5.4 billion—a drop of almost 19 percent. DBRS guesstimated that the group had borrowed as much as $3.5 million to buy the portfolio—meaning that they could cash in their stock and walk away with about $1.9 million. The Toronto and New York real estate markets had also sunk further during 1990. But the analysts were still most concerned about Gulf, Abitibi, and Canary Wharf.

In the meantime, the Reichmanns had begun selling some of their investments. Despite their insistence that they were not worried about cash, they were selling some of the better performers and resolutely hanging on to Gulf and Abitibi. Since some of the companies they were interested in selling were actually partly owned by the public, each deal had its own complications.

One of the first companies the Reichmanns turned their scalpel to was GW Utilities, one of the Gulf spin-off companies. GW accounted for a $1.2-billion holding, or almost 20 percent of the Reichmann family's public stockholdings. It had three major corporate holdings itself: Interhome; the Allied Lyons stock; and almost 90 percent of Consumers Gas, a holding that would fetch more than $900 million on the market. The Reichmanns decided to pay off minority shareholders and make GW a private company. They didn't find it easy to pull off all that deal, however. At the same time, they proposed that Gulf buy the 22.8 percent of Interhome owned by Imperial Oil. Then GW and Gulf would, in effect, trade some assets: Gulf would end up with Home Oil—and Gulf and Home would merge. As for GW, it would end up with Interprovincial, which it would sell. Meanwhile,

Gulf would be selling other assets. Interprovincial was split into two, and both Home Oil and IPL were publicly listed. But the rest of this complicated game of dominoes was never pulled off. Instead, in mid-1991, the Reichmanns canceled the GW privatization plan and said GW's stake in both Home Oil and Interprovincial were up for sale.

The American real estate portfolio, once coveted worldwide, sat for a year without any announcement of new partners. The early 1991 sale of its Allied Lyons stock was easier; GW sold the stock for $900 million, making an after-tax profit of $169 million.

With O&Y redrawing its complicated corporate chart bit by bit, it was hard for outsiders to keep track of which piece fit where. But they could easily see that the Reichmann restructuring had important implications for Canada. The first and most graphic example of this was the Consumers Gas sale. Announced on March 7, 1990, the $1.1-billion deal was finally completed by the end of that year.[8]

The sale of Ontario's gas utility to British Gas had to run the gamut of a public hearing, a provincial election, and an eleventh-hour brainstorming session by Ontario's new NDP government to determine if the province should buy the utility instead. In the process, it became clear that a foreign owner can sometimes be better for a Canadian company than ownership by one of the country's family groups. By happy coincidence, the Consumers sale would prove to be good for both the Reichmanns[9] and for the country.

---

8 The Reichmanns received $769 million in special dividends from GW as a result of the Consumers and Allied sales.
9 For example, in mid-1991, Gulf announced that it was going ahead with a $1-billion joint venture oil project in the Soviet Arctic. Its partners were a Soviet company and British Gas PLC.

CHAPTER FIVE

Going with the Flow

L ionel Dodd is clearly uncomfortable. We're sitting around a table in
his conventional office at Olympia & York Enterprises Inc., where the
only decorative note is an abundance of hockey paintings. We're here to
discuss the Reichmanns' recent sale of Consumers Gas within the context
of O&Y's strategy for the 1990s.[1] Dodd is chief operating officer at O&Y.
However, Dodd is clearly a tier-two player, and he wants that understood.
In fact, Dodd probably does well in his Mr. Fix-It role at O&Y at least in
part because he remains in awe of the Reichmann mystique. His predecessor, Mickey Cohen, headed off to Molson Co. in 1989 when he
realized that with the Reichmanns, he would never be in charge of anything.
Dodd, however, is happy in his role as majordomo. Dodd still says to
colleagues at times that, with the Reichmanns, "the myth is the reality."

In fact, Dodd rarely even says the word Reichmann. It's always "the
company," "O&Y," or simply "the principals." They confer with and listen
to advisers. But "the principals," he says repeatedly, "clearly make the
decisions." Indeed, this control over their own empire sets the Reichmanns
apart from other moneyed families in Canada. Peter Bronfman has Jack
Cockwell, Ken Thomson has John Tory, the Montreal Bronfmans used to
have Leo Kolber and Jimmy Raymond as their corporate kingmakers. The
Reichmanns have no one else making decisions about either their corporate
holdings or any family trusts.

Even though it's not his company, O&Y is clearly Dodd's life these days.
A Regina boy, he was a Big Man on Campus back at the University of
Saskatchewan in the late 1950s and early 1960s. Business manager of the
student newspaper *The Sheaf* and of the campus music directorate, presi-

---

1 Some of the information for this chapter comes from research done by the author for an
  article on Consumers Gas that appeared in the *Financial Times* of Canada in July 1990.

dent of the faculty Commerce Society, an athlete who played football, hockey, and volleyball, Dodd graduated with great distinction from commerce classes conducted in a converted airline building. "Life has changed little from my U of S days," he told a university paper in 1990. "I prepare for meetings the same way as we prepared for classes and exams. The hours have changed little; and I still get taught a lesson from time to time by the best teachers. The biggest differences may be that I no longer have the old classmate fraternity—or work out of an airplane hangar!"

All of which says that Dodd must have been an unusually disciplined student. Obsessed, even. As for the old fraternity, he left that behind thirty years ago when he moved to the University of California for his MBA. Then Dodd joined Ford Motor Company, where he eventually became controller of Ford Canada. Then oilpatch legend Bill Wilder recruited him to join Gulf Canada. Dodd was part of the old middle management team there when O&Y made its successful bid for Gulf Canada in 1985; his performance led the Reichmanns to promote him to chief financial officer of Gulf. Finally, they brought him to head office to give them a hand in other corporate wheelings and dealings.

Despite his nice speech about the good old days in Saskatoon, don't mistake Dodd for a sentimentalist. He was asked to give the keynote address at the Commerce Society's conference on globalization in January 1991, but refused months in advance. He knew he'd be too busy. Dodd kept the date marked on his calendar just to monitor whether he'd made the right call. And sure enough, he was immersed in a board meeting that day.

Consumers Gas was definitely a Dodd deal. Paul Reichmann merely swept in for his customary tour of approval before signing the documents. But the family had never really been happy with owning the company, and the Canadian brokerage community all knew it. Stockbrokers from RBC Dominion Securities, Wood Gundy, Gordon Capital, and every other securities firm on the Street dropped in to see Cohen and Dodd during 1988 about the possibility of a sale of the Toronto-based utility. They were all turned away gently, with some hope but no commitment. Dodd made it clear that he didn't propose to hire anyone to sell Consumers . . . but if someone came up with a customer, that was another story.

Morgan Stanley Canada president Tom Barber wasn't about to put up with a brush-off like that. At thirty-three, Barber still looks like a callow twenty-four-year-old fresh out of a University of Western Ontario business class. Which is what he was only a few years ago when he joined Morgan Stanley's New York mergers and acquisitions operations. And he's not unusual in his personal predilections: he has the usual stockbroker obsessions with a state-of-the-art Jag and all the right accouterments. But unlike many brokers these days, this guy can still afford them. He's proved himself extraordinarily good at brokering billion-dollar deals. In 1988, Morgan Stanley decided he was good enough to head its Canadian operations.

That says everything we need to know about Barber. Morgan Stanley, one of the oldest and certainly most prestigious brokerages on Wall Street, doesn't pick losers. It has conducted its Canadian operations out of its New York office for years, but since Barber opened its doors in Toronto it has consistently snatched a goodly percentage of the Street's big-money business. Its clients include Inco and Nova Corp. And, of course, the Reichmanns. Morgan was happy with its role in the family's corporate restructuring. But the always-hungry Barber knew there would be other work to follow. When he sat down to review the Reichmann corporate chart, Consumers Gas dangled off the bottom of their GW Utilities like an unwanted distant cousin on a bar mitzvah list.

Barber executed a neat two-step that danced around Dodd's reluctance to commit to a sale or a particular broker. He came up with a potential buyer. And to get the buyer's attention, he told them he represented the Reichmanns. As soon as Dodd heard in November 1989 that British Gas, the largest natural gas utility in the world, was interested in buying Consumers, Morgan had the brokerage contract.

British Gas styles itself as the largest integrated gas concern in the Western world. It may have to update its terminology to fit the new East-West relationship, but with assets of $22.4 billion it can call itself anything it wants. And what it wants to call itself is a global company. Sold to the public by the British government in 1986, it's been trying to buy companies abroad ever since. It succeeded in 1988 with Calgary oil company Bow Valley Resources. And since then, it had proved itself a good owner, monitoring operations but letting Bow Valley founder Doc Seaman and his executives run the show. But subsequent attempts to establish its international presence, such as a failed New Zealand takeover, have been less successful.

Barber didn't really have to tell British Gas much about Consumers. It had been shopping for a Canadian gas company for some time and had looked at both of Consumers' competitors, Union Gas and Inter-City Gas. Union was a good company, but its owner had debt problems—including debts to an interested acquisitor within the Toronto Bronfman group. ICG Ontario had been put up for sale as part of a wholesale asset selloff by another holding company, Central Capital Corp., but they wanted too much money.

With Consumers, however, British Gas felt there was real potential. But there was a lot of negotiation to come before it would know if a purchase was on. British Gas opted for mergers and acquisitions specialist Rod Peacock, head of the British office of American investment bank J.P. Morgan, as its adviser and initial negotiator. The six-foot-two-inch Peacock has a name that is Dickensian in its appropriateness; he has a strong sense of self-esteem and doesn't mind flaunting the fact. Barber and Peacock began the first phase of negotiations in November 1989 and met frequently during the next couple of months. Finally, in early February 1990, they had laid the groundwork, and it was time for the two companies to meet each other's emissaries.

When Dodd arrived at J.P. Morgan's London offices, he was introduced to the head of Canadian operations for British Gas, Malcolm Wesley. It was clear from that moment that this would not be a takeover with fireworks and theatrics; if anything, Wesley matched or bettered Dodd in the understatement department. Wesley had been spending one-third of his time in Canada dealing with Bow Valley; a Consumers deal would further increase his stock at British Gas. He wasn't a pushover by any means, however. He later said that he enjoyed the negotiations with Dodd because the Canadian had a style he could respect: tough and unemotional, quiet yet determined. But the negotiations also had the happy tenor that comes when both sides want to make a deal. After the initial dance, it seemed to British Gas that they really needed only to agree on a price.

Then Dodd backed off. Well into the negotiations, GW's board—read the Reichmanns here—decided it needed to be absolutely sure that there were no other potential buyers. Barber prepared a list of possibilities; Dodd recalls, "We looked at about eight firms, most of them Canadian." Among those known to be interested in a Canadian utility was Australian resource firm Fletcher Challenge; British Columbia's Westcoast Energy (which later bought Inter-City); and the Toronto Bronfmans (who, as expected, ended up with Union). None of the others, however, was a serious possibility.

Wesley's boss, Harry Moulson, director of new business development, stepped in near the end to add the corporate weight of British Gas to the proceedings. But the Reichmanns deal only with the head honcho. Once Paul Reichmann had decided that matters were well enough along that he should give the deal his personal blessing, he asked for a special meeting. He met with British Gas chairman Robert Evans for final discussions before signing the sale papers.

With Consumers trading at about $28, British Gas offered the Reichmanns $34 per share for their 83 percent of the company. The Reichmanns were doing well at that price; they had paid, according to Dodd, "in the low $20s" for Consumers in 1986 and would make a $350-million profit on the billion-dollar sale. The offer was also more than 15 percent above the market price. Regulations demanded that they make the same offer to the rest of the shareholders, but nobody really thought there would be any trouble there.

There might, on the other hand, be some fuss from the Canadian government. The deal needed Investment Canada's approval. Even more important in this case was the Ontario government's OK. Consumers Gas was a regulated utility, and the Ontario Energy Board had the right to turn down any new owner. Even when O&Y and British Gas signed the agreements on March 6, 1990, both sides knew the deal might not go through. "All we'd done was ticked past the first minute of the hour," says Wesley. "We still had another fifty-nine minutes to go." Nobody realized, however, just how political the rest of this particular takeover saga would get.

When David Peterson's office handed the Ontario Energy Board its mandate to review Olympia & York's proposed sale of Consumers Gas, it looked as if the provincial utility regulator might cause trouble for the Reichmanns and British Gas. The board was told to look at the sale not just as a transfer of a closely held company from one owner to another, but in the context of the province's stance on foreign ownership. Peterson wouldn't comment on the sale, but made it clear that he generally opposed foreign takeovers. "Every time we sell another of our companies," he told a reporter, "we lose a little piece of our sovereignty."

Peterson would be right, however, only if Canadian-owned companies benefited Canada more than foreign-controlled firms or multinational subsidiaries did. And it was an accepted belief in Canada that this was usually the case; after all, multinationals are known for making decisions at head office. This trend increased during the 1980s, when sophisticated financing for subsidiaries was done more and more with financial guidance from headquarters. But there are other measures of contributing to a community. Research and development is one; creating jobs is another. In fact, Canadian-owned companies were steadily becoming less Canadian in their own financing arrangements and the method by which they decided where to make new investments. Nationalism was making way for transnationalism.

That meant, then, that foreign investment may be just as valuable to Canada as Canadian ownership. In fact, since Canadian governments were in a good position to bargain with companies who wanted to set up in the country, foreign investment could lead to better job security and training and research arrangements than governments could hope for from established Canadian companies looking only at the bottom line.

That wasn't the way most politicians saw matters, however, at the time of the Consumers announcement. Liberal and NDP opposition members in Ottawa and the NDP in Ontario were staunchly against the sale. Connaught Biosciences was mentioned at every turn. Surely, the suggestion ran, we don't want to lose another important Ontario company to an uncaring foreign owner so soon after Connaught. And a utility at that. Although there was no law against a foreigner buying a utility, it had never been done before in Canada.

With a no-holds-barred mandate to debate foreign ownership of utilities, the energy board had plenty of room to maneuver on the issue, should it decide to flex its muscles. At times in the past, the energy board would have done just that. Under its previous chairman, Robert Macauley, it had exceeded its mandate more than once. During Toronto entrepreneur George Mann's takeover of Union Gas in 1985, for example, the board ignored the fact that the deal was essentially unstoppable and launched itself into an examination of the links between Mann's Unicorp Canada Corp. and the Toronto Bronfman family's Edper group of companies.[2]

John Campion, a respected litigation specialist from Bay Street's Fasken Campbell Godfrey, had represented the energy board during that hearing. Campion was again chosen for the board's look at the Reichmanns' sale. He would have a key role in shaping the board's recommendation to cabinet. And Campion was looking forward to giving the foreign ownership issue a

---

2 For more detail on this takeover, see *The Brass Ring: Power, Influence and the Brascan Empire*, by Patricia Best and Ann Shortell.

good workout. It didn't hurt that it dovetailed with his own political leanings: an active Liberal, he was a member of David Peterson's London, Ontario, FOOF[3] set who had emigrated to Toronto but still retained the traditional WASP values of corporate citizenship and duty to community. He identified with the good old days, when London was still an important financial center, utilities were owned within the community they served, and no one could own more than 20 percent of the company.

There were reasons for that belief. A utility, traditionally, hasn't been viewed as an ordinary company. As a monopoly, it owes allegiance to the public, which gives it a license to operate. And it also influences government policy on energy issues, conservation, and research and development. A gas utility also used to have a nation-building role, but these days it isn't involved in exploration or gas development. It merely acts as a delivery service by providing transportation for the natural gas; the money is made by charging a markup on its shipping costs.

But community ownership of its utilities was just one of the many fine old ways that had become anachronistic during the 1980s. A decade ago, Ontario's gas companies were all widely held public companies. Inter-City Gas[4] was the first utility that the Ontario government allowed to become closely held. Consumers merged with the Hiram Walker distillery business in 1981; when it was taken over by the Reichmanns through their 1986 purchase of Hiram Walker, the energy board had just approved the Union Gas sale to Unicorp, and there were no publicly held gas utilities left.

During the 1986 hearing into the Reichmann purchase, the Ontario Energy Board imposed a few rules, particularly that Consumers have an independent board and that some of the company's stock be kept in the hands of the public. That meant that Consumers, the country's largest utility, was the only gas company in the province with any publicly traded stock at all.

Both the Reichmanns and the British buyers realized this four-year-old attempt by the Ontario Energy Board to keep some public ownership of a provincial gas utility could complicate matters when the regulators considered the proposed sale of Consumers. Although the principle of closely held utilities was well entrenched, British Gas could be asked to follow the same rules as the Reichmanns. That meant buying the public's stock at the premium price, then reselling it at a discount.

Still, the deal makers had one point in their favor. The OEB had changed

---

3 Fine Old Ontario Family.
4 Now owned by Westcoast Energy Ltd., which recently changed its name to Centra Gas.

in character with Macauley's July 1988 retirement. He had been replaced as board chairman by Stephanie Wychowanec, a career civil servant who saw her role rather differently from that of the colorful Macauley. The energy board would examine the issues and ask the questions, but it wasn't going to try to set policy on matters outside its purview. It seemed likely that this board would not take a political stand on an issue like foreign ownership. Especially not before or during a summer election.

There were enough politics to go around without the board's participation. And an awful lot of Liberals in the hearing room when the energy board hearings into the British Gas buyout convened in June 1990. The well-connected Campion was only the first of the politicos on the fight card.[5] The real firebrand in the crowd was Maude Barlow, a former Trudeau adviser and activist for feminist and nationalist causes. Barlow had lost an election bid during the 1988 federal election, but had been approached since about running by both the federal and the provincial arms of the party. But she had torn up her Liberal membership card when she took on the job as chair of the Council of Canadians. The council became Barlow's platform for a spirited fight against the Free Trade Agreement. As the OEB hearings began, she had just finished a book outlining her belief that corporate Canada and the Tory party had conspired to introduce free trade for the personal financial benefit of Bay Street and a bunch of Conservative back-room boys—at the disastrous expense of the rest of the country.

One of the few Liberals whom Barlow tagged as being in league with the business-Tory cabal was David MacNaughton.[6] MacNaughton, David Peterson's campaign chairman during the stellar 1988 provincial election campaign, was a Liberal with the best credentials. He was also a proponent of free trade. He had had a happy personal experience with a foreign takeover when he and partner Allan Gregg sold their public relations/lobbying/polling firm, Public Affairs International-Decima, to a British public affairs firm a few years back for several million dollars. That com-

---

5 The weekend before the hearing began, Campion appeared on national television slipping into the counting room after the Liberal leadership vote; he was one of the back-room boys who delayed the vote's results for prime time.
6 Barlow suggested in her book that MacNaughton's tie to a pro-free trade lobby group was paid off by the sale of his company to a foreigner, albeit a British company. In other words, to her mind he sold out his country for personal profit. MacNaughton, of course, thinks the suggestion is laughable. In fact, he was paid partly in the stock of the British acquisitor, and that plunged in price during 1990.

pany then bought New York public relations giant Hill and Knowlton, and MacNaughton ended up as president of Hill and Knowlton Canada.

MacNaughton was approached in January, two months before the announcement that the Reichmanns were selling Consumers, by former federal Conservative cabinet minister Ron Atkey, a partner at Osler, Hoskin and Harcourt, legal advisers to British Gas. Atkey was straightforward about his clients' needs: they wanted a smooth sale, with no sudden reversal from either the province or Ottawa. This was MacNaughton's specialty. And British Gas knew from experience that it needed help in reading the local political winds. In 1988, it had arranged to buy the New Zealand government's oil and gas assets, but public outrage had forced the New Zealand government to reverse its decision. The British company was made to look foolish in one of its first bids to execute its go-global strategy. It didn't intend to look foolish again.

The best strategy was to be open for questions but to stay low profile, MacNaughton's team advised.[7] That suited British Gas just fine. And after extensive "first-day" coverage of the deal by newspapers and the broadcast media, the press for some strange reason didn't pick up and run with detailed coverage of the $1.1-billion sale, the seventh-largest foreign takeover in Canadian history. *Report on Business* columnist Terence Corcoran wrote a couple of good pieces on the issue—both sympathetic to British Gas. On the issue of foreign ownership, he reminded Premier Peterson about the open-door attitude of one of Peterson's favorite gurus, American liberal economist Robert Reich.[8] But the press corps as a whole didn't bite on the story. The *Toronto Star* reporter covering the area was promoted to the Ottawa bureau. The *Globe and Mail* reporter was about to leave journalism and was clearly bored with the story. The *Financial Post* covered the hearings consistently, but its assigned reporter became ill and the paper had to reassign the story, leading to piecemeal coverage.

Barlow did her best to give the sale a profile. Her group lodged a protest against the sale with the OEB, gained official status, and brought in respected economist Mel Watkins as an expert witness to testify that the sale would hurt the gas utility. But despite Barlow's group and an intervention from Energy Probe, the public wasn't much interested either. Munici-

7 The two key team members were Terry Fallis, a government relations expert, and John Lute, an investor relations specialist for Hill and Knowlton.
8 Corcoran pointed out that Reich's work was a major influence on Peterson's Premier's Council, through the economist's association with Toronto-based Canada Consulting Group. Corcoran's other column talked about the fact that British Gas had paid the legal fees for opposition such as Energy Probe and Council of Canadians.

palities had already had their questions answered by Wesley during a series of "information" visits arranged by Hill and Knowlton Canada before the hearing. There were few observers at the hearings; two elderly gentlemen who wandered into the hearing room the day after Corcoran's second column turned out to be the father and a friend of an assisting lawyer.

But one member of the public was passionately interested. Of course, he had his own ax to grind: he was a former Consumers executive, from the good old days when Consumers had been a widely held public company. Chief financial officer for sixteen years until he left for a different job in 1973, Warren Hurst had retired to Gananoque, Ontario, in 1984. He never gave up his interest in Consumers, however. He greatly disapproved of the Reichmann buyout and had appeared before the board during the 1986 hearings.

He didn't make much of an impact that time. But Hurst believed that the Reichmanns would find a utility too closely regulated for their liking. Shortly after the OEB approved the 1986 Reichmann purchase, Hurst approached Mickey Cohen, Dodd's predecessor as Reichmann major-domo, to say if they ever wanted to sell Consumers to let him know. He wanted to try to mount a share issue for the company and put it back in public hands. But Hurst never received a call when his surmise proved correct and the Reichmanns did decide to sell three years later.

When he heard of the British Gas offer, Hurst again said publicly he wanted the chance to mount a public share offering. He said he would match British Gas's price. But he never quite sorted out how he was going to finance the bid. He was convinced that he didn't get a fair hearing on Bay Street because all the brokers were cowed by the Reichmanns. The board listened politely to Hurst, but it became clear that it wasn't going to turn back the clock. Reichmann lawyer Steven Sharpe destroyed Hurst's credibility during his cross-examination. "You've spoken to a manager at the Toronto-Dominion Bank who is prepared to plunk down his $14,000," Sharpe said, sneering at Hurst's ill-fated attempts to gain support. "So you've now got 44,999 shares to sell."

While Sharpe and Campion were both effective at their tasks, British Gas's case wasn't helped by its lawyer, John Roland. He went through his points with a ponderous style and a tedious delivery, alienating the listeners. And he always had to make his point, even when someone else had already made it for him. This hurt him badly in one instance. Campion, as the impartial energy board lawyer, had torn apart economist Mel Watkins's nationalist case against the sale, but Roland built it up again with his ungainly queries. The other lawyers were noticeably disturbed; Sharpe showed his impatience by swiveling his chair away from the board and rolling his eyes.

By the time the three-week hearing was finished, however, it was clear that British Gas had won the battle. The provincial government's anti-foreign investment stance didn't make sense in this instance. Campion and the energy board staff had obviously accepted the idea of a foreign owner, and their report to the board would reflect that acceptance.

British Gas passed the test for all the right reasons. It was doing ten times the amount of research and development that Consumers had done under Reichmann ownership. It knew the utility business. The Reichmanns, in contrast, had never been comfortable with Consumers. They had bought the utility almost by default. And their vaunted financial expertise didn't do much for the business. "It was obvious," said Dodd at the hearing, "that the opportunities which existed in the utilities business were certainly beyond our expertise." In late 1988, the Consumers board had even hired consultants McKinsey and Co. to study how the utility could gain that expertise. That report, however, was preempted by the British Gas offer.

And the nationalists had not made a single convincing argument against a foreign purchase of Consumers. It became clear that as long as the energy board imposed rules demanding that money be invested in research and development and technological innovation, that jobs be maintained, and that Consumers have independent directors, there was no need to worry about foreign ownership of a utility. The original idea that the energy board would take a stand on the foreign ownership issue was diffused because the Reichmanns had not been particularly stellar owners of the gas utility. British Gas would be a better one.

The only real issue left was whether British Gas would be forced to reissue stock in the utility on the Canadian public-equity markets. That was no small matter; the company estimated it would cost as much as $35 million if the energy board forced it to reissue stock immediately. British Gas's managing director, George Langshaw, who represented the company at the hearing, argued forcefully that the company couldn't afford the extra cost. He even hinted that such a demand could queer the deal. For the most part, however, the company was still walking very softly when Wychowanec and her fellow energy board commissioners went off to decide on its ruling.

There was one slip in the carefully orchestrated low profile, however. The day after the hearings finished, British Gas's Harry Moulson, recently back from a lengthy leave of absence, gave an interview in London to *Financial Post* reporter Matthew Horsman. Moulson had been away because of complicated surgery. He knew that the lawyers had advised British Gas to say as little as possible until the energy board ruled on the sale, but his absence had obviously made him a little casual about the situation. He made some offhand remark that the company could walk away if forced to relist the stock. The next day, a *Post* headline broadcast the threat. Wesley blistered his boss by telephone, and MacNaughton's team moved quickly to control the damage. George Langshaw fired off a letter to the energy board, apologizing for the remarks and explaining that Moulson's comments did not represent British Gas's position.

Moulson's blast aside, the plan was progressing smoothly for British Gas. Before the energy board report could be released, however, there was a much more serious blow to the sale. In midsummer, David Peterson called an election. And within days, it became clear that his 50 percent public opinion rating had been an illusion. It appeared that the Liberals might lose the election. David MacNaughton could see both his political connections and a billion-dollar deal slipping through his fingers. As for the Reichmanns' Dodd and British Gas's Wesley, they were more than ever dependent on MacNaughton to somehow steer the deal through a political landscape that they understood less and less.

David MacNaughton is a furtive smoker. He's promised his wife that he'll give up cigarettes. In fact, he's told her that he's already given them up. But he still smokes "on occasion," he says. So he lights his cigarette behind his hand and holds it off to the side, near a giant ashtray that seems to suck in all the smoke and cloak the nasty habit in a hazy veil of silence. MacNaughton smoking is a conspiracy and he automatically draws you in as a silent accomplice. MacNaughton is good at that kind of unspoken agreement. He's made quiet negotiation his vocation and his calling. But as he reflects on events surrounding the summer 1990 provincial election, it's clear that his usual methods of control just didn't work.

This election was different for MacNaughton for a number of reasons. He wasn't in charge; while still an insider, he wasn't even happy with the strategy or team. And he had a billion-dollar conflict of interest to worry about. The decision on Consumers Gas hung in the air as the weeks of the election campaign passed. And as the summer shoo-in began to turn against David Peterson's Liberals, the sale started to look shaky.

The anti-British Gas lobby didn't see it this way. They couldn't get anyone to make the sale of Consumers an election issue, no matter how hard they tried. Although the NDP's Bob Rae had said from the start that Consumers should be publicly held, he didn't want to wade into the issue. But behind the scenes, there was some potential for the sale to surface. Ironically, the possible source of opposition to the deal came from within MacNaughton's own political camp.

The election went very wrong very quickly for the Liberals. By mid-August, they were desperate for a revival of public support. So desperate that they were willing to throw anything to the wolves, even Mac-Naughton's pet project. As MacNaughton recalls it, he missed the Liberal strategy meeting at which Consumers was discussed; he was "out sulking somewhere." Not smart. He heard later that Martin Goldfarb, clutching at any possible straw, proposed that the Liberals come out against the sale of Consumers. All the high-mindedness about letting the energy board make up its own mind was almost sacrificed to the polls.

No decision was taken, but the idea was mentioned and one of Mac-Naughton's employees, a government-relations expert involved in the sale, heard about the meeting from another Liberal campaign worker. He hurriedly contacted MacNaughton, who sprang into action. The idea, MacNaughton reasoned with the campaign strategists, was absurd. Of course, they knew about his involvement with Consumers, but he didn't see how any of them could support such an about-face. Wasn't this just the sort of opportunism that the electorate was mad about? Whether it was Mac-Naughton or simply that the idea didn't ever take off, the Liberal campaign committee agreed. The Liberals weren't going to make Consumers an election issue.

Meanwhile, the NDP was thrilled at what appeared to be a cakewalk. They certainly didn't want to upset the election with an anti-business platform. Better to leave Consumers until they were in government. Which they were, as soon as the results were announced on September 6. David Peterson's last-minute plea to the voters not to bring in the era of red socialism in Ontario was seen for the desperation tactic that it was.

Peterson's warning had found a receptive audience in the business community, however. Socialists! For British Gas and GW, the results couldn't have been worse. All the careful groundwork and months of behind-the-scenes lobbying by MacNaughton's team was suddenly moot.

They had not only to figure out what tactic to take, but find out who would be making the decisions.

First, the tactic. The quiet approach had worked so far, and it seemed like a good idea to keep the sale as much out of the public eye as possible. No point in stirring up passions at a dicey time like this. After all, the sale made practical sense, and the NDP really had little alternative, whatever their private feelings. MacNaughton's team soon realized that the best thing they could do was to try to push through the sale before the legislature reconvened. That way, there would be a much smaller possibility of the sale being nixed at the last minute because of an awkward question—maybe even from an NDP backbencher—about why the government was reversing its policy.

But this wouldn't be such an easy group with which to strike that deal. The NDP isn't used to deals; sometimes, it isn't even interested in deals. Still, Bob Rae was a realist about the situation. He knew the matter would have to be settled one way or another fairly soon; he knew there were no other real bids, notwithstanding Warren Hurst's good intentions. And the energy board report, when it arrived on his desk, favored the sale. It asked only that British Gas reissue public stock within two years.

Consumers was only one of a number of unfinished pieces of business Rae had inherited from the previous government's agenda. There was the matter of Varity Corp., the renamed and heavily subsidized former Massey-Ferguson farm equipment company. Varity had announced its intention to move to the United States after accepting millions in federal and provincial grants on the basis of being a Canadian company. Rae had raged at this cavalier attitude toward the company's responsibilities to the province. Now he had to cut a deal of some sort.

There was also the Liberals' $55-million pledge to Toronto's Ballet-Opera House; there was the NDP pledge to nationalize car insurance; there was a whole list of social, health-care, environment, and education promises. How the NDP dealt with these first holdover issues would indicate how it would be judged by the electorate. And the way it dealt with Varity and Consumers in particular would be used by the business community to take a measure of the man and the government.

Marc Eliesen had been watching the Consumers story unfold from the catbird seat as deputy minister at the province's Ministry of Energy. Eliesen had arrived at the ministry shortly after the sale was announced. But he hadn't had an active role in the government's mandate to the energy board.

The relationship between the Ministry of Energy and the energy board only confirms that there's no politics like bureaucratic politics. The board prides itself on being separate and distinct from the ministry; and the staff at the two organizations have very different ideas about how the province's utilities should be run. Eliesen certainly had his own ideas about Consumers. He thought that the energy board had been too quick to accept British Gas's limits on conservation and research and development, for example. He wanted to see more job guarantees and more money spent.

With the NDP in power, Eliesen was about to get his chance to get involved in the affairs of Consumers Gas. He was a Liberal appointee, but he had been chosen for his past record as a senior provincial bureaucrat rather than for his political leanings. A quick look at his résumé marked Eliesen as an NDP loyalist. He had been Ed Broadbent's director of research and then a deputy minister for NDP governments in British Columbia and Manitoba. Eliesen's most high-profile position, however, had been his stint as chairman of Manitoba Hydro during the Howard Pawley government's tenure. The main criticism of his role at Hydro was his intense partisanship.[9]

The energy board delivered its report to Rae in mid-September. British Gas, true to strategy, presented a worried face to the press about the public share issue. It was still planning to push for an extension. It was in, however, for a whole new round of negotiations.

Bob Rae had enough to deal with the morning after his election victory. Molding a cabinet out of a string of inexperienced politicians; learning how to use the levers of power; reassuring the world that Ontario had not changed overnight into a Communist enclave. He and his party had been against the Consumers deal, but they needed expert help on this decision. By the time the report arrived, Rae's transition team had handed the Consumers file to Eliesen. The deputy minister invited Wesley and his advisers to the ministry to read the report the afternoon of its release. Then he set out the new ground rules. The government wanted more from the buyer. It wanted jobs, research guarantees, and a commitment to conservation and cogeneration.

9 Eliesen was appointed chairman and chief executive of Ontario Hydro by Bob Rae in June 1991.

Wesley and his colleagues left fairly satisfied. They had their own private agenda, and this suited it just fine. They had been holding some extra promises in reserve. They could actually live with giving a lot more than had been demanded in the report; certainly much more than their strict stand at the energy board hearings.

But British Gas didn't realize that Rae's office had given Eliesen a second set of instructions. Eliesen was to negotiate with the potential buyers, but at the same time, he was to chair a second set of meetings with officials at Treasury and Ontario Hydro. This high-level team would look at the feasibility of the province buying the gas company.

The option was never likely. Ontario simply didn't have the money—it could have borrowed it, but that would have added too much to the provincial debt. But it had to be looked at, to satisfy the more radical members of cabinet, and to satisfy Rae and the others that there was no way to implement their preferred option. Certainly, the idea held its appeal for Eliesen, given his background at Manitoba Hydro. The staff at Ontario Hydro couldn't believe the government was serious, but they soon got the message: this deputy minister of energy would be taking a close interest in their organization.

British Gas managing director George Langshaw showed up again for the negotiations with Eliesen. Malcolm Wesley's father was seriously ill, and Wesley had been jetting back and forth to England to be with his family. His father died just before the negotiations were complete, but Wesley was back within a day or two, to find MacNaughton confident that the deal with Ontario would go ahead.

Eliesen, as a seasoned bureaucrat, knows how a politician likes to have an issue handled. The options should be clearly presented, with accompanying justifications for whichever position is chosen. Yet somehow an experienced bureaucrat can usually manage to present the options in such a way that the official's favorite looks more appealing. In his meetings with the Ontario cabinet's priorities and planning committee, and then with the full cabinet, Eliesen presented both a Plan A and a Plan B. But it became clear that the provincial buyout had a number of problems. The government couldn't very well buy one of three gas companies and leave the other two alone. There might also have been a conflict with Ontario Hydro over the pricing of two different forms of heating. And British Gas was painted as an extremely cooperative, sensitive buyer. Eliesen later said that he personally had favored British Gas.

The sale to British Gas satisfied another item on Rae's political agenda:

showing that the socialist hordes could deal with the business community. The week before the Consumers Gas announcement, Rae had gone to New York City to convince Wall Street that Ontario was in stable, financially sound hands. He needed to: Ontario was entering its worst recession in history and he had to protect the province's credit rating with the foreign institutions who hold most of Ontario's bonds. Going ahead with the sale of Consumers to a foreign buyer—a sale already recommended by an independent quasi-governmental commission—would win points in New York. And Rae, while a strongly partisan NDP, prides himself on his intellectual rigor. He had recently read a *Harvard Business Review* article by Robert Reich, which suggested that it wasn't nationality that mattered, but interventionist government policy to ensure that all companies were good corporate citizens.[10] And he had a healthy disregard for the Canadian business community's sentimental attachment to its home country and province. He understood that it didn't matter to the Reichmanns that Consumers was located in Toronto. They would spend their money where it best suited their own corporate and familial needs. And it made sense for Olympia & York, just as it made sense for the Toronto-Dominion Bank, to diversify outside the country rather than to pump money back into such a small market.

Rae also understood that British Gas was offering to do things with Consumers that the Reichmanns never would, simply because it looked at the utility business in a different way. Since this was British Gas's main business, it did more research in the field. And it wanted the Canadian operation to be a model of foreign investment, in order to smooth the way for future purchases elsewhere. That was a happy situation for any new government.

Still, Rae had to go against party policy to approve the sale. He had to reject the traditional NDP nationalist stance and say that selling a utility to a foreign buyer was a good thing. It was tough for some members of his cabinet to swallow. But by the time of the second priorities and planning meeting a week after the negotiations began, it was a done deal.

When he heard the news, Wesley was smug; through all the frustration and game-playing and his own personal sorrow, he was finally about to see the end of this deal. He was surprised, however, to hear that Eliesen had been

10 Reich, as mentioned earlier in the chapter, is also a favorite of David Peterson's.

conducting a full-scale government buyback study even while negotiating with him. But there were smiles all around on the acquisitor's side. British Gas had completed a crucial foreign diversification. And David Mac-Naughton had shown Bay Street that he could still deliver the goods, even without David Peterson in power.

And now there were only a few minutes left on the clock. British Gas made its formal offer to shareholders, and by December 1990, it owned 97 percent of the company.[11] As for the Reichmanns, they now had a billion dollars to smooth their corporate restructuring.[12] "I have to resist any temptation to be flippant," Dodd said when asked by the energy board what he would do with the money. Despite the common belief that the money would go straight to Canary Wharf's bankers, Dodd insisted that the billion would be spent in Canada.

The Reichmanns planned to redeem $500 million of GW's commercial paper, and pay down a credit line it had with the Toronto-Dominion Bank. And $250 million would be funneled into consolidating their energy holdings. That included a purchase of an additional stake in Interprovincial Pipeline from Imperial Oil. So the Reichmanns sell to a foreigner, but buy something else from a foreigner; a wash in foreign-ownership terms. Dodd didn't add that this aspect of the deal was purely accidental.

Perhaps the happiest deal maker of all, however, was Bob Rae. He had shown with this deal that interventionist government can work in Canada. Ontario couldn't realistically afford to add to its debt load by buying the company, but it could force British Gas to increase its research and development commitments and provisions for job safety in order to gain government approval of the deal. In the months ahead, he would put the same belief into practice again and again: when business proposed to back out of its commitments to Toronto's SkyDome Stadium; when Dofasco announced the closure of Algoma Steel; when de Havilland was about to be sold to a foreign consortium.

Rae didn't always win. And he wasn't always right; his interventionist, high-debt spring 1991 budget caused Bay Street to march on the provincial legislature and soured the relationship with the country's business community. Worse, it sent a message to foreign investors that Ontario was not

11 By mid-1991 British Gas had still not been able to sell Consumers' Telesis oil and gas subsidiary, one of the federal government's few additional conditions for the sale. The reason was simple: there were $4 billion in oil and gas assets for sale in Canada. Investment Canada wasn't pushing the matter. British Gas also had not yet decided to reissue the Consumers stock; it has until the end of 1992 to do so.
12 GW recorded an after-tax gain on the sale of $201 million.

committed to dealing with its debt problems. But with the Consumers deal, Rae had taken a clear stand for a melding of business and community interests. In doing so, he deliberately ignored his own party's platform on foreign ownership. Rae's message: he knew the tide of business events couldn't be fundamentally altered by government. But he wanted, as much as possible, to control the flow.

CHAPTER SIX

Call Me K.S.: Hong Kong Money

Richard Li is a surprising young man. Not because he is so cosmopolitan, so self-assured at twenty-five. That, after all, is to be expected in a prince of international commerce. It is rather his well-thought-out and strongly held beliefs about Canada that are remarkable. This is no cardboard cutout young billionaire. Of course, Li, the second son of Hong Kong titan Li Ka-shing, has had all the grooming and requisite schooling to enable him to discourse eloquently about the rapid shifts in the nature of business amid today's geopolitical revolutions. But there is both a drive and an intellectual spark that carry the listener along with Li's line of reasoning. His is an impressive performance. A performance that it would be difficult for most of the scions of Canadian moguls to equal, certainly.

Li is passionate about Hong Kong, his base, and about Canada, his adopted and sometime home. He doesn't understand why other Canadians—he always refers to himself as Canadian—don't channel their obvious feeling for their country into building international business ties. That seems to him like the basic formula to make the country prosperous and assure that it doesn't fall behind the spiraling pace of technological change. The Asian marketplace, he points out, is growing by U.S. $3 billion every week.

That pace of development demands people with technical skills and management skills. Canada has many of those skills. Li has touched down in Toronto in mid-March partly because he's just arranged for a group of Canadians to join one of his family's companies, a telecommunications venture in Hong Kong. "I have right now eighteen families moving to Hong Kong in the next sixty days, piloting a new project," Li Jr. proudly explains. "And these are very senior professionals." On the other hand, Li feels that

Canada isn't taking full advantage of the expertise offered by Asian immigrants. As he puts it, "Maybe there could be a better use of Asian immigrants to bring expertise in here, so that Canada can go and conquer new markets."

Li is undeniably a product of a coddled and elite upbringing. Not many fourteen-year-olds are packed off by momma and poppa to private school in California, more than 7,000 miles from home. Fewer still by the age of twenty-four have an executive assistant handling their mail, travel arrangements, and the myriad details of everyday life in the jet stream of international business. But Li seems suited to the life, as deserving of his position as anyone could be. There is only the occasional slip into arrogance: during a luncheon meeting at Chiaro's, an elegant restaurant in Toronto's King Edward Hotel, Li twice snapped his fingers to summon the waiter.

Richard and his elder brother Victor, who is all of twenty-seven, are the sons and heirs of Li Ka-shing. K.S. to friends and business associates, Chiu Yan (Superman) to much of the Chinese population in Hong Kong, Li Ka-shing is the island's richest and most influential business person. There has been some business community buzz about which son will inherit control of Li's $4-billion empire. (That's his personal net worth; his businesses are valued at about $40 billion.)

Richard certainly has the higher profile back in Hong Kong at the moment. While Victor sticks to real estate development, Richard has been trained as an investment banker and is now spearheading his family's move into satellite television throughout the Pacific Rim. Recently, Richard has been traveling west to London even more than he travels east to Toronto. And that's a lot: during the first nine weeks of 1991, Richard Li had taken eleven trans-oceanic business flights.

This might sound like an arcane piece of business trivia, but it isn't. The peripatetic habits of Richard Li should be of interest to all Canadians. His family is the most high-profile of the Hong Kong immigrants, and that immigration represents an important element of rejuvenation for the Canadian nation. It is new money and new talent, something this country was built on. Except that none of our waves of immigration have had such a uniformly high level of education, and so much money. And such a looming, definite deadline as the 1997 reclamation of Hong Kong by the Chinese government in Beijing. "Our group is only one of many multinational groups in Asia outside of Japan," says Li. "They are in Canada, they're looking, they're here. I see them everywhere."

The way Canadians deal with the Li family and all the other Hong Kong immigrants says much about our country's future. Young Richard doesn't understand the standoffishness and plain intransigence of many Canadians about opportunities for international investment. He refers to a recent exchange with a senior old-line Canadian businessman. The executive insisted that Canadians had to adapt to free trade with their major trade partner, the United States, before they could cope with other types of opportunities and challenges. Things must happen in phases, he added; Canadians needed time to adapt to and accept immigrants and their joint ventures. When Li asked how long it would take to make that transition, the executive replied that it would take another four years or so. That doesn't make sense to Li, who is used to the frenetic pace of Hong Kong. "To me, four years would mean you miss the opportunity," says Li. "The world changes about fivefold in four years."

Li must also know, although we don't discuss it, that there is an element of blind fear at work here. Not everyone is happy with the arrival of the Lis and other immigrants. The city of Vancouver, for one, was in an uproar in 1988 and 1989 because of their real estate holdings and new developments. Magazine covers were splashed with the label HONGCOUVER. And that is just part of a larger xenophobia in Canada toward immigrants. Especially Asian immigrants.

This doesn't mean that we should bend any rules for Hong Kong immigrants, or unthinkingly accept any customs they bring. It does mean that we need to understand the reasons that they are choosing Canada as a basis for investment and immigration. And when we start to look at the reasons, they are startling in their familiarity.

The Lis have much in common, after all, with the Reichmann family. Both are immigrants who chose Canada because it was a safe, secure country with an open door. Both are attracted to its real estate and natural resources. And they operate their businesses in very similar fashions. They are private whenever possible about their affairs. They make long-term connections with a few financial institutions, but will reach out all over the world if need be to finance a particular project. Most of all, they are building for future generations.

And they have great financial power. When Li Ka-shing bought a Hong Kong utility a few years back, it took only seventeen hours to negotiate the deal. And one minute to negotiate a $192-million loan from the Hongkong and Shanghai Banking Corp. (Li happens to be a shareholder, director, and one of two deputy chairmen of the bank). It's no wonder, with that type of control, that when K.S. Li moves money out of the country, Hong Kong jumps. Li said once, "The tallest tree attracts the most wind"; the Reichmanns would certainly agree with that sentiment.

The Hongkong and Shanghai Banking Corp. picked up the pieces when the Bank of British Columbia fell apart in 1987. But Li Ka-shing's major connection with Canadian financial institutions is in Toronto, through a long-time relationship with the Canadian Imperial Bank of Commerce, and a more recent joint venture with Gordon Capital Corp. His two other main Canadian holdings are resource-based: a control position in Husky Oil of Calgary, in concert with CIBC and Nova Corp., and a collection of real estate holdings, mostly in Vancouver.

Husky is Li's largest overseas investment to date, and he's had some trouble with it. The company hasn't lived up to his expectations at all, and Nova Corp., with other financial problems, is selling its portion. Li has resisted the idea, but he might end up selling out of Husky, too.

If he does, the money he receives won't necessarily be reinvested in Canada. For a Hong Kong-based investor such as the Li family, nothing is presumed and nothing is static. As he plans for the future of his family, Li knows he must expand beyond Canada in investment terms. The negative reaction to his real estate plays on the west coast has shown him he can go only so far here. In recent years, the group has looked on the United States as a more and more attractive place for potential investments.

He began the push southward by arranging a joint venture with Gordon Capital on a U.S. $3-billion junk bond purchase from a floundering California savings and loan company in 1990. That deal eventually fell through; but Li is ready for another entrée, and ideas cross his desk every day.

In April 1991, Richard Li told a Calgary conference on doing business with the Pacific Rim that "my family and my company have made the initial phase of our investment in Canada." The progress of and prospects arising from these first steps by one Hong Kong family into Canada make it clear that the Li family has much to offer Canada. The question now is what will happen in Phase Two. At this point, each of their investments has been beneficial to the country and to the family. But each is now in flux. What's not as clear is what, in future, Canada will have to offer the Lis and their compatriots.

When the money lenders at Canadian Imperial Bank of Commerce decided more than two decades ago to lend money to developer Li Ka-shing, they made one of the smartest decisions in the bank's 124-year history. Li never forgot that the bank had supported him when he needed it; CIBC became one of his favorite financial institutions.

In 1974 the banker-borrower relationship became a partnership when the bank and Li formed merchant bank Canadian Eastern Finance Ltd. (CEF). Starting small, with $7.9 million in capital, it bankrolled real estate deals in Hong Kong. In 1986 a new holding company, CEF Holdings, was created so that the group could diversify into corporate finance and venture capital lending throughout Asia. Li's companies provided about 30 percent of the merchant bank's business.

The relationship became profitable in Canada as well, when CEF financed Li's Husky takeover in 1984. And when Li became the successful bidder for Vancouver's Expo '86 site in 1988, CIBC was brought in as a minor partner. In fact, by the mid-1980s it was rumored that Li was the bank's largest individual shareholder, squeaking in at just under the authorized 10 percent limit on individual stockholdings in a Canadian bank. But Richard Li says those 10 percent shareholding stories are false. Yes, the Li family owns stock, but nowhere near that much; the investment "is not a big deal," and certainly not the group's only Canadian stockholding. "K.S. has denied that, and [Donald] Fullerton [CEO of CIBC] has denied that at the same time," Richard Li says.

Gordon Capital Corp. must be every bit as thankful as CIBC for the connection between Li and the bank. Back in the mid-1980s, CIBC was looking closely at entering the brokerage business. At the time, the bank thought it would build its own brokerage operation.[1] And it decided that one of the best ways to become a big player on Bay Street was to hook up with maverick brokerage firm Gordon Capital on a few special projects through a jointly controlled merchant bank.

At first, CIBC wanted to own 25 percent of the new merchant bank, named Gordon Investment Corp. (GIC). Ottawa, however, limited its holding to 9.9 percent.[2] That was all right, though, because as part of the arrangement, the bank brought along as investors a few of its favorite clients: Canada Life Assurance, Japan's Yasuda Trust, and of course Li Ka-shing.

---

1 See Chapter One.
2 Recently, it has successfully lobbied Ottawa again to increase its holding to a 24.9 percent non-voting interest in GIC.

Gordon clients also became partners in the merchant bank, including General Electric Capital Corp., the Kuwaiti Investment Office, and Conrad Black's Hollinger Inc. The structure is a bit complicated: Gordon Capital partners own half of GIC; GIC, in turn, owns half of Gordon Capital. The other investors own the remaining half of GIC. With $500 million in capital, Gordon partner and GIC founder Neil Baker was given a wide-open mandate to make money and expand abroad. So began a partnership that would provide Gordon with the wherewithal to look beyond Bay Street to deal making on Wall Street.[3]

For years, Jimmy Connacher, the intense, driven patriarch and controlling force at Gordon, would stare out his office window at King and Bay streets in Toronto and out across Lake Ontario. "The biggest market in the world is on the other side of that pond," he'd rail. So much money, so close, yet he couldn't get at it. And that frustrated Connacher, who is a man used to getting what he wants. During the 1980s, he had turned Gordon Capital from a small firm catering to institutional clients into the most aggressive powerhouse on Bay Street. By 1990, Gordon brokered an average $1 billion in trades daily—15 percent of the Toronto Stock Exchange's volume. At the same time, Gordon was hitting its head against the limitations of the Canadian stock marketplace, which was becoming more concentrated and less vibrant.[4]

Gordon had run an office in New York for almost twenty years, but it was the standard Canadian third-tier entry, capable of selling only Canadian resource stocks to Americans when resource stocks were in fashion. During the late 1980s, Gordon opened a big, new office on the top floor of the General Motors building in Manhattan. It's filled with American brokers selling American stocks. But it's still not an entry in the big Wall Street stakes. Connacher needs access to the big New York deals in order to take Gordon into the 1990s as a New York broker with Canadian roots.

After two and half years during which he looked at about fifty potential deals, GIC president Baker brought Connacher the deal that he thought

---

3   Baker, a long-time partner of Jimmy Connacher's, was an early adviser to Canadian moguls Peter and Edward Bronfman. Originally a silent partner who bailed out Gordon during a cash crunch during the 1982 recession, Baker joined the firm full-time in the mid-1980s and thought up the merchant banking idea.

4   Gordon's role in revolutionizing Bay Street during the 1980s is detailed in *The Brass Ring: Power, Influence and the Brascan Empire*, 1988, by Patricia Best and Ann Shortell.

could take Gordon into the United States in a big way: a $3-billion junk bond portfolio. Although this was too big for the investment bank to handle alone, it couldn't risk the money it would lose if it didn't pull off the deal. Gordon's management turned, naturally enough, to one of the richest men around: Li Ka-shing.

By this time, the connection between Gordon and Li had an added family tie. And it showed that Li's loyalty to the Bank of Commerce stretched only so far. Victor had worked briefly in CIBC's real estate department, but when Li Ka-shing wanted his second son, Richard, to learn about the world of finance, Li bypassed the Commerce and arranged for him to train at Gordon. Richard says that the decision for him to go into investment banking was a happy marriage of his own interests and a need for investment banking expertise by his father's group of companies.

He also proudly states that he applied and was accepted on his own merits by two major New York banking groups, much larger and "much better known investment brokerage in the world than Gordon Capital." He would have preferred either New York firm, perhaps as a precursor to a stint at Gordon. In classic inheritor form, "I would rather work in a place that is only my connection rather than my family's connection." But he didn't have a choice. The family's plans were for him to train at Gordon, then return home.

Richard bought a partnership at Gordon Capital, the securities firm— separate from Li's investment in the merchant bank GIC. Around the firm, Richard's partnership was referred to as his birthday present from K.S. Richard Li adjusted well to the rough-and-tumble world of Gordon, enjoying the race-car circuit frequented by a few of the partners. Some partners dubbed him Little Richie, and he received his share of criticism. No finger snapping here. One insider says, "People were not going to kiss ass for a few million bucks."

That seemed fine with Richard and his father. When Richard returned to Hong Kong in early 1990, he was assigned responsibility for the GIC investment bank holding. Shortly thereafter, GIC, with the Li family as a partner, found the deal that could take it into the United States market.

Columbia Savings and Loan of Beverly Hills, California, was one of hundreds of small financial companies caught in the vortex of the United States savings and loan crisis in the late 1980s.[5] Columbia, however, was newsworthy even in this gathering of rogues and finaglers. Its chief executive officer, Thomas Spiegel, had abandoned the traditional S&L role of mortgage lender and deposit taker to become a big player in the junk bond market. Michael Milken, the evil genius and junk bond king from stockbrokerage Drexel Burnham Lambert, was a friend of Spiegel's; by 1989, Milken had sold Columbia U.S. $5 billion in junk bonds. When federal regulators moved in to force the company to reevaluate its holdings in early 1990, the bond portfolio was worth at most U.S. $3 billion. The company was U.S. $350 million in debt, and federal regulators were hovering at the door.

Washington had two choices. It could allow Columbia to sell off the bond portfolio at a sizable discount and cover its gargantuan loss. If it went that route, the federal deposit insurance corporation would have to put hundreds of millions of dollars into the company. The second choice was to move in and liquidate the company, which would leave the government holding the bonds. Under that scenario, it would double the U.S. $4 billion in junk bonds the government was already stuck with from other failed S&Ls. And it would still have to cover the company's losses.

Opinions were divided about which route was the best one. But the federal regulators, overcome with so many other problems, chose not to bother outlining which type of deal they would approve when, in mid-1990, Columbia placed the junk bond portfolio on the auction block in a desperate bid to avoid liquidation by Washington. Bidders included corporate raider Carl Icahn, Salomon Brothers, Citicorp, and Bankers Trust. And one Canadian company: Gordon's investment bank, GIC, in concert with Li Ka-shing. On July 25, Columbia announced that the Canadian investment bank had won the bidding with an offer of U.S. $3 billion, slightly higher than the bond's latest evaluation.

GIC and Li were paying top dollar. But they weren't really paying that much, it turned out. GIC and three of Li's companies planned to split a 10 percent down payment on the bonds—U.S. $150 million each. The desperate savings and loan company was willing to lend the group the remaining 90 percent for 10 years, at a reasonable 10.5 percent interest rate. In the meantime, if the bonds fell in value by 7.5 percent or more, the group could simply forfeit its U.S. $300 million down payment and walk away. The whole deal would be structured through a special company set up in the

---

5 The information in this section is based in part on research done by the author for an article that appeared in *Toronto Life*.

United States, called Gordon America Limited Partnership. The last two words are especially important: if the company defaulted on payments, neither Columbia nor the United States government would be able to demand money from the deal's international backers.

If, on the other hand, the bonds rose in value, GIC and Li stood to make a lot of money. For starters, by selling part of the portfolio, they could pay the savings and loan company the money they owed. And they would still have a lot of bonds left. A very sweet deal, and one that rested on a belief that the United States economy would bounce back from recession. GIC and Li were betting on the next decade. Suddenly, Gordon was a name in the United States. It had proposed a daring, brilliant ploy. And the international investment community had its interest piqued by Li Ka-shing's obvious interest in the United States. As for Bay Street, it was in awe. This was way beyond anything a Canadian broker had tried before. "It's too early," cautioned one banker at the time the deal was announced, "to call it the deal of the nineties."

It certainly wasn't the deal of the 1990s from K.S. Li's perspective; maybe the deal of the month. Richard Li says the group sees at least two potential deals this large every month. Many of these are from the United States, and Li's group had been actively scanning them. In 1989, Li held real estate in the United States valued at only $24 million. A paltry sum, especially when compared to the billions he has committed to Canadian developments. The United States was the logical place to expand from his Canadian base.

But only at the right price. Most of the American deals Li's group looked at were too expensive. Or they didn't like the "Sell American" nationalism they encountered in places like Texas. And they wanted only investments that fit with their overall corporate strategy. By 1990, that included high-growth areas such as telecommunications as well as real estate and natural resource companies. As Richard says, the plan "isn't investing in the U.S. for the sake of investing in the U.S. If it's a good deal, we'll go ahead."

In fact, Li had been shown the Columbia portfolio sale by another broker by the time Gordon called with the idea. So once the Lis decided they were interested, it didn't take long to make their own in-house assessments. "Our consideration period for that deal," says Richard, "was two weeks." And that wasn't because they took Gordon's word about the junk bonds' value. A Li team of advisers did its own in-depth assessment of the portfolio. After all, with a 6 percent ownership in GIC as well as its half-interest in the deal itself, it would have the largest individual stake in the success or failure of the idea.

Li's people said yes to GIC because they saw the same opportunity as Gordon: access to the United States business community. The fact that they wouldn't have to spend any real money was an enticement. But what really excited them about the Columbia portfolio was that it included 300 bond issues from 176 name-brand American companies—names such as RJR Nabisco, McCaw Cellular, and Eastern Air Lines.[6] These firms had all raised money for acquisitions or mergers by issuing debt in the junk bond market during the 1980s; now many of them were in need of investment advice and, in some cases, massive corporate restructuring.

For Gordon, it was an inside track on a lot of deals. "Suddenly," says one Gordon insider, "you have seventy-five very attentive listeners and another hundred you have a reason to call." It had a chance to be a big-time broker in the United States. The incentive for Li was similar, from an investment perspective. These companies, when restructuring, might need a joint-venture partner. Or someone who could buy some assets they had to sell in a hurry. It was like a key to the door of corporate America. At the time, Richard Li told reporters, "We look at this investment as a window into corporate America and further investment opportunities." The next spring, he said that the investment "would have provided us with interface with these companies directly." In both cases, the partners planned to rachet their role as debt-holders into a position of power during the coming restructuring of corporate America.

Gordon began preparing for its new role, interviewing junk bond analysts and merchant bankers. They were also using New York public relations firm Adams and Rinehart to arrange press interviews and Washington lobbyists to keep them in touch with the government's reaction, since the sale still had to be approved by Washington's treasury department before it could go ahead. Gordon badly wanted that approval. It didn't flinch when Iraq invaded Kuwait in August, and junk bond markets plunged 5 percent within a month amidst the uncertainty created by the Gulf conflict. Baker had included a prescient "war" clause in the agreement. But Gordon didn't

---

6 The implosion of Canadian Robert Campeau's empire had precipitated a crisis in the junk bond market in early 1990; Campeau was in Columbia's portfolio when the Canadian–Hong Kong group decided to take advantage of that collapse.

want to abandon the venture just because the bonds had dropped in value. It was just too important to the brokerage firm.

The attack on Kuwait and its effect on the United States economy separated the very eager Gordon from the more balanced Li group. Richard Li told an American reporter on August 30 that his family might withdraw from the deal because of the economic conditions caused by the Gulf invasion. With oil prices rising and the United States economy still in a slump, the United States didn't look so good to Li. But for the moment, the group hung together.

Then suddenly, the deal was in danger from another source—Washington. The partners had done their homework before making the offer. They had the support of Columbia's financial advisers, First Boston Corp., and well as the California savings and loan regulators. Meanwhile, their Washington lawyers kept close tabs on the federal approval process. As the summer waned, however, all of their reports became less and less positive.

Then, three weeks before the Columbia sale was to close, Gordon partner Tom Allen and a few other partners were summoned to Washington. There, they heard that Tim Ryan, director of the United States Treasury Department's Office of Thrift Supervision,[7] was about to announce the deal was off. While the S&L regulators hadn't outlined any guidelines for the bidding, they had decided that the GIC-Li bid left too much risk with Columbia, and ultimately with them. New thrift legislation passed in August by Congress didn't allow the S&Ls to keep their junk bonds, and that was a possibility with the GIC deal. Ryan told the public his decision on Monday, September 10.

Gordon found itself back at square one. The partners had to bid all over again as part of a general bid open to others. They immediately began to renegotiate. As one insider said, "Gordon hasn't been known to sit back and—what's a nice expression?—twiddle its thumbs." During the next several weeks they tried a number of alternatives on Ryan's office, hoping to satisfy federal regulators by slightly increasing the cash component of their bid or giving Columbia a partial benefit if the bonds did well in succeeding years. That's what the regulators said they wanted.

But in fact, the regulators changed the rules as the year wore on and Columbia's financial position degenerated, and it became clear that Washington would probably have to seize the company and add it to all the others whose assets were in its clean-up agency, the Resolution Trust Corp.

---

7   The department in charge of managing the failed savings and loan companies taken over by the United States government.

The managers at Resolution Trust made it clear it didn't want to end up with the junk bonds if they could help it—and that's what could happen if the value of the bonds fell far enough and GIC opted to walk away. So they demanded a deal without that contingency.

And in the end, not even Gordon could make the deal work. In January 1991, they walked away. The Canadian broker was not going to eat America. Part of the breakdown was that Li Ka-shing was not going to give too much for the opportunity the junk bonds represented. Richard Li jetted back and forth between Toronto, New York, and Hong Kong during the intense negotiations. "It was a nightmare of negotiations, lawyers' discussions," he recalls of the aborted deal. "We worked very hard on it and we drew our line and if the line was beyond a certain risk factor we would not go in."

The Canadian broker has been left hanging in limbo, its Canadian business stable but unexciting and its future in the United States still up in the air. Connacher is planning to retire in a few years, and it's unclear who will run Gordon when he's gone. Some people on Bay Street are looking to Li Ka-shing to play a larger role.

It's possible. Especially if Gordon does succeed in expanding outside Canada, perhaps through acquisition. Then the Li family could end up with a larger hand in what would essentially be an American brokerage firm with a Canadian base. Unfortunately, in the meantime the dynamic brokers at Gordon Capital are stuck talking about what could have been rather than conquering the big bad world. One Toronto fund manager says, "They're beginning to sound like a bunch of wannabes."

As for Li, he was actively considering a world of investments. What the group will do next, says Richard, is "hard to predict." One increasingly likely possibility in 1991, however, was the sale of its position in Husky Oil—its largest single Canadian investment.

When Bob Blair tells the tale of his first meeting with Li Ka-shing, the story tumbles out in typical Blair style: lots about his company, Nova, and very little about the people involved.[8] He starts with Nova's operations in China, which necessitated a Hong Kong office back in the early 1980s. The office was set up to explore the market in the People's Republic of China

---

8   The information in this section is based in part on research done by the author for an
    article that appeared in the *Financial Times* of Canada.

for pipelines and petrochemicals. The company's representative, a metal-lurgist named Dora Kwok, worked hard to establish the business base through Hong Kong. Li was among her contacts, and she made sure the boss met him when Blair came to town. Beyond that, Blair doesn't re-member any details of a connection that would result in one of his most important business deals. "I don't keep a very good chronology of this in my mind," he rumbles in his oft-noted Scottish burr.

Nova still does business in China, but it doesn't have a Hong Kong office any more, ironic considering the Li family's feeling that Canadians need to reach out to make international business contacts. But then, it's also quite possible that Li Ka-shing has seen more than enough of Bob Blair and Nova by now. Not that there's any bad blood between the two. Just an important but less-than-successful investment that has become a somewhat painful question mark for both the iconoclastic Canadian company chief and the legendary Hong Kong magnate.

Blair characterizes Li as "a folk hero in his own time," and he likes the idea that people have suggested that he and Li have a common approach to business and life. "Other people have remarked that we have certain similarities, although he managed to be more successful financially," Blair says with a laugh. "I don't claim that success." With a little prompting, however, he'll explain the parallels: "We share the same point of view, such as building for the long term and playing things straight." This meeting-of-great-minds idea fits with his self-image as a member of an international stratum of "philosophically inclined" executives. Blair keeps in touch with these chosen peers through handwritten letters about Nova's activities and his own mindset. The latter is usually left of center on political policy issues, quixotic, and definitely out of sync with the Calgary oilpatch and the Canadian business community. In fact, it's difficult to imagine anyone comparable to Bob Blair. A short, stocky man with a shy yet pugnacious manner and Captain Kangaroo bangs, he is not popular close to home. "I admit to being called a loner. I don't try to be a loner. I think all that means is that I've got to go my own way," Blair says with a trace of pride. "I don't travel with the herd all the time."

His is an almost corporate New Age approach to life—an approach also reflected in his ergonomically correct office, his aerobics classes, and his honorary posting as professor of environmental design at the University of Calgary. Blair, whose business thrives on the production of ceiling tiles, garbage bags, and plastic spoons and forks, and the production and sale of fossil fuels, sees the environment as the issue of the 1990s.

He didn't have the typical small-town Canada exec-in-the-making upbringing. In his own right, however, Blair can claim to be a son of the oil patch. His father, Sydney, was a researcher on the Athabaska tar sands project back in the 1920s. He also worked in Trinidad and Scotland, before returning to Canada and eventually running Bechtel Canada. Bob was born in Trinidad and still speaks with an accent acquired during his years in Scotland. He didn't enjoy the time he spent with the American Brahmins at prep school Choate, but he credits that experience with making him into a Canadian nationalist. After graduating from Queen's University, he worked at Bechtel Canada, then ran another United States subsidiary, Alberta and Southern Gas, before landing at what was destined to be his life's work, Nova, in 1970.

Back then, the company was called Alberta Gas Trunk Line, a small provincial gas pipeline company with a quasi-monopoly on gas transmission. It was set up in the early 1950s by the provincial Social Credit government to ensure that control of Alberta's natural resources didn't fall into the hands of foreigners. Blair fancied himself something of a nationalist and convinced the government to support the company's expansion into Northern Alberta, a historic bid against a team of multinationals for the right to build an Alaska pipeline.[9] These days, it transports 80 percent of natural gas marketed in Canada.

With the ascendancy of Peter Lougheed, Nova became almost an instrument of the province's industrial policy, moving into the petrochemicals industry with government support and guidance. Many people thought it was a crown corporation. And it was widely believed that this would soon be Canada's most powerful multinational itself—and a very nationalistic one at that. In 1978 it had purchased Husky Oil in a pitched battle with Petro-Canada and Occidental Petroleum. During the 1980s, Nova moved into just about every industry that Blair could think of: cellular telephones, trucking, steel, and more.

But in 1986, Blair did something very strange for your average gardenvariety nationalist: he flouted a government law prohibiting the sale of control of an oil company to foreign interests, in order to make Li Ka-shing

---

9   The pipeline, like many of Blair's ideas, is still a pipe dream. It cemented a long-time friendship with a number of Dene natives, however; Blair still goes to a reserve in Alberta for R&R.

his partner in Husky. Given Nova's role in Alberta life, that made K.S. Li a stakeholder in a Canadian myth.

Li didn't have the average Canadian exec-in-the-making upbringing either. He arrived in Hong Kong from Chiu Chow in Guangdong province in southern China at the age of eleven and within two years was supporting a widowed mother and two siblings. He was running a plastics company by the time he was out of his teens—flowers, watch bands, toys—and by twenty-three had his own business, with a $2,000 stake. But Li's legend was made by his real estate dealings; he had an uncanny ability to move in before the boom and leave before the bust every time, rather like the Reichmanns. Next, Li diversified; but his investments fared better than the Toronto brothers'. In 1979—at the time the Reichmanns bought Abitibi-Price, their first non-real estate holding—Li bought one of Hong Kong's British trading houses, or hongs: Hutchison Whampoa Ltd.

By the mid-1980s, Li's major companies (including Hutchison Whampoa and Cheung Kong)[10] accounted for 10 percent of the Hong Kong stock exchange's capital. These days, it's closer to 15 percent of the island's equity.

With China and Britain earnestly negotiating over the island's fate in 1984, Li's Hutchison gave shareholders $256 million in cash through a special dividend equal to one-quarter of its equity. Since much of that went to Li, it naturally sparked rumors that he was on the way out. He may be a hero, but that didn't stop the criticism. As *Business Week* commented in February 1985, "The local press accused Li of trying to milk the company to line his own pockets." It turned out they were massively overreacting.

Li wasn't leaving. But he was looking to make a substantial investment outside the country. Something that would set his two sons up, just in case. He'd talked with Blair in 1984 about a small investment in Nova's oil company, Husky Oil, but the federal National Energy Program made this a difficult proposition. In 1985 they talked about potential joint ventures in China instead. But the change to a Canadian government with a pro-foreign-investment stance in late 1984 suddenly made Canada a likely possibility for Li's money.

10 Cheung Kong (Holdings) Ltd. is a property developer, but also a holding company and Li's top company. It holds part of his trading company, Hutchison Whampoa Ltd. Cheung Kong is also Li's means of controlling Hong Kong's largest utility, Hongkong Electric Holdings, as well as Green Island Cement Co. Through these companies and a few more minor ones, Li has holdings in construction, communications, shipping, and retail firms, as well as energy companies (including Husky).

By 1986, Blair badly needed a partner at Husky. Nova was a majority shareholder in Husky, so whatever happened at the oil company either helped or hurt the gas pipeline and petrochemical company's bottom line. In 1986, Husky was definitely hurting Nova. Blair's aggressive expansion plans for the oil company meant it needed money; the commodities cycle of the early 1980s meant Nova didn't have the money to give. Oil prices were low and staying low, and Husky's earnings were set to tumble in 1987. "In 1986, Nova was at the bottom of the cycle," Blair later told a reporter. "If our back wasn't against the wall, it wasn't sitting very far off the wall."

Bill Richards, the former president of Dome Petroleum, claims some of the credit for the deal. He was on contract to Li, at a rumored $1-million retainer, to find potential investments. "I've shown Li just about everything in Canada," he said at the time. Blair downplays Richards's involvement, however. No matter who the matchmaker was, Li liked the idea of an investment in oil. Rumors of the deal began to float, as well as some incorrect rumors about a merger of Nova and Texaco. Nova stock rose as a result of the rumors.

Li's managing director at Hutchison Whampoa, Simon Murray, and a team of analysts met with Blair and his board in Calgary and in Hong Kong. There, Blair presented the one-page investment proposal. Li had a month to decide. He took four weeks and two days, including a final eight days of round-the-clock meetings in Hong Kong. In December, he let Blair know he was in.

First Li would pay Nova $453 million for 43 percent of Husky, the same stake that Blair's Nova would hold. Li's son Victor would buy 9 percent of the company. CIBC was a part of the plan, of course. Its Hong Kong joint venture with Li provided the financing, and it bought the remaining 5 percent of Husky. Each side would name half the directors; they would share control of the company that way, since the board had to approve all major decisions. (Nova used Li's money to buy out Husky's minority shareholders.) Li and Victor came to Calgary for a press conference, and Blair hosted both a lavish Li-meets-the-oilpatch reception and a private cocktail party in his home. In Hong Kong, Li had a large Santa and sleigh pulled by huskies rather than reindeer strung across the front of Hutchison's headquarters building.

It was nothing more than a back-door foreign takeover according to the nationalists, no matter how many times Bob Blair said it wasn't. The CIBC and young Victor Li (twenty-two at the time) were only in there to make it look as if Husky were still controlled by Canadians, they argued. Nova's partnership position didn't satisfy those who thought Canada should maintain control of its energy assets.

In fact, Blair and Li were applying their own interpretation of the government's oil ownership policy. Ottawa allowed only financially desperate companies to be taken over by foreigners—a policy introduced by Tory energy minister Pat Carney earlier that year and reiterated by her successor Marcel Masse the month before the Husky deal. Now Masse had to decide whether to swallow Blair's explanation. And if his officials knew anything about Chinese business families, they knew there was no real separation of assets among the generations. What is the son's is the father's. Li had said he gave Victor the money to make the investment. Of course, he told him to vote independently.

But Blair had paved the way, using all his political connections. Mulroney's office knew about the Li deal ahead of time; Blair and Husky president Art Price walked Masse and Ed Broadbent through the deal two weeks before they signed the papers, and the Liberals also knew the details of the proposal. The joint control of the board satisfied the government's demand that corporate control not pass to a foreign group. And Blair the nationalist believed in the rightness of his idea. He even defended the move by saying it made Husky more Canadian to have Li arrive, insisting that it was better than the previous "migration of Husky shares not owned by Nova into the U.S." Investment Canada eventually agreed; the deal was okayed the following spring.

And despite the nationalists' fears, the Li purchase didn't set off a chain-reaction sale of Canadian oil companies to foreign interests. Instead, the oil business became increasingly unattractive during the late 1980s. By the end of the decade, there were precious few takers for any oil company. Especially Husky, as it turned out.

It seemed like a good deal at the time. When they signed the deal, Husky shares were trading at $9.75. Blair offered shareholders $11.80 cash or Nova stock; they took the cash. In the meantime, oil stocks rose by one-third in Canada during the spring of 1987. Li's people thought the price of oil had bottomed out in 1986 at U.S. $15 per barrel. Besides, he liked Canada. He told the press conference that he wasn't interested in the United States. "But we looked across the Pacific and saw the high growth rates of the economy and the huge amounts of capital investment that is available. And we think that may be the most important part of the deal."

The partners committed to invest up to another $1 billion in Husky during the next few years. Li also talked about making other investments in Canada. He wasn't exactly clear what he'd buy; one time, he speculated about a supermarket chain. Another time, he was interested in Dome Petroleum—and he and Blair did take a look. Turbo Resources was another rumored candidate, but again, no bites. In 1988, they looked at Texaco Canada, but its United States parent wouldn't sell.[11]

Husky president Art Price, asked about Blair's and Li's different slants on Husky, cannot begin to answer. "You could write a book," he says enigmatically. Basically, however, they worked well together: Blair brought the political, social, and Canadian economic perspective to the table, and Li the foreign investors' broader view.

Husky, however, was a disappointment. Price sold some assets and bought others and hung on for the big payoff. Husky's east-coast drilling plans didn't pan out and its concentration on heavy oil didn't help matters, since oil prices stayed low. Husky lost $36 million in 1988; it made money the next year, but not enough. It seemed Husky must be viewed as a long-term proposition. The partners spent $400 million to acquire Canterra Energy from Nova in 1988, but never invested the rest of the promised $1 billion. Still, Li was willing to be patient—something he wasn't used to in Hong Kong. "Nova is more interested in near-term financial performance than Hong Kong is," says Price. The Li family, he added, can better afford to wait for a return on their investment until the mid-1990s. It turned out that it was the Canadian investor who couldn't wait for a turnaround at Husky.

Li's presence in Husky had been great for Nova and Blair; it had given the company some needed oomph in a bad time. But when Nova's petrochemical markets turned around in 1987, Blair proved that he hadn't learned any lessons about caution from having been up against the wall in the past. Polysar was a bad buy for Bob Blair. He bought at the top of the commodities cycle again, and by 1989, Blair's Nova was a company with $8 billion in assets and $4 billion in debts—$1.4 billion of that from the Polysar takeover. Li's managing director Simon Murray put his finger on the sore point: "If you have long-term vision but short-term cash-flow problems, life can become difficult."

Nova also had some very impatient shareholders; Nova is a widely traded

---

11 Imperial Oil bought Texaco Canada in 1989.

company, and as a result of the Polysar takeover it had attracted the interest of a number of stock arbitrageurs in New York. These guys eat companies for breakfast and spit them out before lunch. After Blair made an egregiously optimistic forecast for Nova's earnings—he predicted $2 a share but the earnings came to only 64 cents for each shareholder—more than 10 million Nova shares traded in a single day. Blair announced a plan to sell $500 million in assets and finally arranged to sell one of its most valuable assets—Polysar's rubber division—in May 1990. Even so, from a 1988 high of $14.75, Nova stock was selling at $7 at one point in 1990. Shareholders smelled blood.

Ironically, as Nova contemplated slipping out of the Husky knot, the oil company was finally beginning to look healthy. Debt had been lowered and Husky had added to its oil holdings through the Canterra purchase. Blair's son Jamie, the head of Husky's international division, was hoping for that big oil play somewhere else in the world to lift the company out of the doldrums. Even without it, one analyst valued it at $3.4 billion in 1989. It wasn't showing the type of return Li Ka-shing was used to, but it had potential.

However, Nova couldn't satisfy shareholders with potential. It looked, says Price, at "a host of ideas" to prove that Nova had part ownership of a company that shareholders just weren't giving the company credit for in the stock price. But it didn't have the earnings to make shareholders sit up and take notice and oil prices were too low to make them happy about its so-called "strategic" value as a long-term holding. That left just two options: a public sale of Husky stock, to make Nova shareholders realize what a 43 percent shareholding was worth these days, or a sale by Nova of some or all of its Husky shares.

By 1989, the rumors had already begun that Blair wanted to sell Husky, and that Gordon Capital was shopping around Nova's interest in the oil company. Blair, a seemingly almost unwitting master of circumlocution, didn't say yes; but he did say he'd "never say never" to a sale. In June, Li was in Canada accepting an honorary law degree from the University of Calgary. When asked whether his share was on the block, he was emphatic. "No," he said, "we have a very good percentage of shares, and don't see any change."

A year later, there was no resolution. "We have to work together constantly," said Blair in late 1990, "to ensure we're taking into account each other's point of view." But both Blair and Li were finding it difficult to dance with a partner who was doing a different set of steps.

*

The thought of selling Husky seemed to stick in Bob Blair's craw. For months and months he had trouble actually saying the word *sell.* He'd go only as far as saying that "at good value we'd be prepared to relinquish our shareholder position—if our partner is OK." And he couldn't, just couldn't, bring himself to talk about whether Li also wanted out of Husky. "Such thoughts," he said in early 1991, "are a bit intimate. We don't talk about how we feel about each other kind of third hand."

Nova's holding in Husky is seen on Bay Street as a "tough sale." A next-to-impossible sale in fall 1990, according to Eleanor Barker, an analyst at Sanwa McCarthy Securities, who has followed Nova and Husky for years and whose clients made a lot of money on Nova's purchase of Polysar. The only hope, in her mind, was that the Gulf conflict would drive up oil prices and make the company a bit more attractive. Of course, prices went right back down again. Shell talked of buying "some assets" at one point, and there were rumors that there was almost a deal of sorts in 1990—one of those complicated asset spin-offs that are designed for unsaleable companies, where each side ends up with some cash and some stuff they don't really want. By autumn 1990, Blair said he had "seen a hundred" possible restructuring plans for Husky. But nothing so far.

Meanwhile, Nova ended up restructuring yet again. Diversification is out of fashion; Blair wants to create two companies, one for petrochemicals and one for pipelines. While it's around, the Husky stake will be tagged onto the pipeline company.

Li has held on for five years, watching oil prices slide and Nova's interest turn elsewhere. He has also put up with shareholder criticism at home. At the 1989 annual meeting of Li-controlled Cavendish Investments—which holds part of the Husky shareholding—a shareholder specifically criticized Husky's poor returns, and Simon Murray agreed. "The short answer for Husky is the oil price has not performed over time the way we anticipated," he said, "so it's going to be a waiting game. And I would be misleading you if I said we were happy with that situation." Still, Murray was publicly supportive of the company through 1989 and 1990.

By 1991, however, Husky's future hung in the balance. Hutchison Whampoa's annual report featured a two-page spread on the oil company and two prominent pictures of the Canadian flag. Li rated only the same number of photographs himself. But behind that boost there was some politicking going on.

The turning point for Li and Murray was the Gulf War. Eleanor Barker was pleased by the $10 increase in light crude and doubling of heavy oil prices, but it made Li's group nervous. Especially when prices slid wildly after the war. They began to think they were in the wrong business. "It's a tough game—a big man's game, and it's becoming a bigger man's game," Murray told a reporter soon afterward. "That means the smaller you are, the more vulnerable you are. It's all very well for Exxon to blow two billion and forget where it went. We can't have that kind of trouble.

"If somebody walked in and said, 'I will give you good money for Husky,' we would certainly look at it," he added. "But that's not the same as saying we're looking for a buyer." After resisting the idea of a sale, the Hong Kong investors were finally considering it, since Blair seemed determined to restructure or sell Husky. "That, to some extent, puts pressure on us—whether we join them or find somebody else to replace them . . . all those sort of things come on to the table," Murray explained to the reporter.

That sounds fairly clear and straightforward. But not to Blair. "I wouldn't think that was right," he said of the reports that Li wants out. He labels it a theoretical discussion blown up by the newspapers. "I don't think that—it wouldn't be my understanding that he's out looking for buyers." Most telling, however, is his postscript. "We just don't talk about that . . ." Finally, however, Blair could no longer avoid his fate. In late June 1991 Husky was publicly put up for sale, and Blair announced he would be retiring as soon as the company's restructuring was approved by shareholders.

And Blair acknowledges that Li can't be happy with the fate of his largest foreign investment to date. "I think he'd be very charitable to me if he said he was happy, because we haven't made a lot of money for him and others of his investments do quite well." In fact, there was little market for Husky. Barker estimated at the time of Nova's mid-1991 announcement that Nova wanted about $900 million for its holding; she valued it at $500 million. As for Li's other plans in Canada, Blair hasn't a clue. "I've not heard him comment lately." The meeting of the minds seems to have gone awry somehow.

All of this is not good as far as Canada is concerned. Husky was a linchpin investment for Li. And although he has said in the past that if he ever sold he would reinvest his money in Canada, a sale might now fit with his United

States investment plans. "Sometimes you can get a better investment and maybe you change," he said in the *Globe and Mail* in 1990. Besides, he doesn't want to seem too big a wheel in Canada. When he bought his Husky stake, he said that he liked Canada because the politicians treated him like "an ordinary person." But Li and his son Victor had since found out that in Vancouver, they were not thought of as ordinary—and they were not really very welcome. Any move by Li to move out, whether as a result of Husky or experiences with other investments, is worrisome. As his one-time adviser, Bill Richards, said with great optimism when he bought into Husky: "K.S. has long coattails."

Victor and Richard Li grew up thinking of Vancouver the way some Canadians think of cottage country. The family had a summer home there, and from the time they were toddlers the boys flew in on a frequent basis. So it wasn't at all unusual that Victor would end up in Vancouver when, in 1986, K.S. sent him to Canada fresh from an engineering course at California's Stanford University to establish the three-year residency needed for Canadian citizenship.

It was also natural that Victor should become involved in real estate development in Vancouver. Property investment was also something that he had been familiar with since childhood. K.S.'s empire had been founded on real estate, after all, rather like the Reichmann family fortune in Canada. Much of Hong Kong's wealth, in fact, is based on land development; 60 percent of the stocks traded on Hong Kong's Hang Seng stock index are property companies.

And by this time, the Li family already had substantial real estate holdings in Canada. K.S. had dabbled a bit in United States markets such as Phoenix and Denver but the investments hadn't panned out, victims of the oil bust of the 1980s. Canadian investments were more successful. One of K.S.'s first purchases had been Toronto's Harbour Castle hotel back in 1981. Li paid an estimated $100 million plus and resold at the height of the Toronto property boom in 1989 to a Japanese group for $185 million. But much of his property portfolio—a collection of apartment buildings and office towers—was on the west coast, where he had been investing since 1968.[12]

12 More information on real estate holdings and other Hong Kong investments in Canada can be obtained from the following books: *China Tide: The Revealing Story of the Hong Kong Exodus to Canada*, by Margaret Cannon, HarperCollins, 1988; *Hong Kong Money: How Chinese Families and Fortunes Are Changing Canada* by John DeMont and Tom Fennell, Key Porter, 1988; *The Hidden Establishment* by Brian Milner, Viking, 1991.

Then, on April 29, 1988, the Lis won the right to develop the largest urban renewal project in the country. Vancouver's former Expo '86 site, also called B.C. Place and Pacific Place, covers one-sixth of downtown Vancouver. For this, Li and a few partners paid $320 million, with the payment spread over twenty years. Of course, he would be spending billions more: $2 billion was cited as a best guess at the time of bidding.

The money, the impact on the downtown area, and the symbolism of the international exposition site meant that this deal was bound to be controversial. In fact, it was a political boondoggle long before Li won the bidding. Li wasn't Premier Bill Vander Zalm's personal favorite for the project; that honor went to his buddy, British Columbia businessman Peter Toigo. Also competing were various other important Vancouver business executives, including Expo '86 chairman Jimmy Pattison, financier Sam Belzberg, former retail czar Charles (Chunky) Woodward, developer Jack Poole, and Edgar Kaiser, Jr., the former chairman of the Bank of British Columbia.

But once Li did win, the press questioned his relationship with cabinet minister Grace McCarthy. The Li family had hosted McCarthy during past trips to Hong Kong. This is common in Hong Kong, but raised eyebrows in Vancouver. One realtor even suggested that this was a payback by the province for the Hongkong and Shanghai Banking Corp.'s 1987 bailout-cum-takeover of the Bank of British Columbia.

All the fuss was not helped by Victor's own private business dealings. After working in CIBC's real estate department in Toronto for a short time, Victor headed for Vancouver to monitor the family's real estate holdings. A few months after the Expo announcement, he came under fire in Vancouver for his involvement with a condominium development in the False Creek area of the downtown. The condo units were offered for sale in Hong Kong only, with ads announcing the sale in the *South China Morning Post*. Residents there lined up for the opportunity to buy, and all 216 units sold within three hours.

Vancouver residents, who had been shut out, felt the Hong Kong buyers planned to flip the units for a good price. A few did, but most were looking for either a long-term investment or a place to live when they arrived in town. Victor, however, made a public apology. "I made my biggest investment about six years ago when I became a Canadian and a British Columbian," he said at a special press conference. "I want to emphasize again it is always our intention to be a good blue-chip Canadian company."

Unfortunately, the condo incident set off waves of bad feelings that affected all the Hong Kong immigrant investors in British Columbia. Xenophobia is never far from the surface at the best of times, but this time, it resulted in an extraordinary statement by Premier Vander Zalm. A month after the condo disaster, Victor Li's New Year's weekend Whistler ski plans were cut short by a startling news report. Vander Zalm had told reporters that he wanted to reopen the eight-month-old Expo deal. He wanted assurances from the Li family that there would be no quick resale or flip of the land. Victor Li hurriedly met with Vander Zalm at Fantasy Gardens, the premier's theme park. After that, Vander Zalm calmed down. Of course, he said, he understood that a deal was a deal.[13]

Victor went public to combat any rumors of flips or foreign sales at the Expo site, even though the property was still awaiting city approvals and was a long way from any development. He promised that the units there would be advertised twice in the Vancouver media before they went on sale, with two potential lenders listed in the ads. Then Vancouver residents would have a twenty-four-hour head start on other buyers. (This was later extended to a two-week head start.) This time, a sensitized Victor did himself proud. The public censure was all of Vander Zalm, for bowing to racist sentiment.

There is still, however, an anti-Li wave of envy and prejudice in Vancouver. Essentially, the anti-Li forces insisted that the Hong Kong magnate had paid far too little for the project that will change the face of downtown Vancouver. The payment of $320 million spread over fifteen to twenty years equals, by the province's own estimate, only $140 million had it been paid upfront. And it could cost the government as much as $50 million to remove toxic waste from the property. Li decided to share the project with a few friends.[14] Victor Li told a reporter these minority partners were brought in for reasons that were not financial. "If you want a celebration party, you'd better bring in enough shareholders to have a party. It's no fun celebrating by yourself." But many Vancouver residents felt they weren't invited to the party. And they resented Li having a party in their city.

Stanley Kwok, former head of the province's development team for the Expo site and Li's point man for his bid, is now head of Concord Pacific

13 Vander Zalm sold Fantasy Gardens to a Taiwanese investor in 1991; his involvement with the investment's sale would lead to his resignation as premier and leader of the Social Credit Party in B.C. Grace McCarthy had already resigned as a cabinet minister at that time; she later ran (unsuccessfully) for the SoCred leadership.
14 K.S. Li bid in concert with fellow Hong Kong investors Chen Yu-tung and Lee Shau Kee as minority partners. Several other friendly investment interests were included for small percentages, including CIBC.

Developments, the company in charge of making the empty expanse of land into a multi-billion-dollar collection of offices, housing, hotel accommodation, and shopping. An architect who emigrated from Shanghai to Hong Kong, then seventeen years later landed in Vancouver in 1968, Kwok chooses to let the enemy defend Li's Expo lands purchase. He dismisses all questions about the Li group's payment for the land by handing out a newspaper article. Dated April 29, 1988, it is by *Vancouver Sun* columnist Vaughn Palmer, a consistent critic of the Expo bidding process.

Palmer claims in this piece, however, that it is the province, not Li, who is getting the bargain. After all, B.C. paid only $60 million for the land in 1980; and land prices slumped after that before rising later in the decade. Palmer termed the $1.5 million per acre for raw land fair, especially since Li and his partners will be carrying some of it for many years before development—paying interest on borrowed money for land that isn't making any money. And he pointed out that the government will be receiving another $80 million during the next two decades as the project is developed.

That matter disposed of, Kwok makes it clear that he's much more concerned with the land's development rather than the storm of protest over its purchase. Once Concord Pacific had completed its plan for the site, more objections were raised. The city council dismissed it as "too elitist" and demanded a less architecturally ambitious, more "friendly" reconstruction. Three years, two city councils, two building directors, two directors of social planning, and 176 public meetings later, Kwok still hasn't broken ground on the 7,600 residential units and 3 million square feet of office and retail space. At the time of writing, he was awaiting development permits for an autumn 1991 start on the first building.

Once that threshold is crossed, scores of other property owners in the area will also begin plans for development in conjunction with the Expo site. Almost every other development plan of Vancouver, in fact, is tied up with or at least influenced by the Expo land project. It's a symbol of the future in this city that would like to fancy itself an international financial center, given half a chance.

But just as Expo '86 itself sold Vancouver as a Pacific city, the Expo land project illustrates its limitations as an international center. When dithering over the developer's proposal, a city official explained the care being given to the planning process. The Expo site, he said, is "a symbolic piece of property." But Vancouver hasn't paid enough attention to the symbolic messages it has been sending out to international investors.

It's much more than just the Lis. In Vancouver, it's called the Asian

Invasion. There is a culture clash between the Asian immigrants, with their large "monster houses" and their money and their fast-paced life style, and the locals. Normally laid back, Vancouverites have been getting steamed about the newcomers. They feel they're being pushed around simply because people with money are moving into the neighborhood. The local graffiti is a play on the Ugly American syndrome: "Asians, go home!"

Kwok draws the comparison to Americans when explaining that it's a fashion these days to blame Vancouver's problems on the Asians. In fact, there are strains from increasing urban crowding and immigration. About 60,000 people arrive in the beautiful city annually, 80 percent of them from other parts of Canada. Yet the immigrants catch all the flak. "It's not necessarily a large number," Kwok adds. "It's just that they don't look the same." And Vancouver is still hardly crowded by any standards, even Canadian ones.

Of course, it's easier for an outsider like myself to condemn the Vancouverites' attitude. But people can't sell their city as an international trade center in the making and then protest when immigrants arrive or foreigners buy their real estate. And Canada is gaining from this wave of investment-oriented immigration. We gain both money and management skills.

Many of those who arrived with the first waves of Hong Kong immigrants a quarter of a century ago are now valuable citizens, part of the community fabric. The second wave, a result of the 1974 Sino-British agreement to hand over the island by 1997, was more oriented to eventual immigration by the next generation.

So it doesn't matter if we call it immigration or foreign investment. In a generation, we won't notice the differences between established and new Hong Kong Canadians. Even when parents stay on the island, the children often attend Canadian schools. And in Hong Kong, the younger generation was not born in China and has a very different outlook. "Their values are a fit within this universal culture and are only incidentally Hong Kong," says former Canadian high commissioner to Hong Kong Maurice Copithorne.

But we may not gain these skilled, moneyed citizens and such a happy cultural and economic fit after all. We shouldn't be so smug about all the attractions of living and investing here. For we're seeing something we hadn't expected: people packing up and going home.

It's called reverse brain drain. Here the immigrants' degrees and qualifications are questioned; they don't speak the language like a native; they can't make as much money. "The present generation of Hong Kong people is about money," says Yao Wei, a former Chinese diplomat now acting as an adviser on Hong Kong immigration into Canada. "Let's face is, it's make the money while you can." The cellular phone is the ultimate Hong Kong money-making tool: portable. The people are portable too. The Hong Kong nickname for emigrants to Canada who leave a family behind is "astronaut." More and more astronauts are returning to mission control. Copithorne, more cautious, says the people will naturally flow back and forth. "The water's a bit muddy." Yao Wei is more definite in his assessment: "Right now, more people are going back."

Richard Li, for all his passion for Canada, is a good example of that pattern. Even Victor divides his time between the two countries. Right now, Richard is spearheading his family's plans for a satellite television system linking more than forty countries and 2.7 billion people in Asia. Their trading company Hutchison owns one-third of a satellite called AsiaSat and has reserved half its capacity. After high-profile, hard-nosed negotiations with the Hong Kong government, the group launched the service in April 1991, six months ahead of schedule. There will be four English channels and one Mandarin channel.

Which brings up another telling point: there's nothing binding the Li family's money to Canada. After their rather dismal experience with Husky, the failure of their joint venture with Gordon Capital and the sclerosis of the Canadian economy argue against a big push here.

And there isn't much chance right now to work on long-term relationships, like the Lis' twenty-year partnership with CIBC. Time is a precious commodity in the Hong Kong psyche. Investors there move in seven-year cycles; entrepreneurs can double their capital in seven years; speculators in as little as three. So the remaining six years before the island is handed over to the People's Republic of China is almost a lifetime in Hong Kong business terms.

Of course, the money has to go somewhere. Even without the constant threat of 1997, the country just isn't big enough to hold all that wealth. Its live-today philosophy doesn't encourage research and development spending or technological developments, either, and it's not close enough to many markets. Although the Li family plans to spend hundreds of millions of dollars there during the next few years, Richard Li, when talking about the failed Columbia S&L deal, makes a simple but salient point: "Basically, Hong Kong is too small for us already."

There's Asia. If Hong Kong investors are looking for low-cost labor, they can choose among China, Thailand, Malaysia, Sri Lanka, or India. Asian countries. Singapore has become a very attractive destination, and the government there is doing everything it can to encourage investment and immigration from Hong Kong. Li is there, as are most of the big moneymen. It offers the same language, the Chinese culture, and the free-market ethic. There is no tax on offshore profits. It's also a three-and-a-half-hour flight from Hong Kong, not a thirteen-hour, forty-minute trans-Pacific marathon to reach the nearest coast of Canada.

And there's the United States. Traditionally, Hong Kong's ties were with Britain and the Commonwealth, Taiwan's with the United States. As a result, there are 60,000 Canadian university graduates in Hong Kong. But those days are gone; the Lis and others are now educated in the United States, and many Hong Kong investors feel there is more money to be made south of the forty-ninth parallel.

Canada also used to be more cooperative about immigration. The United States Congress is considering an amendment to its immigration laws to set up an investor category, much like Canada's and Australia's. Should this pass, it's likely the flow of immigrants and investment will be diverted, at least in part, to the United States—unless Canada shows itself to be more attractive and welcoming. And the United States is actually less restrictive about some aspects of its visas. It allows investors to delay settling for up to fifteen years; Canada demands settlement within three. On a recent trip to Hong Kong, Prime Minister Mulroney was lobbied on just this point.

Hong Kong investors know the societal problems in the United States and are attracted to Canada's stability and quality of life. But they don't like Canadian taxes and don't understand why we have a medical insurance plan. They don't necessarily equate quality of life with a broad-based standard of basic necessities.

We shouldn't let that influence our policies, of course. But we should realize that during an economic downturn here, Hong Kong investors could do the same thing that Canadian investors often do: divert their investments south. There is more danger that their money won't return. Says Yao Wei: "The pull can be very strong." In spring 1991, Kwok, who is also on Cheung Kong's board, was ruminating about Li's plans for overseas developments. They would occur, he said, "wherever the opportunity lies. The next project could be here, or it could be in the States."

If a Canadian were asked to describe the perfect immigrant, the description might run something like this: someone with skills to help this country grow and prosper. Someone with enough money to start a business or invest in our companies. Someone who could broaden our cultural horizons and bring a new flavor to our cultural mosaic. By that measure, the Hong Kong immigrants are the perfect new Canadians. They have the same entrepreneurial skills as many of the postwar immigrants, but also the money to take advantage of those skills. Canadians' rejection of these ideal immigrants leads to the scandalous conclusion that Canadians don't really want any immigrants at all. As a senior government official said about the Jews in the late 1940s, it seems that none is too many.[15]

This is not only close-minded and prejudiced, it is simply wrong-headed. "Few Canadians recognize the debt they owe to immigrants who now import $5 billion plus into our economy," pointed out *Globe and Mail* economics columnist Peter Cook in an August 1990 article. Without this "financial transfusion," Cook added, the Canadian current account deficit would be larger than it is and Canadian interest rates higher. We need their money. One of our real problems is our small population. Our home market is too small. We don't have enough capital interested in long-term investment. We need a higher percentage of educated Canadians attuned to the demands of the technological era.

Hong Kong investors provide all of those things. The island is our largest source of immigrants—28,000 in 1990, twice the number from any other single country. And twice as many Hong Kong residents were still choosing Canada at that point over any other destination (Australia, also popular, was rejected by many as being too racist). Last year 13,000 Hong Kong youths came here as foreign students.

They bring money; Hong Kong is the homeland of more than a quarter of our business immigrants—5,300 in 1989—triple the size of the next largest group. Under the federal investor-immigrant program, they must invest a minimum of $150,000 if they locate in less popular provinces, $250,000 if they choose British Columbia, Ontario, or Quebec. In 1988, Hong Kong investment amounted to $2.4 billion; in 1990 it was $4 billion. Between 1986 and 1988, that type of investment flow created 3,000 Canadian jobs in the garment, electronics, and plastics industries.

These families are taking a risk. Not all the businesses are successes. In 1991, immigrants were worried about spending their money here on busi-

15 The 1982 book *None Is Too Many: Canada and the Jews in Europe, 1933-1948*, by Irving Abella and Harold Troper (Lester and Orpen Dennys), outlined how Canadian immigration policy during the 1930s and 1940s was designed to keep Jews from immigrating to Canada.

nesses that might fail because of the Canadian recession. But they also face a risk at home. "You make more money in Hong Kong, sure," points out Yao Wei. "But how long is that going to last?" The most recent example of the fluidity of Hong Kong business deals is the planned seaport and airport for the island. The first big post-Tiananmen project, it has become bogged down in fighting between China and Britain, a fact that sends shivers through the island's population.

In a funny way, in fact, Hong Kong immigrants and Canadians share a certain lack of control over their economic future. The people of Hong Kong don't have any control over the future of their homeland: over who will govern them and what that system of government will be. That breeds rootlessness and selfishness. In Canada, we don't have a lot of control over our finances; we desperately need money in this country. That causes resentment, envy, a dog-in-the-manger mentality. We lose sight of the fact that we want these people for more than their money. "Gumption," says Copithorne. "That's what we look to our immigrants to provide. They don't inherit our views and prejudices toward what can be done. They break the customs." These days, that helps broaden the Canadian outlook, he adds. "It's a significant contemporary influence. It's helping us to shape our economy toward the demands and needs of the world."

Of course, Hong Kong immigrants can be insensitive to and impatient of Canadian ways at times. They are used to a noisy, frenetic environment, for instance, and disdain more laid-back ways. "Let's be fair," says Yao Wei. "Hong Kong people, they should at least be sensitive to the issues here." To encourage that, he helped plan the Canada Week celebrations in Hong Kong in May 1991. Much of the interchange was about business—and it wasn't just the usual tales of gold in the street. For instance, Ken Georgetti, president of the British Columbia Federation of Labor, was asked to speak at a symposium on Canadian investment. The tactic was that he would calm Hong Kong investors' fears about labor unions in British Columbia and help explain the difference in management styles in Canada to which Hong Kong investors must adjust. One of Georgetti's challenges: explaining why it takes fifteen hours to turn a ship around in Hong Kong's port and thirty to forty-five hours to do the same job in Vancouver.

Brian Mulroney was also at the Canada Week sessions. His visit was designed to deliver a strong message of support for Hong Kong: he didn't visit China and refused meetings with Chinese officials. Instead, he met with Hong Kong business leaders and spoke about Canada's unity question, trade, and investment. Mulroney's message was mixed. At one point he seemed to be on a mini-election tour as he told a television interviewer that the opposition parties in Canada may not be as open to Hong Kong immigration as he has been. And he told a Chamber of Commerce gathering that "we will be with you for the long haul."

But Mulroney turned down requests for looser rules on entry visas and said immigration would be within set global guidelines. He may not have to worry about too much demand. "I hope the Canadian government will look with an objective eye at the comparison between investments in the U.S. and Canada," an investor with Canadian holdings told the *Globe and Mail*'s correspondent, Edith Terry, after Mulroney's speech.

Hong Kong is mercurial; its mood swings are more dramatic all the time. It could be swinging against Canada. When Li Ka-shing bought his Husky stake, Bob Blair said that the Hong Kong entrepreneur openly talked about his choice of Canada for the investment. His explanation: Canadians had treated him well in past dealings. "He feels in the long range," said Blair, "that ours is a stable, reliable, civilized, peaceful society." Canadians would do well to reflect on the simple home wisdom proffered by Li to students at the University of Calgary in 1989. "Always remember," he said, "that your greatest asset is your reputation."

CHAPTER SEVEN

The California Roll

There is a ritual to entering a Japanese executive's office or meeting room. Cards are exchanged with a bow—very important. The guest must sit in the chair furthest from the door. There are four chairs, often black leather, arranged two by two, straight across from each other and separated by a table, usually square, usually topped with brown Arborite. Tea is served, the office lady bowing and scraping. There is an exchange of civilities. Unfortunately for the Westerner, the Japanese executive normally doesn't move beyond that. He maintains his *tatamae*, or false front, for the entire conversation. Frustrating, but after a while the Canadian visitor grows comfortable with the rhythm of pleasantries. In order to go beyond the platitudes, there must be many meetings.

Matters can move much more quickly even at the first meeting, however, if the Japanese executive is familiar with the visitor's company and business. That makes it easier for the Japanese to "define the question" and focus on business opportunities. Then, mutual interests and a series of searching questions may lead the Japanese business associate to venture an opinion or a judgment.

When I met with Toshihiro Matsuki, managing director of C. Itoh and Co., he cut through all the formality and careful evaluation of mutual benefit. There was still the traditional introduction, but that made what came next even more shocking. Once Matsuki began to speak, he gave me his *honne*—his real thoughts. I could have been sitting with Lee Iacocca. In fact, for bluntness, Iacocca has nothing on this guy.

Matsuki had been one of forty-six Japanese business leaders on an investment mission to Canada in the autumn of 1989. I was talking to him in March 1990, and the group, led by Mitsubishi Corp. president Shinroku Morohashi, had just published its findings. They were politely favorable, but not as glowing as the report of an investment mission of four years earlier. In Tokyo, I'd been hearing the same sweet nothings from everyone I'd interviewed so far: Canada is a lovely country, so big, so many resources — but it really has nothing special to offer. Matsuki was saying the same thing, but more bluntly: the mission had been poorly organized, the wrong points had been emphasized, and the Japanese had left without learning what they wanted to know about the Free Trade Agreement.

Then came the stunner. "The governments of many provinces were trying to explain that the quality of your labor is better than Americans'," he said. "Without really using a direct expression, I think that also means that you don't have many black people. And that, I think, was the point that really you wanted to explain to us." That he would think this was our message shows a huge communications gap. We had obviously done a bad job in our presentations. It also shows that Japanese perceptions of Canada are invariably within an American context.

Now, this outrageous comment was not coming from a neophyte. Matsuki has been doing business in Canada for twenty years, regularly visiting British Columbia because of C. Itoh's lumber interests there. Certainly, he's been trading with Canada long enough to know something about our training and education systems. He showed that when he added that although the provinces were trying to promote the quality of the labor force, "we do not look at Canada as cheap labor or high-quality labor."

Matsuki's comment threw me for a loop until, many months later, I read the authorized translation of Japanese politician Shintaro Ishihara's bestseller, *The Japan That Can Say No*. Ishihara is also uncommonly blunt; he is, however, a popular politician who is said to represent a viewpoint common to many Japanese. And he mentions racism as an underlying flaw in the American system. A class system based chiefly on race is responsible for the poor education and training of much of America's work force, Ishihara contends. He also believes that American attitudes toward the Japanese reflect this same racial prejudice. It's a short leap of logic to realize that Matsuki was merely imbuing Canadians with the same brand of veiled but endemic Western racism.

The Japanese don't find this attitude particularly shocking. Indeed, they themselves have often been criticized for their own discrimination against other races. And the group that came to Canada on the Morohashi trade mission are a particularly like-minded crew. They are all corporate executives, closely tied to the ruling Liberal Democratic Party (LDP).

The trading houses were, of course, well represented on the mission.

They each had a number of representatives on board. Mitsui, Marubeni, Sumitomo, Nissho Iwai. There were consumer products companies, such as Sony, and resource manufacturing concerns, such as Daishowa Paper, Kawasaki Steel, and NKK Corp. And of course officials from the Bank of Tokyo, Japan's Ministry of International Trade and Industry, and the Japanese business organization, the Keidanren.[1]

Matsuki isn't as sympathetic toward Canadians as many of his counterparts in Tokyo, in part because he has had at least one unpleasant experience with the Canadian government: some years ago, Canadian competitors lodged a complaint with Revenue Canada that one of C. Itoh's subsidiaries wasn't paying its fair share of taxes. That still nettles him. Make no mistake, however, he still prefers Canadians to Americans. Matsuki believes that he can trust Canadians not to divert promised supplies to domestic markets—we don't have the domestic demand, so our exports are more important to us. "Then again, they [Canadians] take care of the foreigner much better than Americans." He respects Americans as more competitive, more aggressive than Canadians. But he likes Canadians better. They are not as open as Americans, but they are easier for him to trust.

Of course, these stereotypes all hinge on the relative power held by the United States, Canada, and Japan in terms of our international trade positions. Canada, as usual, has little power but many needs to fulfill. Japan is our second-largest trading partner. Our trade balance with Japan is twice as large as Canada's trade relationship with Great Britain and five times that with France. In fact, Canada's trans-Pacific trade has been higher than our trans-Atlantic imports and exports since 1983. Aside from its importance as an export buyer, Japan is Canada's third-largest direct investor—direct means money spent on a significant holding in a business or real estate, as opposed to money spent on investment holdings in our stock or bond markets.

But Canada isn't a big deal for the Japanese. They're very concerned with increasing their investment in the United States and (more recently) in Europe and within Asia. Canada, in contrast to all these other places, neither offers a sizable market nor poses a threat that they may be shut out unless they establish beachheads from within. So Japanese investment in Canada, although big by our terms, has represented only 2.5 percent of all Japanese foreign investment for two decades. During the same period, Japanese investment in the United States doubled from 20 to 40 percent of

---

1   A federation of business company associations, more or less equivalent to the Business Council on National Issues in Canada.

its foreign investment. The Japanese weren't happy with the era of Pierre Trudeau and the Foreign Investment Review Agency. They stayed away after a very unfavorable 1976 trade mission report.

The trade missions clearly set the tone for Japanese investment here. Its total $4-billion investment in Canada to date is double what it was in the mid-1980s. The government claims that change is largely due to a glowing report by a 1986 trade mission much like Morohashi's. The missions have had little impact on the types of investment made, however. Japanese business here so far has either been to buy resources or to set up distribution and merchandising facilities for products shipped from abroad to Canadian subsidiaries of Japanese firms. And those subsidiaries usually exist because of the restrictions on American imports imposed before free trade.

The Japanese have their own reasons for not being all that enthusiastic about free trade between the United States and Canada. They look on it with what one American observer describes as "reserved skepticism." For them, the ease of moving between the two markets is outweighed by the significance of the United States decision to make a commitment to a North American trading bloc. That type of regionalism, they fear, could quickly turn into a we-they mentality: North America vs. the Pacific Rim.

Canada's one card to play in this global trade gamesmanship is our relationship with the United States. We are like a courtier trading on his access to the king. Our diplomats decided during the free trade negotiations that it would be to our advantage to convince Japan that we can help it in its delicate negotiations with the United States. At the same time, our trade officials were setting up the Free Trade Agreement as a way to entice other investment, using Canada as a less threatening, a "nicer," base from which to deal with the United States market. This notion has a particular appeal for the Japanese.

Of course, this free trade marketing strategy could backfire on Canada. Japan could look at the trade agreement and decide that the Canadian market could easily be serviced from the United States. No need to put more money in Canada, when the United States can be made happy by new investment there to supply the peripheral Canadian marketplace. Canada could be, to a large extent, abandoned. Not only would this mean no new investment, but there's a chance that the distribution and marketing centers could be closed.

So during the 1989 trade mission, it was crucial for Canada to create the right impression on the Japanese. Unfortunately, we failed. We weren't prepared, even though we'd wanted the visit ever since Brian Mulroney had lobbied former Japanese prime minister Noboru Takeshita for another investment mission during Takeshita's Canadian visit in January 1988. For one thing, Ottawa had trouble handling eager but ill-prepared provincial officials. "Each province did not know how to welcome the mission," recalls Matsuki. "So they all referred to Ottawa. Ottawa sent a manual to all the provinces. So all the provinces welcomed us with the same manual."

The Japanese were struck, in fact, by the power of the provinces. The visiting executives were divided into two groups during the mission, and between the two were obliged to visit almost every province. "I think," says Matsuki, "this is what you call the political compromise." They didn't understand why they were forced to do so much traveling. The many stopovers did give them an opportunity, unfortunately, to note the inconsistencies between federal and provincial policies.

The Japanese left feeling that they didn't get enough information on subjects such as taxation, the country's economic environment, and the actual contents of the Free Trade Agreement. This must, they decided, have really been a friendship mission rather than a serious investment briefing. "We had many welcome speeches, many luncheon parties, and many dinner parties," recalls Matsuki. "We did not have much time for questions." With his lumber interests, Matsuki wanted to know all about the softwood lumber dispute between the United States and Canada—the politics, the detailed negotiations, the prospect for future adjustments to the eventual agreement.

"I understand that in Ottawa there were some people who actually worked for the [free trade] negotiations," he added. "If they could explain what happened and what America said and what Canada said, it would have been very [interesting]—a live report. The point is, we want to know [about] the political influence or political relationship between Canada and America." That, Matsuki and his more reticent Tokyo counterparts all agreed, is the one question that must be answered before the Japanese will make any further investment decisions.

Canada's clumsy handling of the Morohashi mission was a serious mistake. The diplomatic corps knew it; during 1990, they tried to patch up their error by dispatching free trade experts to Tokyo to call on members and fill them in on details about the Free Trade Agreement. Part of the problem was beyond their control, however; in autumn 1989, it was still too early to know exactly how the trade agreement would work.[2] No one was

2 See Chapter Nine for a discussion of free trade in operation.

sure what the American attitude toward Japanese subsidiaries in Canada would be.

External Affairs had the right take on the way to get the attention of the Japanese, however. Just mention the word *America* and see their polite indifference turn to genuine enthusiasm. The Japanese are obsessed with the United States, even more than the Americans are obsessed with the Japanese. And the only way that Canada is going to be able to benefit from Japanese investment in any significant way in future is to correctly gauge and aggressively capitalize on that mutual obsession.

The Americans and the Japanese are both masters of control. Their love-hate relationship is based on an uneasy balance of power. The Americans conquered and continue to dominate the Japanese militarily; the Japanese dominate economically. The unease underlying their constantly shifting relationship, however, emanates from a more complicated cultural gap. The Japanese admire America's culture but also cherish their own. They deplore the smug shiftlessness of American society. The Americans want Japan's money but have difficulty dealing with Japanese mores. Yet at the same time they admire and are adopting some elements of Japanese culture. All this is a bit like the historical relationship between Old World and New World, back when the cultured Old World was Europe and the moneyed New World was America. Only it's not that simple.

The best anyone can hope for here is a synthesis of the two cultures. Even Shintaro Ishihara promotes this idea: Japan and the United States are the two nations that will shape the future, he says in *The Japan That Can Say No.* "The United States is a Western model of modern civilization, Japan an Eastern version. They are different but not incompatible; confrontation is not inevitable. Bearers of great traditions, both countries are now challenged to reach a higher level of human accomplishment." Ishihara's next sentence focuses this challenge: "In the new age, economics will be preeminent."

A telling, if small-scale, example of this cross-cultural fertilization is the recent announcement that Japan Air Lines' new nonstop service between Washington and Tokyo, which began March 31, 1991, would feature the world's first-ever in-flight sushi bar. During a three-month test run, Japanese sushi chefs served passengers in first class and executive class from a specially constructed nine-person sushi bar. This Oriental addition to the more mundane Western-style air fare was made possible by new technology in the carriage and storage of fresh food. Typical Japanese innovation: able to capitalize on technology for any conceivable market. But it's just as likely that the American passengers will enjoy the raw fish and rice; sushi is popular the world over, in its original form and with United States-inspired adaptations. The most well known among the latter is the California Roll. This delicate morsel is named after the state where it was created, which just happens to be Japanese visitors' favorite among American states. And it serves as a fitting metaphor for what is happening to sovereignty worldwide these days: a melding of ideas and customs through the revolution in global communications.

The Americans and the Japanese have created that revolution. For the most part they haven't, however, yet managed to come to terms with each other's customs and use them to reach a new level of accomplishment. So far there's much more mindless copying than true understanding and innovation. And the relationship also illustrates the nationalistic tensions that still shape our cultural and political beliefs and, by extension, our economic policies. There's a real danger that these tensions could escalate into an unfortunate power struggle among polarized trading blocs, a struggle from which relatively powerless countries like Canada can emerge only as losers. To gain any benefit from the relationship between the two powers, we must understand the ingredients that make up the metaphorical California Roll.

Yutori is an ideal state for which all Japanese yearn. It incorporates contentment, release from angst, a feeling of freedom. Ideally, it was achieved through religion; more usually, it was sought over history through merging oneself with a richer, more powerful, more stable social entity. At one point in Japanese history, that would have meant securing a place in a powerful feudal clan; ten years ago, it would have meant securing a position in a large, powerful corporate structure. These days, the youth of Japan are trying a new path to *yutori*—one more familiar to their American contemporaries. Contentment through consumerism.

The young men and women known as Japan's *shin jinrui* ("brand new man" or, more literally, "new human species") come to Tokyo's Shibuya district to shop. The *shin jinrui* are seen as trouble by many of the older generation—too lazy, too unmotivated, too demanding, too American. Their break with traditional Japanese values and goals is much more complete than merely the propensity to spend. But their material demands are the same as those being made on a more moderate scale by all Japanese consumers. They can pay for a better life style. The streets of the business district are lined with the BMWs and Jaguars of those who can afford the astronomical parking fees, or *gaisha*, needed to keep a car on some of the world's most expensive real estate—the equivalent of U.S. $400 monthly on average, $600 in the Ginza district.

Before 1985, foreign cars were considered ostentatious and somehow unpatriotic. Then the government gave its blessing to their purchase and even launched import promotion schemes. When a commodity tax on the vehicles was removed in 1989, registrations of new foreign cars jumped by 35 percent. BMW and Mercedes-Benz capitalized on this change in attitude with aggressive marketing programs and a push to open local dealerships, leaving less astute car manufacturers in the dust.

Even those who can't afford *gaisha* are buying what they can. Just about every "office lady" who rides the subway system to her parents' suburban home carries an Yves St. Laurent handbag.[3] The list of other favorite purchases includes TV sets, washing machines, VCRs, fridges, and European designer clothing. "Japan's rich. It took a while for it to sink in," says Paul Summerville, the Canadian in charge of research at the Tokyo office of British investment firm Jardine Fleming. "But people have more money in their pockets now—and they're demanding more."

The Japanese are also seeking happiness abroad in packages of two and three weeks. The United States is a big tourist destination, with California the biggest draw. The Japanese are also crazy about cowboys. Beef quotas were loosened a few years ago, and the Japanese are developing a taste for steaks. Japan's largest beef company, Zenchiku Ltd., bought the 77,000-acre Lazy 8 ranch in Dillon, Montana, a few years back for U.S. $12.6 million in order to satisfy that taste. Ever since, mini-vans full of gray-suited executives armed with cameras pull up almost daily to catch a glimpse of their own private piece of the Wild West.

This is all officially approved policy, in moderation of course. A number of Japanese think-tanks with business and government links have been counseling more basic structural reforms to the economy to enable Japan to better fit in with the world around it. The most famous study, the 1986

---

3   Yves St. Laurent was ubiquitous in spring 1990, but by summer 1991 these handbags were passé. Louis Vuitton, according to one Tokyo resident, had become "the luggage of choice." The hot item of the day, however, was the Lanvin "Kelly" bag, named after Grace Kelly. With a retail price of $3,500, it has a two-year waiting list among university-educated working women in Tokyo. In Japanese-English idiom, or "Japlish," it's described as perfect for "high-sense shopping."

Maekawa Commission report, also suggested more openness to foreign companies. Along with this comes a push to lessen the power of the domineering *keiretsu,* an interwoven system of industrial groups.[4] They also see the payoff of all this cultural adaptation. A 1988 report on internationalization and cultural friction by the Japan Economic Research Institute calls economic friction "the labor pains of Japan" in emerging as a dominant international power.

There is a patina of American culture everywhere in Tokyo. English signs in the subway, a likeness of Michael Jackson on a three-story electronic billboard above a cluster of shops in the Roppongi district, mirror-glass office buildings cheek-by-jowl with Shinto shrines. And, everywhere, Western dress and Western music. But it is only a thin coating. To the Japanese, the Americans are still largely incomprehensible aliens. One local Tokyo nightly news report begins its American section by using the theme song from "Mission: Impossible."

That refrain seemed particularly appropriate during the spring and summer of 1990 as the two governments engaged in their Structural Impediments Initiative (SII) talks. In Tokyo, the message was that after years of stalling, Japan was giving in to American demands on all fronts. In Washington, the message was that the Japanese were being intransigent toward valid American demands. In early March of that year, Prime Minister Toshiki Kaifu flew to Palm Springs at President George Bush's request, and the pair agreed they needed a deal. By late March, their negotiators had put one together. The Japanese government would buy American super-computers; it would bend its tight rules for pulp and paper imports; it would eventually open the retail industry to competition; and it would increase its spending on public works—with bidding open to foreigners.

In response, the United States would leave Japan off the congressional hit list of trading adversaries, the so-called Super 301 "bad boys"—all countries targeted for retributive measures. The United States would not erect tariff barriers against Japanese products that they felt were cheaper because

---

4 A group of cartels dominated Japanese commerce before the Second World War. They were disbanded by the Americans, but regrouped and re-emerged as the powerful *keiretsu.* A pyramid of companies, a *keiretsu* arranges for inter-corporate investments and mutual financings and stakes out market shares for products in particular businesses. A *keiretsu* will contain a chain of companies—an auto company, for example, and its parts suppliers as well as its banker.

of domestic subsidies. The Japanese also pushed the United States on its own internal structural problems. Especially the deficit. Americans can't stand that type of holier-than-thou judgment, especially since they're so used to playing the role of judge, but they did promise to raise tax revenues, reduce the budgetary deficit, work to increase individual savings, and improve education and training programs. It's questionable whether the United States will deliver on its promises. Some economists feel the Japanese missed a unique opportunity to push the United States harder and further.

To execute all their concessions, the Japanese government would have to tear down the protectionist distribution system that has been in place for more than a hundred years and that was reinforced by the postwar reconstruction that was designed to supply the country with basic necessities while building businesses. Letting retail chains expand means putting tens of thousands of elderly shop owners out of work at a time when care for the elderly is becoming an increasing problem. Allowing the sale of cheap imported rice means abandoning the Japanese farmer. Both actions mean hurting the traditional Liberal Democratic Party's political base. Worst of all, it means going against the grain. It means, in short, doing things the American way.

The Japanese government was in a bind. It knew that it needed to make these reforms. But Kaifu didn't have the political support to make drastic changes to the country's economic structure. He is seen as a weak leader; since his predecessor Takeshita resigned as a result of a stock scandal, Kaifu has always been Hobson's choice. His support is shaky even within his own Liberal Democratic Party. So Kaifu and his handlers used the American trade demands to help the reforms gain acceptance. He isn't the first Japanese leader who has taken that path to reform. "That's a well-known approach in Japan," says York University's Japan expert Charles McMillan. "Foreign pressure often helps the administration to deal with otherwise intractable domestic concerns."

Having made the commitment in March, however, Japan stalled on a final SII agreement through the spring. Political analysts were divided on the reasons why. Some said that the foreign pressure tactic hadn't worked well enough against determined pressure groups fighting the changes within Japan. The government is preeminent in most areas of economic planning and social policy because it is executing policies that have a national consensus behind them. But it flounders when particular groups are openly against changes, such as land reform or restructuring the distribution system.

Some Western analysts didn't accept the "weak Kaifu" theory; they thought Japan was deliberately stalling. Japan's unwillingness or inability to make a final commitment placed the talks on shaky ground more than once. Finally, Bush and Kaifu had to do some political jockeying to reach common ground only days before the July 1990 Houston economic summit. Japan agreed to spend U.S. $2.77 trillion on public works during the 1990s; to crack down on bid rigging, monopolies, and unfair business practices; and to go ahead with retail sales reforms. At the summit, Kaifu worked hard to make a connection with Western reporters, speaking off the cuff and even jokingly donning a Stetson at a media barbecue.

Ironically, any changes either country could make would be to their benefit. If Japan adapts its distribution system and public works bidding, imports more rice, or allows retail chains, prices will fall. "A lot of people are saying that this will only lead to growing efficiency in the Japanese marketplace, which will be the last thing the Americans could want," muses Patrick Cirillo, a research analyst for the Centre for International Studies in Toronto, who closely tracked the SII talks.

Kaifu's control problems make it clear that politics and human nature are the same everywhere. Business is another matter. The Japanese simply have a different attitude toward business. Their system is centralized, organized, and closely controlled. Japanese management style is admired worldwide as efficient and effective. Companies have developed strategies for product development, and companies are willing to commit the money to ensure the process works. The Japanese spent 20 percent of their gross national product — U.S. $550 billion — on new plants and equipment in 1989. That's more than Canada's total GNP; two-fifths of that money was raised on the Tokyo stock exchange. Japan, a smaller economy, recently bypassed the United States in capital spending. Most of that money went to replace old operations with new robotic plants. The Japanese plan to spend much, much more on entirely new operations by the mid-1990s. Japan already has two-thirds of the world's industrial robots and is constantly adding to its supply. A survey of more than 1,200 senior executives conducted at a 1990 meeting of the Geneva-based World Economic Forum ranked Japan first at turning innovative ideas into competitive products. (The United States ranked third.)

In Japan, companies, through their *keiretsu,* support one another in times of need. They plan long-term approaches to new markets in concert with government policy makers and are committed to investing money in their country's long-term economic future. They are the first to admit that their fortunes have been made applying the research discoveries of others, and they are concerned about changes to international laws on patents and intellectual property rights. The Japanese want to make their own R&D advances. They're spending about one-quarter of their capital expenditure annually on R&D. And they're even hiring American scientists and computer experts. As a result, many of the research breakthroughs are now coming from Japan, including a new generation of home appliances incorporating computer chips that use "fuzzy logic" to make decisions about what to vacuum or how to wash a garment, for example.

Hiring Americans underlines that the Japanese recognize that their more harmonious yet more conformist culture hasn't yet developed its basic research skills. There are other drawbacks to the Japanese way. In fact, there is also a dark side to all this central planning. The system is rigid and entry is tightly controlled. Successful companies are off-limits to foreign buyers.

The same World Economic Forum survey that praised Japan's ability to develop products also called it the most unfair player in world markets. In Japan, foreign takeovers are not illegal, but they might as well be. "That kind of question is deeply rooted in Japanese culture," says Mitsuo Sato, senior managing director of the Tokyo Stock Exchange. "To Western people, particularly to Americans, a corporation is no more than a kind of tool to make money. To the Japanese, the corporation is something more than that. Hence, we have a kind of mental attachment to the company." A good explanation, but it doesn't account for the fact that the Japanese buy companies in other countries while keeping foreigners out of Japan.

Another explanation of the virtual ban on foreign takeovers is that powerful outside groups within the Japanese economy would weaken the Japanese *keiretsu.* The dominance of the *keiretsu* is dependent on enormous levels of economic control by top holding companies over their subsidiaries, at the expense of minority shareholders. Edith Terry, Tokyo correspondent for the *Globe and Mail,* stated in a 1990 series of articles that with Japanese strength in foreign markets, the *keiretsu* system will force a battle between Japan and the West over their starkly different forms of capitalism.

In its most sinister incarnation, the closely intertwined Japanese corporate system also has allowed for insider trading of stock by corporate and government officials; bid rigging for public works; and the recognition and institutionalization of the *yazuka*, organized crime groups that run the country's day-labor pools with a strong arm, as well as a plethora of strictly illegal operations. In the United States, there is a so-called revisionist school of thought that argues that Japan cannot be treated as a free-market player in negotiations. Instead, these economists and Japan-watchers say, it must be dealt with through "managed trade"—that is, tariffs, import restrictions, and other such measures.

American and other foreign employees of Japanese corporations are not always treated very well. The often-admired Japanese management systems fail on this point; the Japanese can be arrogant and intolerant to outsiders. In their United States operations, Japanese firms have a bad reputation for freezing out local managers rather than trying to fit them into the corporate culture and for keeping all real power at head office.

Recently, Japanese firms have acknowledged this. With the aid of head-hunters in the United States and Europe, they're working to change their corporate style abroad. A labor shortage at home gives them more reason than ever to adapt their mores to the local work force in host countries. Having American managers in their American subsidiaries increases cultural frictions in the short term, but will ultimately smooth out the differences between the two countries' very different corporate styles. The Japanese call the strategy *dochakuka*, which means becoming part of the local earth.

It's difficult to cooperate successfully with a group you don't really like— or that doesn't like you. The Japanese still have some very negative judgments about American society. A *Newsweek* poll taken at the time of the SII talks showed that they categorize Americans as lazy (66 percent of respondents), addicted to drugs and alcohol (93 percent), too ethnically diverse (57 percent), not interested in enough long-term investment (55 percent), and too greedy (53 percent). This is particularly significant given the Japanese penchant for shading the truth to make it sound more pleasant.

Each country thinks it is friendly toward the other. Another poll taken at the same time showed that two-thirds of Japanese feel friendly toward the United States and 75 percent of Americans think they're personally friendly toward Japan. That contrasted with each side's guess about the feelings of the other: 70 percent of Japanese feel Americans look down on them, while 48 percent of Americans think Japanese look down on them.[5]

The bias and the prejudice are deep-seated and seem to be growing. Americans are looking for an enemy these days. Rather than a military enemy, they've found an economic one. The richest man in world, aside from heads of state, is railway and real estate magnate Yoshiaki Tsutsumi, whose empire is worth about U.S. $16 billion. He's one of four Japanese among the top ten on *Forbes* magazine's wealth list; there are three Americans in this exalted position.[6] Even so, much of Japan's wealth is corporate, rather than personal pools of capital. At least 20 percent of the world's largest multinationals are Japanese. And the number keeps going up, not down.

In 1990, Americans felt they had a right to be paranoid about the Japanese. And the media fueled that paranoia. When Mitsubishi Estate bought Rockefeller Center in New York, a local Fox network news report broadcast pictures of the bombing of Pearl Harbor—and pointed out that Mitsubishi had made parts for the Japanese fighter planes. (This suggestion of an aggressive Japanese acquisitor was patently untrue: the Rockefellers had shopped their property around to a number of Japanese companies as well as to the Reichmanns and other foreign groups.)[7] A New York TV station also ran an ad for Pontiac dealers that played on the same theme. "Imagine a few years from now. It's December and the whole family's going to see the big Christmas tree at Hirohito Center," it stated. "Go on. Keep buying Japanese cars." On screen, white letters on a black background proclaimed, "Enough already."

Japan-bashing was a feature of a number of print and broadcast ads. An American Oldsmobile dealer ad compared heights of Japanese and American men. "That's why our car is built for our size families," it intoned, "not theirs." Meanwhile, workers at Japanese-owned car plants in the United States have for some time been making cars that rank higher in quality than

---

5 Source: *New York Times*/CBS News and Tokyo Broadcasting System.
6 The Reichmanns were also in the top ten in 1990, as well as a Swedish family and a South Korean entrepreneur.
7 They did, however, discriminate on the basis of taste, refusing to show their information to Donald Trump.

American cars. Pictures of samurai in magazine ads and on magazine covers stirred fears of where the next product "war" would be.

The February 26, 1990, cover of *Fortune* presented a fascinating picture of American angst on the eve of the Kaifu-Bush SII summit. Titled "Fear and Loathing of Japan: Why it's growing/Why it's dangerous/What to do about it," it parodied the classic *New Yorker* drawing of New York dominating its readers' view of the world. The *Fortune* cover showed Tokyo, represented by buildings bearing the signs Seiko, Fuji, Nikon, and Sony and by a threatening red car set to drive across the Pacific Ocean to New York at the other end. Canada and Mexico were represented by pale pink blobs of land stuck off at the ends of the picture; no other countries appeared.

The hysteria was in part fueled by Japanese purchases of American entertainment companies. Sony Corp. of America, run by Akio Morita's younger brother Masaaki, bought CBS Records in 1988 and Columbia Pictures in 1989. And in 1990, Matsushita Electric Industrial Co. bought MCA Inc. for U.S. $7.1 billion—the largest-ever Japanese takeover of an American company.[8] Among all this Japan-phobia there were few actual facts. Great Britain, not Japan, was the largest foreign investor in the United States during the 1980s, spending more than U.S. $100 billion. Moreover, the top three companies exporting to the United States are British. Honda, the top Japanese exporter to the United States, ranks thirteenth worldwide in exports to the United States.[9]

In the United States there was also a public uproar about Japan's lobbyists and its funding of American think-tanks. Politicians and journalists charged that Japan was attempting to subtly influence—read subvert—American policy making. This at a time when the United States was turning to Japan to bankroll a foreign policy agenda that the United States can't afford.

The United States is obviously overreacting, but there are very good reasons for the Japanese to tread carefully. Akira Suzuki, a strategist at Morgan Stanley and Co. in Tokyo, points out that as much as 15 percent of corporate Japan already has operations situated in the States, and Japan also relies heavily on American exports. "They went to the United States like corporate immigrants," he says of the large Japanese firms. "To pay for their American citizenships, they've got to be more American."

---

8   This had a Canadian repercussion: MCA is a major shareholder in struggling Cineplex Odeon Corp. of Toronto, together with the Montreal branch of the Bronfman family.
9   Source: *The Economist.*

The Japanese believe that part of their problem with the United States is simple public relations. They are more used to behind-the-scenes lobbying than front-and-center statements of their national goals, but they are now trying to explain their economic and political vision more clearly to the American audience. In 1990, Japan's Ministry of International Trade and Industry (MITI) published its first-ever decennial look at future economic trends. The MITI report (translated into English) projected radical changes within Japan during the 1990s. It forecast a trilateral (North America-Japan-Europe) power base and said Japan would of necessity become more active in dealing with international affairs. It would use its money to "emulate the role the United States played in world development after the Second World War."

Ironically, the United States is not far behind Japan in the area of unfair trade practices: it ranked third in the World Economic Forum survey. Most damning of all, the United States was cited as the most complacent country about its economic future. Ishihara's book contains a ten-page list of items that the United States needs to fix, everything from allowing consumers less access to banking machines to a ban on the export of Alaskan oil to stronger gun control laws. Even less partisan observers of the world scene agree that in order to save their industrial structure, Americans must become more committed to long-term investment, with lower initial returns for the company but payoffs for the entire economy in product innovation and technology training. They must be more willing to support other companies in times of need, more committed to an effective public education system. In fact, more Japanese.

Even when the Japanese had their own domestic economic setbacks during 1990, American fear of their domination remained. A January 1991 cartoon in *Forbes* showed a typical white-collar American watching a business news broadcast. The announcer's message: "Rumors of a buyout of the entire American economy by the Japanese sent the stock market soaring." The *Forbes* cartoon was surprising, given the bad year Japan endured during 1990. In fact, many Westerners felt the joke was on Japan at last. The Tokyo Stock Exchange had dipped and dived all year, endangering the capital base of many financial companies. Inflation and interest rates rose, the yen fell, stock speculators were badly damaged, and many institutions had to ease off on their foreign investments.

Still, the market's fragility was merely a temporary setback to Japanese expansion, as shown by all the money pumped into research and capital improvements. The consumerism and the stock speculation can be viewed as the natural adjuncts of good economic times. "The economy has come into its own, so people are more ambitious about their demands," says Paul Summerville. "But at the core, Japan remains unchanged."

As does the United States. Its involvement in the 1991 Gulf War showcased its continuing reputation as the unbeatable international enforcer. Japan sent no troops to that engagement, only money. At the same time, there was another international arena in which the United States badly needed Japan's money: Eastern Europe. Support for the newly capitalist nations was an issue at the time of the 1990 SII talks and remained one during 1991. Japan already had a growing interest in the European Community and in 1989 invested U.S. $14.2 billion in Europe, twenty-eight times its 1980 level of investment. It had been concentrating on western Europe, taking a generally low profile on eastern European calls for financial aid and investment. Still, a capitalist eastern bloc is seen as a base for less-sophisticated manufacturing and an eventual market worth pursuing. And Ishihara among others sees the opportunities in areas such as Siberia. "Eastern Europe and the Soviet Union," he proclaims, "will ultimately be part of the global network of Japanese technology." The lure, he adds, is natural resources. And there is the vast market for Japanese products. This isn't yet official Japanese policy. But investors are beginning to examine the idea. And Europe's gain, unfortunately, would be Canada's loss.

Makoto Toda was certainly favoring investment in Europe in the spring of 1990. Toda is what is known in Japan as a "salaryman," a middle-level manager, in his case at the country's largest life insurer, Nippon Life Insurance. As the general manager of the international planning department, Toda is in charge of the giant Japanese firm's foreign investments, which account for about 5 percent of its total holdings. Nippon Life, as the largest single shareholder on the Tokyo Stock Exchange, is of course particularly vulnerable to the periodic plummet of the Nikkei stock index. Despite the Nikkei's severe plunge in early 1990, Toda was sanguine. During the final week of March 1990 (the week of all year-end accounting in Japan), Toda was busy meeting with the dozen investment experts from around the globe who report to him. They had not gathered to fret about the falling fortunes on the Nikkei, or to worry about how it would fare during the next twelve months. Rather, they were studying their global investment strategy for the next five years. Why worry about the billions already lost, after all, when there were billions yet to be won?

Nippon Life, like most other financial institutions in Japan, thinks that many of the billions will be won in the coming decade in stock markets—and they're making many of those stock investments in Europe. A third of Nippon's U.S. $8.6-billion international stock portfolio was in Europe by the end of 1989; that's slightly more than its American shareholdings. "If we are to become more sophisticated investors in global asset management, we must stress stocks more," Toda explained. "We want to invest more in European stocks to get more capital gains, because we want to pursue total returns." The other Japanese institutions are all following similar investment plans—all, of course, with the government's blessing and encouragement.[10]

One Japanese fund manager's European investment plans may seem to be of little interest to Canadians, but they indicate a very important shift in money and power away from Canada. Moving into European stocks means moving out of North American bonds. For years, Japanese insurers were pushed into international bond markets because their government's regulations didn't let them pay dividends to policyholders from capital gains on stock investments. Now this is changing. As a result of a deal with the Ministry of Finance, Toda and his counterparts have begun to shift their investments into the stock market. In the next decade (around the time they are ready to sell stock and make capital gains they wish to pass on to policyholders), the investment rules will be more formally altered. In the meantime, the companies can position themselves to take advantage of the coming change, all accomplished through quiet consensus leading to unruffled adaptation. The Japanese way.

The change will do more than just ruffle the Canadian financial scene. At the end of 1989, Nippon, for one, had placed 52 percent of its U.S. $15.5-

---

10 In the spring of 1990, Toda was the point man on the fate of American stockbrokerage Shearson Lehman Hutton. Nippon Life owned 13 percent of the American brokerage, which was in trouble from lack of business. Both Shearson chairman Peter Cohen and James D. Robinson III, chairman of Shearson majority shareholder American Express, flew in for emergency meetings. As a result of one of those high-pressure discussions with Robinson, Nippon agreed to help shore up Shearson through a few joint ventures and Toda invested U.S. $200 million in American Express as well. Soon after, Cohen was gone. Toda was fascinated with the American-style corporate morality play; it was so different from the Japanese way of doing business.

billion bond portfolio in North American bonds, more than one-third of
that in Canada. Japanese investors such as Nippon are Canada's main
creditors, holding $44 billion in Canadian government bonds—10 percent
of all Canadian bonds and half of those held by foreign investors. Unfortunately, the Japanese don't usually buy Canadian stock. When they do, it's
as a venture capital play rather than a serious element of their stock
portfolios. Canadian stocks are perceived as resource-dominated and
chancy.

Japanese investors buy our bonds because we're a high-risk nation,
owing to our government debt. This means we'll pay them a high return for
their money. A good deal from their perspective, since they see us as a stable
nation, Quebec's sovereignty aspirations notwithstanding. More stable
than Third World countries, which are the only ones offering interest rates
comparable to Canada's and Australia's. So foreign investors, especially the
Japanese, tend to make a good deal of their bond investments in these two
former British colonies. They jump in, particularly when they feel that
Canadian bonds are a bargain in relation to United States bonds. And they
stay as long as rates remain high. But they'll jump out just as quickly if an
interest rate drop increases the price of their bonds, giving them a quick
profit.

That became very clear in mid-January 1990, when Bank of Canada
governor John Crow pushed rates down a notch by artificially flooding
Canadian money markets. There was a large-scale international selloff of
Canadian bonds, orchestrated in good measure by the Japanese. As a result,
the Canadian dollar fell from U.S. $0.8649 to $0.8585 in a day and a half. By
week's end, the dollar had fallen as much as 3.5 percent in value against the
American dollar; by mid-February, it had gone as low as a 4.4 percent drop.
Crow hurriedly moved back into the market, bolstering the dollar and
jacking interest rates back up.

Even with Canada's high interest rates, there was a lot of competition for
Japanese money during 1990. Much of it was in Japan itself, where companies needed more money and their own interest rates rose. By June,
Japanese institutions had purchased 60 percent fewer foreign bonds than
they had the previous year. Even the ever-popular Europe was hit. Europe
didn't turn out to be the investors' paradise it had been touted as—nor did
the investors turn out to be quite as long-term as they had planned. And the
United States government was disturbed to find that after seven years of
voracious investing, the Japanese were selling more United States bonds
than they were buying. They kept their holdings in high-rate Canadian

bonds at about the same level, but shifted from long-term holdings to short-term Canada bonds—easy to sell on short notice.

A worried Michael Wilson arrived in Tokyo in November 1990 to talk up Canadian bonds to anyone who would give him a hearing. His meeting with Prime Minister Kaifu was canceled, but he met former prime minister Takeshita and the governor of the Bank of Japan, Yasushi Mieno, as well as Finance Minister Ryutaro Hashimoto. He also spoke to the heads of a long list of banks, insurance companies, and brokerage firms.

At every meeting, Wilson mentioned Canada's energy resources at a time when the Japanese were being hit by high oil prices immediately after the invasion of Kuwait by Iraq. But mainly, he reassured investors that Canada wouldn't be lowering its interest rates, even though it was in a recession that had no end in sight. A Tokyo businessman told the *Globe and Mail,* "Wilson's been going around to everyone and saying, 'Don't sell Canadian bonds.' "

While Wilson was in Tokyo painting the brightest possible picture of a Canada eager for Japanese investment, however, his version of events was belied by a major investment setback on the part of a number of Japanese steel companies and banks. They were in a legal fight with Quintette Coal over the price they should be paying for Quintette's northeast British Columbia coal. And Quintette was playing by American-style rules.

The Japanese were a key link in British Columbia's plan to mine coal in the northeastern corner of the province during the early 1980s. The British Columbia government desperately needed to help the province work its way out of the 1981-82 recession, so it subsidized a new rail link and port, allowing Denison Mines of Toronto to start up Quintette, and Teck Corp. of Vancouver to start the neighboring Bull Moose mine. A consortium of Japanese steel companies agreed to pay more than $100 per tonne for the coal and to be minority partners in the mine. As a result, an international consortium of fifty-six banks financed the project, which opened in 1984, just minutes before the price of coal went down the toilet.

Quintette never made money. In 1985, Denison wrote off its entire $240.7-million investment in the mine. But it continued to operate the mine for a lucrative $5 million annually. The next year, the Japanese quietly asked to renegotiate the substantially above-market price they were paying for Quintette coal. Their contract allowed for this type of renegotiation, but Quintette wasn't having any of it. Instead, it sued its partners-cum-customers.

The two sides agreed to an international arbitrator, and the Japanese even agreed to have the three-year negotiations take place in British Columbia with an all-Canadian panel. Finally, in 1989, the panel ruled in Japan's favor and suggested a compromise price of $75. But Quintette didn't accept the ruling; it appealed to the British Columbia Supreme Court. It lost again, in early 1990. By this time, coal was trading for only $63 per tonne.

This wasn't, of course, the first time the Japanese had lost money on a foreign investment. They had good reason to believe, however, that Quintette had government backing; suddenly the government was nowhere to be seen. And along the way, Quintette's management and lawyers did some pretty nasty Japan-bashing. Meanwhile, the international bankers were essentially carrying Quintette. On June 13, 1990, Quintette went under the protection of the Companies' Creditors Arrangement Act to restructure $750 million in debt. The creditors weren't buying. The fifty-six banks— including a number of Japanese banks—made that clear in December. By February 1991 they'd replaced Denison as operator with the other north-eastern mine operator, Teck Corporation. Teck's mine, unlike Denison, had always run at a profit, even after prices dropped. And it had renegotiated the price the Japanese were paying without protest or publicity, showing that it knew the cardinal lesson for dealing with the Japanese: losing face is worse than losing money.

Quintette's type of nastiness wasn't even whispered about during the 1989 investment mission, of course—even though all the visitors knew about it. The Canadian diplomats also ignored a few tricky questions about the environment, such as public protests by environmentalists over mission chief Morohashi's planned $1.3-billion pulp mill in Alberta. The Mitsubishi-Honshu Paper Co. joint venture is building one of the world's largest pulp mills in northern Alberta, and federal officials had spoken out against it because of its potential effect on the ecology of the Athabaska and Peace rivers.

The environment and Quintette were important issues to the visitors, since most of their Canadian investments are in resource industries. For example, Daishowa Paper Manufacturing Co. owns the old Ottawa Valley paper company Reed International and is also building a $1-billion pulp mill near the Mitsubishi mill in Peace River, Alberta.[11] Toshihiro Matsuki, whose company, C. Itoh, also has lumber interests, asked about changes in Canadian environmental laws while meeting with federal officials in Toronto. "I was told I did not have to worry about that," he recalls. "I know the true story. But you did not want to touch on that matter." The Canadian officials were either naïve in believing the Japanese didn't know the environment was becoming a big issue in Canada or condescending in thinking that the Japanese would accept excuses or partial explanations.

Besides wanting to present a positive image to the mission, the Canadian government and the provinces had another agenda for their guests. They needed to explain that although all investment was equally welcome, of course, some types of investment were more equal than others. Canada wants 1990s-style investment: high technology.

Back in 1986, we'd actually asked for some high-tech investment. The Japanese had responded with platitudes about how Canadians are good at developing technology in very specific fields—often related to resource management—whereas the Japanese are masters of manufacturing and distributing technology for the mass market. They implied that there might be room for some kind of industrial cooperation and technology exchange. But nothing happened, because nothing really could happen.

The Japanese are high tech. And they like to keep their high technology advantage at home. Less-skilled, lower-priced labor is used in mass production facilities abroad. They've developed that strategy throughout the Pacific Rim and are now expanding production both in the United States and Europe. There are exceptions, of course. In 1989, for example, a Japanese company bought Ottawa-based Lumonics, a Canadian high-tech laser company with a good product but a bad balance sheet. The reason: they could pick it up cheaply, making it worth the effort. And after a decade of courting Nippon Telegraph and Telephone Corp., Northern Telecom sold the Japanese telecommunications giant its first order of Canadian switching equipment.

But all this high-tech talk was more than a little puzzling to the Japanese. High tech in Saskatchewan? In Nova Scotia? Why? Yet each province valiantly trooped the visitors through laboratories and pitched their value as future centers of high-tech industries. "Everywhere we went the provinces were really expecting investment in the fields of electronics or biotechnology and high technology," recalls Matsuki. "Nobody talked

---

11 Daishawa also came to the rescue of the cash-starved Quebec Nordiques and now owns 18 percent of the hockey team.

about natural resources . . . We have an interest in British Columbia. [It seemed that] you are not welcoming any investment in that field."

Not true. We'll take whatever investment we can get these days. For instance, we're pushing for Japanese auto plants, even though these do not create jobs that will improve the skills of our work force. Here Canada has followed the American model: import quotas combined with duty remissions and local incentive grants for new plants. And it has worked: three Japanese companies have production facilities in Canada, and there are six joint ventures with auto parts companies. But that shouldn't be confused with an industrial policy to take Canada from the manufacturing to the technological age. This is not high-tech stuff, just assembly-line production for a local market.

Aside from our trees and mines, the one thing the Japanese have been interested in is our real estate. No wonder. Japanese land is so expensive that at the height of their land price spiral in 1989 they could have bought all of Canada by selling the grounds of their Imperial Palace in Tokyo. Besides, the Japanese think Canada a beautiful country. Especially the west coast. Especially Banff.

Oh, they like Prince Edward Island as well, home of red-haired Anne.[12] But PEI has long had in place rigid foreign investment rules (for foreign, read non-Islander). Banff, however, has none of these restrictions. During the 1980s, Japanese investors bought two major hotels, including the famous Banff Park Lodge. Japanese signs began appearing in the tourist town. There were so many Japanese tour groups that the federal government passed legislation stating that 30 percent of the rooms in hotels in Banff National Park be set aside for Canadians every year.

At the same time, four hotels and lodges in Whistler, British Columbia (including Nancy Greene Lodge), were sold to Japanese buyers. Urban hotels are also a popular purchase. Japanese groups own the Coast hotel chain in British Columbia and Alberta, the Pan Pacific hotel in Vancouver, the Sheraton in Hamilton, Ontario, and the Prince and Westin Harbour Castle hotels in Toronto.[13]

The bottom line here is that when the Japanese think of Canada, they

12 The Japanese have long been fascinated with Anne of Green Gables. Young Japanese couples go to Green Gables to be married, and one of the northern islands in Japan now has a replica Green Gables as a tourist draw.
13 The latter was purchased from Li Ka-shing at the height of the Toronto property boom.

don't think of a major industrial or trading power with whom it behooves them to negotiate seriously. They don't think of a giant market for their goods, with serious opportunities for domestic production. They don't think of a cheap local labor force that makes it enticing to set up plants. And they don't think of high tech. What they think of are mountains, trees, and a vast expanse of beautiful countryside.

And Canadians have done little in their actual performance to change the foreign view of the country as a resource economy. But we have a skewed idea that because we're a G-7 first world nation, we have some right to be a high-tech nation. We don't have much to offer for a joint venture, which only leads the Japanese to view our approach as an invitation to set up shop with some carte blanche assurances of government support.

It's all a question of control. The traditional equation has been that the Japanese have the upper hand. Fact is, we've precious little reason to demand equality in a partnership, let alone control. When we do, without the money or skill to back up our demands, we end up looking simply foolish. And we risk seriously alienating our Japanese bankers.

Douglas Kennedy, a Canadian now working for the American investment banker Morgan Stanley in Tokyo, takes a pessimistic view of Canada's chances at benefiting from even the best results of the United States-Japan relationship. "After all, the California Roll is an American invention," he said, picking up on the metaphor, "and none of its key ingredients are found in Canada. The possible exception is crabs—and Canadians are crabby enough already." The situation doesn't have to be this way, he adds, but it is Canada that must adapt. Like the United States, in our commitment to our economy we must become more Japanese.

The Morohashi report was polite, but not encouraging. Canada "extends a warm welcome," Morohashi wrote; the investment environment is "stable and positive," the "potential for increased investment over the long term is high." But it was lukewarm compared to the 1986 group report. There was no commitment to investment, no assurance that Canada was the route to take to the United States.

Ottawa knew it had failed. The Japanese were not satisfied with our answers on the Free Trade Agreement. It's still not clear to them—nor apparently to us—whether a Japanese firm setting up in Canada will be subject to trade barriers in the United States. They're not convinced that setting up in Canada will be good enough to satisfy American demands for local investment rather than imports into the United States market. And otherwise, they have no reason to bother coming to Canada.

Four months after the report's release, Ottawa dispatched an official from External Affairs to Tokyo to answer more detailed questions on free trade to try to stir up some interests among mission participants. As he was flying over the Pacific, Mulroney's Meech Lake Accord was falling apart. By the time the Canadian Airlines jet landed in Narita Airport, the deal was dead and there were a lot of questions hanging in the air about Canada's future.

When he rose to speak the next day, the official was terrified that he would be grilled about Meech Lake and the stability of Canada. He needn't have worried; no one asked a single question. The Japanese just don't pay that much attention to Canadian affairs.

Of course, if Quebec separates there will be an effect on Japanese interest in Canadian bonds—we'll be less stable. But the effect will soon pass as long as we are still in some sort of loose association. To the Japanese, we're already part of the North American trading bloc. The only questions are how we fit with the United States, and what advantage they gain in North America from dealing with us.

In October 1990, the Business Council on National Issues sent its own investment mission to Japan. It included top bankers, brokers, and heads of industrial companies. The contrast to the Japanese mission here was marked: there were no meetings with Prime Minister Kaifu. The group, in fact, couldn't even gain access to top government officials or businessmen. Few members of the Japanese investment mission even showed up to meet the Canadians at specially staged receptions. Morohashi was particularly noticeable by his absence. "The effect of the latest Japanese trip report," remarked *Globe* correspondent Edith Terry, "may be that Japanese attention will drift elsewhere."

Prime Minister Mulroney attracted some of that attention once again when he arrived in Tokyo in May 1991 to open the new Canadian embassy. The business contingent with him—including Molson Company's Marshall (Mickey) Cohen, Royal Trustco's Hart McDougall, and Tom D'Aquino from the Business Council on National Issues—at least met top government officials and business executives. But the meetings were purely protocol; the trip had no substance other than to wave the flag.[14]

A few weeks after Mulroney returned from his Tokyo trip, the bottom

14 Mulroney garnered poor press back home during the trip after he made a partisan attack on Ontario premier Bob Rae. He said that Japanese business leaders were anxious about the NDP's election victory and the provincial budget. But one of the Japanese businessmen with him said the matter hadn't been discussed. In Tokyo, however, no one even heard about the gaffe.

fell out of the Canadian argument for Japanese investment. The United States accused Honda Canada of exporting cars that had too many Japanese parts, from Alliston, Ontario, to the United States. According to the United States Customs Service, the cars had less than the 50 percent material, labor, and processing required under the Free Trade Agreement. If the Americans could prove their case, the Japanese would be forced to pay an additional $20 million in import duties. Honda Canada, which exports 80 percent of the 100,000 cars built annually at its Alliston plant to the United States, said it was being falsely accused. The matter was still being hotly debated as this book went to press. But the outcome of the dispute was beside the point. By raising the specter of a potential shutout, the United States was sending Japan the message that investing in Canada was not the same as setting up plants south of the forty-ninth parallel.

In his Tokyo office in March 1990, Matsuki waved a copy of the Morohashi report in the air and shook his head. "This report introduces the budget of each province and such and such. So what? Maybe I'm wrong. Maybe this is the necessary step that everyone has to start with. I have been visiting Canada many times in the last twenty to thirty years. That's why I'm not representing the others' opinions." In other words, as an informed observer, he thought the whole exercise quite pointless.

That's really too bad. Canada needs the Japanese; we need their money, we need their technology, and we need to learn from their vaunted management techniques. We should grab every chance we can to benefit from their investment and learn from the best parts of their culture. We should be willing and happy participants in the California Roll meshing of Western and Eastern economic cultures. We have a great chance to do it, hanging on to the coattails of the United States.

It's even more unfortunate when we have such a chance and blow it. While I was in Tokyo, a meeting with another member of the investment mission sparked my interest in Moli Energy, a British Columbia company that had a unique high-tech joint venture with a major Japanese trading house. Here was a chance for international success. It turns out, however, that after a checkered history, if Moli succeeds at all it will be because of the Japanese. If nothing else, the story of Moli Energy shows how we can learn from the Japanese. Let's hope we get more chances.

CHAPTER EIGHT

The Holy Grail Technology

The imperious man in the power position smoked and ruminated; everyone else listened. Masao Ikeda is senior executive managing director, at Mitsui and Co. Ltd. in Tokyo, and everything about our meeting that mid-March afternoon reflected his exalted rank. We were in Ikeda's barn of an office, rather than the standard cramped, anonymous meeting room. Three courtiers danced nervous attendance on Ikeda; I was glad for the support of a hired guide. Ikeda's guttural tones and habit of leaving his sentences hanging made communication stilted, but he had a good command of English. And he was willing to talk. He talked about his experiences with the United States, where he had worked, and Canada, which he had recently visited as deputy chairman of the Keidanren's investment group. He talked about his feelings nowadays toward North American investment by Mitsui, his U.S. $60-billion trading firm. He talked some platitudes, and he talked some sense. And through it all, there was the underlying feeling that we were all partaking in a formality every bit as ritualized as traditional Noh drama. Where Toshihiro Matsuki had been the exception, Ikeda was playing by the rules. His *tatamae* was firmly in place. Once again, the *gaijin* visitor was being introduced to the typical Japanese business face: generous, honorable, astute, conservative, and essentially anonymous.

Then suddenly, a crack showed in the facade. I asked an off-the-wall question, drafted on the run from a vague memory that Mitsui had just made an investment in a small, British Columbia-based company called Moli Energy Ltd. Why, I wondered, had Mitsui decided to bail out the obviously troubled Moli? That was the end of Ikeda's smooth pattern of talk and smoke. Ikeda's agitation at being caught without an answer bordered on theater of the absurd. As for his aides, they began buzzing and flapping their wings in distress, thumbing through briefing books, pointing out notations, proffering explanations rapidly, softly, respectfully. A Japan-watcher told me later that it would be routine for the staff members to formally tender their resignations after leaving a man of Ikeda's standing unprepared for any potential question from a visiting journalist—although they probably wouldn't be accepted.

All the information was exchanged in Japanese. I had not arranged for an interpreter in this instance, but I left the tape recorder running. I didn't need to understand the words, however, to realize that I had committed a diplomatic gaffe. When, after a painful pause, Ikeda reverted to English, he didn't mention Moli Energy and I didn't press the matter. Twenty minutes later, however, my guide and I reconnoitered outside by the garden of the Imperial Palace, down the street from Mitsui's Chiyoda business district headquarters. She carefully listened to my tape and diligently translated the Mitsui executive's exchange with his subordinates. Ikeda had been assured that Moli was but a small tendril in Mitsui's overseas investments, and he should not be concerned by his lack of knowledge of the company. Moli was a troubled company that Mitsui had stepped into in Vancouver, and if things turned out as expected, Mitsui should end up doing well financially from the move.

It's a good thing someone expects to do well from Moli Energy. The late Norman Keevil, Sr., the entrepreneur who backed the rechargeable lithium battery maker from its 1977 conception until his death in autumn 1989, never made a penny on it. Neither did any of the other private investors nor the numerous small public shareholders. Certainly not the British Columbia government, which spent about $30 million on the company, or Ottawa, which backed Moli for $6 million.

Yet Moli was the best of all possible bets: a high-technology company born of Canadian ingenuity, with a great product, an eager export market, and enormous potential. After a dozen years and $120 million spent on developing its battery to the point at which it could be mass-produced, however, it fell victim to quality problems and a lack of staying power on the part of its Canadian investors. Enter the Japanese, who bought the company's assets on the cheap in return for a commitment to continue the company's research and production in British Columbia.

Hugh Wynne-Edwards, who headed Moli through its darkest days in 1989, says the company is a classic example of Canadians at their worst and the Japanese at their best. "It had a very good chance of success. It had one of Canada's most gifted entrepreneurs and promoters as its champion, who understood technology and was comfortable with the people. That was an enormous plus. It had a very good research team. No question. It was in pursuit of a holy grail technology. What it didn't have was the management expertise necessary to succeed. If you look at what the Japanese do and what Moli did, they're almost opposites. The net net is unless we learn how to innovate, we're not going to be here." And effective innovation needs good management. Canadian research and development tends to be all research and precious little development. This provides a good fit for the Japanese, who are masters at development, design, and engineering. Especially when Canadians don't know what to do with what they've found. "Being able to wander through a country that prides itself on individual creativity is attractive to the Japanese," Wynne-Edwards points out. "And when you can pick up research products for a nickel on the dollar, it looks marvelously cheap." Perhaps, after his experience at Moli, Wynne-Edwards is a bit cynical. But it's the Canadians he shakes his head at; he speaks of the Japanese view of Canada with unalloyed admiration: "The Japanese look and see a garden, and they pluck all the vegetables."

Wynne-Edwards brackets the story of Moli Energy; he was there at the end and back at the very beginning. In 1977, Wynne-Edwards was head of University of British Columbia's geology department. Over in the physics department, a few scientists were working on a method of creating rechargeable batteries that used lithium as an energy source. American research scientists were working on the same idea, but the electrode material needed to offset the lithium element of the battery was expensive and had to be synthesized in the lab. Rudi Haering, head of the physics department, asked Wynne-Edwards whether any potential natural source of encasing material existed in the province. Haering had been experimenting with molybdenum disulfide, which was a "layered compound" whose complex chemical makeup meant it could absorb the shock of the energy released by the lithium. Wynne-Edwards provided him with some samples and pointed out that one acceptable type was mined in British Columbia. Haering also told Wynne-Edwards that he was looking for some sort of backer, an entrepreneur who also knew enough about science to understand the potential for the battery; at that point, Haering and his confreres were trying to develop a rechargeable battery for use in an electric car. Haering wanted to meet Keevil, a neighbor of Wynne-Edwards's. Wynne-Edwards arranged the introduction.

Norman Bell Keevil was a legendary mining man, a member of both the Toronto and Vancouver business elite, and a multimillionaire. But he was trained as a scientist. The son of a British horse trader, Keevil was born in Saskatoon in 1910 and graduated first from the University of Saskatchewan, then in 1937 from Harvard with a doctorate in geophysics. He had a promising academic career, completing postgraduate work at both Harvard and MIT, and teaching at Harvard, Saskatchewan, and finally at the University of Toronto.[1] He began consulting to supplement his professor's income and after the Second World War converted submarine tracking technology to try to detect mine sites from the air.

Keevil's magnetic airborne detector found a copper mine in Temagami and after failing to convince others of its potential, he staked it himself in 1954. Four years later, Keevil proved he could be just as agile in business, parlaying his first million into control of five mining companies worth $35 million. Teck Corporation was at the center of those maneuvers, and through Teck Keevil spent the next decade acquiring about eighty mining companies. He was labeled Evil Keevil for his acquisitive, even predatorial style. But he proudly adopted the moniker, displaying it on his team's hockey sweaters at the annual Prospectors and Developers Association hockey game in Maple Leaf Gardens.

Keevil and his family moved from Toronto to Vancouver in 1972, although he always maintained a Toronto residence. He was a mine developer rather than a typical Vancouver promoter, however, and Teck became a powerhouse in the industry.[2] Keevil's companies produced gold, silver, copper, molybdenum, zinc, and niobium. Teck also invested in a pump to bring drinking water from the ocean; a superconductor; oyster farming; and genetic engineering. By the late 1970s, Norman Keevil, Jr., was taking a leading role in company management, and his brother, Brian, was involved in venture capital subsidiary TDK.[3]

But at sixty-six, Keevil wanted to do it all over again. He wanted another scientific discovery. He was fit, vibrant, and still a visionary—"a hip shooter and a cowboy," according to one admiring miner who sold out to

1 Keevil's Second World War research included studies of mustard gas, Vitamin B2 and the effect of vision in bright light, isotopic tracers in explosive reactions, and the use of radioactivity to calculate the earth's age.
2 Roland Michener worked at Teck both before and after his term as governor general; he was chairman in the late 1970s.
3 During the 1980s Teck became part owner of the much-disputed Hemlo gold mine in northern Ontario. It also took control of $2-billion mining company Cominco, moved into oil and gas, and developed northeastern B.C. coal. Despite debt problems, it remained a relatively stable, secure company.

Keevil in the late 1970s. "He had amazing vision and wisdom and technical judgment," recalls Wynne-Edwards. "He understood better than 90 percent of the population that if you didn't get a major piece of technology, you were not going to be a world player."

Moli was a natural. Keevil's mines were among the major producers of molybdenum. He understood the science and saw the enormous commercial potential for the lithium battery. The battery industry, particularly in North America, was stuck in the past. It had started with lead acid batteries and moved to nickel cadmium, but any research into alternative energy sources was being done in California jet-propulsion labs rather than by the battery manufacturers. Yet lithium gave far more energy per unit weight than nickel cadmium. It would make a more efficient battery, with the promise of twice the performance. The American scientists had developed non-rechargeable lithium batteries; the UBC group built on that idea.

Haering worked in concert with two other scientists in his department: Jim Stiles and Klaus Brandt, and the patents were registered by the trio.[4] Brandt recalls the appeal of their original electric car battery: "It sounds so wonderfully Canadian; vertical integration from raw material to high technology for export. That was a story that's politically easy to sell." And Haering, he adds, "knows a little bit about selling too." Keevil bought. By the end of 1977, he had invested $25,000 in a brand-new company called Moli Energy.

The Molicell battery was a still a laboratory experiment. "We were very very far," says Brandt, "from anything that looked anything like a battery." It took them almost five years to come up with a prototype. By that point, the plumetting price of oil and the recession had changed their strategy, as it did with so many corporate paths in this country. Electric vehicles were suddenly not as fashionable. So the Moli scientists decided instead to concentrate on developing a smaller battery, to link to the increasingly important miniaturization of consumer electronic products. Happily, the same raw materials worked in the more compact form. Suddenly, Moli was part of the high-tech revolution, working hand-in-hand with the computer chip.

"It's a holy grail technology," explains Wynne-Edwards. "If you look at what has happened since the invention of the chip, the downsizing has reached the point where the largest thing on a portable piece of electronics

---

4 Haering retired in the mid-1980s, but remained a consultant to Moli and Dr. Keevil. Stiles eventually left to join Sherritt Gordon in Alberta. Brandt remains at Moli.

is the battery pack."[5] By 1984, after seven years of research, Moli had finally
developed a size AA battery cell that it could show to potential customers.
Of course, concentrating on consumer electronics meant that Moli needed
a link with Japan. But Moli never really had to pursue the Japanese. As soon
as they heard about the battery, Andrew Ito and Mitsui arrived at Moli's
door.

Andrew Ito was intrigued by the glowing local press reports about Moli.
Ito, a Canadian-born entrepreneur, was Mitsui's project development
specialist in Canada. That gave him plenty of scope: with $3.2 billion
revenues in 1989, Mitsui is the largest Japanese trading company in Canada.
It's larger than Molson, Stelco, or Domtar. A man with an eye for the main
chance, Ito immediately saw the potential for the Moli battery in the
Japanese electronics industry. "My gut feeling," he says, "was that this was
something revolutionary." And he knew that for once, the Canadians had
something that had not yet been developed in Japan or the United States.
Ito, in fact, paints himself as a champion of Canadian technology. "I don't
think the Japanese have the high-tech field cornered," he says. "The only
problem is we [in Canada] don't have the population and we don't have the
money."

Ito met the Moli scientists, whom he mentally dubbed "the three
musketeers," and began to court Stiles. "I couldn't even get his name right,
he was so close-mouthed," he chuckles. He made the dance card when
Stiles asked for a few introductions to people attending a convention in
Japan. At this stage, Ito had no real desire to meet Keevil. He wanted to
know exactly what these people had to offer before dealing with anyone
with Keevil's negotiating reputation. And Keevil wasn't running to meet Ito
either. Teck had an arrangement with another Japanese trading house for
its northeast British Columbia coal development, Bull Moose. For a while,
Keevil thought he could ratchet that into a Moli deal as well and believed he
should deal with the same trading house if possible. In 1985, Brian Keevil
went to Japan to check out the possibilities. While there, he also met with

---

5   Keevil tried to do all the right things. In September 1983, he hired Irvine Hollis, the
    president of Duracell Canada, as Moli president. Hollis had actually tried to convince
    Duracell to buy Moli; when he didn't succeed, he joined the young company. This
    would give Moli the marketing presence it needed. A marketing expert at the top seemed
    exactly the right move for a company about to move from the laboratory to commercial
    production. But it was too soon to turn Moli over to the marketers and Hollis left in
    1985.

Mitsui. It became clear that Mitsui was the prospect with the most potential.

Mitsui, meanwhile, had to decide to take on this somewhat risky product from the Canadian inventors. Andrew Ito lobbied hard. "Fortunately, we had an ex-battery company guy in Japan who was intrigued with the technology, and he created interest within Mitsui in Japan." Even better, the technology interested one of Mitsui's best clients. Nippon Telegraph and Telephone (NTT), one of the largest companies in the world, wanted as powerful a source of energy as possible for its increasingly popular portable cellular phones. Mitsui agreed to act as Moli's agent in Japan and matched a $2.5-million investment by Teck to help Moli move toward mass production of the batteries. Once it made up its mind, recalls Ito, Mitsui wanted product "yesterday, so to speak."

Now Moli had a real problem. It didn't have the batteries to fill the orders. "Myself, not knowing too much about batteries, I thought this was a piece of cake going into production," says Ito. "That's where we made our mistakes." Keevil—Dr. K to the scientists at Moli—went into overdrive. In classic Canadian entrepreneurial style, he turned to the government for financial support. And what Canadian government wouldn't have jumped at the chance? After all, Moli had announced the battery cell that would change the world. British Columbia couldn't resist. In 1984, British Columbia was willing to do just about anything to create jobs. And Moli hit all the buttons: it was homemade high-tech, with promising export markets and the backing of one of the province's most successful entrepreneurs. During this period it was always described as a showcase company for the province. Keevil made his influence count. Without British Columbia money, he was considering an Ontario location for the production plant. Teck's venture capital subsidiary, run by his son Brian, was located in Toronto, and Moli's engineering and commercial types favored the idea.

British Columbia premier Bill Bennett killed that plan with a sudden show of largesse. In 1985, in concert with Ottawa's Western Diversification Program, Bennett announced that the province would provide a $25-million loan to Moli. This was no government handout, however; it was a five-year loan, with interest at market rates. Added to this was $25 million raised from the public, through a stock market listing and public share offering at $8 per "unit."[6] It was billed by Dominion Securities and

6 Each unit consisted of a common share, a warrant, and a $1.60 tax credit. The warrant allowed shareholders to buy another share for each warrant held, at $10 each, before January 1990. No warrants were ever exercised.

Pemberton Securities[7] as the most significant public offering ever in Canada for a company with no actual product.

The Moli plant was built at Maple Ridge, a town in the Fraser Valley about one hour's drive from Vancouver. But it wasn't just a matter of building a plant. The three musketeers and their colleagues had to design all the one-of-a-kind equipment. "The only thing that Moli was able to purchase off the shelf," says Brandt, "was a used labeling machine." The jump from handmade experimental batteries to mass production was their own little version of the Industrial Revolution. And like any revolution, the jump to large-scale production produced its own share of chaos. Equipment designs had to be changed, then changed again; costs mounted. "It was a laboratory product. It was a can with some very neat physics in it," says Wynne-Edwards. "But it hadn't been designed for a matching production process, and the production process hadn't been worked out."

The plant opened on September 20, 1987. Theoretically, Moli should have had the capacity to build 100,000 battery cells a week. But practically, it wasn't able to produce a fraction of that amount—and it was going to lose money on each one it built. "When the premier cut the ribbon in September '87," says Wynne-Edwards, "as far as I can tell it was already evident that the plant wasn't going to work."

Moli's crucial strategic error was rushing into production before it was confident of its product. It was worried about the competition. While the American experiments had been in research labs rather than within industry, in 1986, Japanese firms began pouring money into research on lithium batteries. "All the large Japanese battery companies, without exception, became competitors," says Brandt. One Japanese company spent $50 million over a half-dozen years, but reached only the rudimentary laboratory stage that Moli was at by 1984. Others seemed to be further. There were announcements in the trade press of batteries that had been developed and would soon be on the market, including some hoopla from one of the Sony group of companies in 1987.[8]

The traditional nickel-cadmium battery makers, suddenly faced with the prospect of hot new Japanese competition, quickly made some long-overdue improvements to their own batteries. Changes that, according to

7 Both companies are now part of RBC Dominion Securities Ltd.
8 As of early 1991, however, Moli remained the only firm with any commercial rechargeable lithium battery.

Brandt, "could have been done decades before." By the end of the 1980s, the nickel-cadmium variety ran longer and held their power for a longer period of time. Keevil and the Moli scientists felt they had to jump in soon or they would lose the day. They didn't know whether they had a two-year lead or a six-month one.[9]

The mass-production plan was Keevil's call. As a miner, he was used to sinking his money in up front; it made sense to him to build a plant that was big enough to satisfy what he saw as a huge demand down the road. And he had marketing consultants who were urging that he actually break ground for a second plant as the first one was rising. Keevil simply wasn't versed in how to manage an innovative manufacturing company. The research people didn't fight Keevil's decision; they took no part in management decisions, even though they knew that the battery should be tested before going into full production. "R&D remained R&D," explains Wynne-Edwards, "and when the manufacturing decision was made, the R&D people almost washed their hands of it. That was somebody else's problem." Moli went from making fifty to one hundred batteries a day to full-scale factory production without any basic, necessary market trials. "The cells tested very well in the lab," according to Wynne-Edwards, "[but] it doesn't matter how much you test a product under laboratory conditions. That's not what people do with it."

The plant was divided into three sections. In the back, the chemicals were manufactured. In the middle, the electrodes were made. In the front, the actual cells were assembled, packaged, and shipped. This was the high-tech end of the plant, with the state-of-the-art equipment. They originally set up the front with the capacity to produce 33 million batteries a year; even that was only one-third of the plant's planned capacity. But they couldn't get near that goal. In fact, as they installed the equipment, they were continually forced to readjust it.

By 1988, NTT was waiting for Moli to fill its order for 5 million batteries. But Moli couldn't boost production to fill it. With a plant capacity for 100 million battery cells a year, they struggled to produce one million a year. And the equipment problems and mounting interest on the British Columbia loan meant they lost money on every battery produced. Keevil and Mitsui looked seriously at the production problems and decided the solution was more money. Keevil put on his cowboy hat and lassoed the investors one more time. He told British Columbia and Ottawa it would be

9 They had already started research in association with NTT on a second-generation battery that would be faster and more powerful again. That research goes on.

a while longer before they saw results and asked them to renegotiate their loans on a more favorable basis. And early in 1988, Keevil approached large private investors. He was obviously still treating publicly listed Teck as his private fiefdom; it kicked in another $2.5 million. Mitsui matched that. He raised several million through private placements in England and the United States. And Alcan signed on with $10 million in return for just under 20 percent of the company.

Alcan's involvement was Wynne-Edwards's doing. As vice-president of research and development at the Montreal-based aluminum giant, he was convinced that Moli could eventually produce the type of battery he wanted for an aluminum-powered car. Wynne-Edwards had joined Alcan because he wanted to help repair the gap in industrial R&D in Canada.[10] His role there included encouraging outside investments in seed companies, and his favorite idea was that a car could be built of aluminum and also could run on the electricity generated by aluminum. Moli fit nicely into this research niche.

Although a number of investors made commitments to Keevil, they were attaching some conditions to the money. So the fund raising dragged on through the middle of 1989. Meanwhile, Ottawa and British Columbia had a consultant take a look at the company. It saw the problems, but felt that once they were fixed the company would take off. And with a promise of money if not the money itself, Moli was spending $1.7 million monthly on production. Finally, in late 1988, Moli began shipping batteries.

Big mistake. They didn't quite mention to the Japanese that there had been a few problems with defective batteries during the testing process. The scientists called the problem "venting." A layperson would call it an explosion. The battery was releasing all of its energy at once. As Brandt points out, there was a simple explanation for the reaction: "You get a lot more energy in a smaller package, and it becomes harder to control." The minor glitch happened when the batteries were recharging, so the Moli scientists decided it must be something about that process. They did a few tests, made a few adjustments. They always managed to iron out the individual battery cell's problem. But they didn't solve the production defect. Finally, they just hoped it would work itself out. "The first market trial was with NTT, the largest company on earth, in Tokyo," says Wynne-

10 In the meantime, during a stint at the Ministry of State for Science and Technology, Wynne-Edwards had helped to reorganize federal funding of scientific research, setting up the Natural Sciences and Engineering Research Council and the Social Sciences and Humanities Research Council.

Edwards with a sad shake of his head. After eleven years of research, the Moli batteries were innovative and powerful. But they had neither of the two attributes that the Japanese prize above all else: quality and control.

Moli was taking a risk in shipping its batteries without full-scale testing. Unfortunately, the decision blew up in management's face—that is, after it had blown up in a customer's face. He was your basic nightmare: a Japanese racketeer. In Japan, the substrata of society that organizes betting and prostitution and other sordid activities—their Mafia—operates in a very businesslike fashion. And like other business people, they need the latest technology. This particular gentleman acquired one of NTT's portable cellular phones, equipped with a Molicell battery. And on August 10, 1989, that battery pack exploded, burning this rather dangerous customer. "This was a very difficult customer to deal with," says Wynne-Edwards, "in terms of embarrassment."

The media reaction was difficult to deal with, too. The explosion was in all the papers the next day, and even worse, on the six o'clock television news. For NTT, the bad publicity couldn't have come at a worse time. It had just experienced the ultimate loss of face: its chairman had been forced to resign because of his involvement in the Recruit insider-trading scandal.

The Japanese press blamed Mitsui. Mitsui was Moli's Japanese representative, and it actually assembled the cells into the battery packs after they arrived in Japan. But it was Moli's fault. The company was shipping defective battery cells to Japan.

Moli's reaction didn't help either. It couldn't afford to launch its own product recall, so NTT had to do the recall itself. This placed Mitsui in a very delicate position with NTT. In Japan, Moli was described as a "Mitsui group company," and that's the way NTT viewed the situation. The tiny British Columbia company had disrupted the delicate balance of power within top Japanese business circles.[11]

Alcan's money had finally arrived the previous June, and around that time an ailing Keevil had convinced his old friend Wynne-Edwards to take on the CEO role at Moli. Wynne-Edwards left Alcan and made a brief foray to the west coast, then headed for a cottage in Quebec before officially

---

11 NTT also had to settle a lawsuit with the customer.

starting at Moli after Labor Day. When he heard about the NTT recall, the vacationing soon-to-be CEO was relieved. He knew the company was losing money on every shipment and thought a breathing space would be good for the company.

Wynne-Edwards knew there were problems that needed solving at Moli—"or I wouldn't have come." But he thought that the recently completed refinancing meant there was money in the till; he didn't know that the company had been spending the cash before it arrived. And he certainly didn't calculate the extent of the damage that one exploding battery pack could wreak. "I didn't realize that it collapsed the tent."

"My understanding when I took the job was that the company had been refinanced, most of the problems identified and fixed." Still, he cut short his holiday, arriving at the plant on August 22. Then he realized that the battery recall meant that Moli had only debts, angry investors, a flawed product, and no hope of selling anything for some time. "By the time I got here it was too late," he says. "I was like a surgeon at the operating table. You did what you could but the damage had been done."

The staff and executives at Moli—both the marketers and the researchers—were shielding themselves from the desperate state of the company, Wynne-Edwards says. "There was nobody in there who was being dishonest, it's just that you go on papering things over and papering things over and papering things over." He made them look at the numbers, at the losses on each shipment. He was never sure if Keevil understood the extent of the problem. That's a common management problem in a technology business, he adds. "The people who are running the money and the people who are doing the research think they are communicating, but they're not."

The problem at Moli was no longer the product recall. It was the money. The battery cell defect was finally tracked to a particular piece of prototype equipment, designed by the scientists and manufactured on contract. Once found, it was easily fixed. But Moli would not have the opportunity to tinker any more, to try to scale their manufacturing up to the break-even point.

In September, Wynne-Edwards found he had $33,000 left in the company, and it was using up about $1.4 million monthly. At that rate, it had essentially already spent the $20 million pledged the previous year. Wynne-Edwards had thought that cash would be available for future operations. Instead, "as fast as the money was being raised it was going down the tube."

Venture-capital investment is based on trust. Once the trust is gone, there's nothing left. That was the psychological damage inflicted by the Tokyo explosion. Investors had poured in $120 million over eleven years, with no revenues to show for it. They were already wary. From the beginning, "all the analysis done showed an absolute hockey stick of revenue," comments Wynne-Edwards. "What happened, of course, was that Moli kept moving the base of the hockey stick." Wynne-Edwards soon discovered just how hard Keevil had pushed people for the 1988 refinancing. "He'd at least cracked people's arms if not broken their ribs," says Wynne-Edwards, "to get the money out of them." The resentment they hadn't voiced to Keevil came through loud and clear when Wynne-Edwards arrived at the door. "The Canadian investors saw it as disaster," he sighs. "And ran for the hills."

On September 13, he proposed a drastic salvage plan to the British Columbia government. Wynne-Edwards wanted to spend another $30 million. He would remove the product from the market for two years and run product trials. He would ask for more than $20 million from the Japanese, $5 million from British Columbia, and $6 million from the other major shareholders. Keevil, who listened to the presentation by phone, immediately pledged a million as a personal investment. But no one else came forward. Two British Columbia cabinet committees turned the idea down flat. The province could never have allowed Moli to shut down and work on its battery. It had supported the company for the jobs. "What drives public policy in Canada is employment," says Wynne-Edwards. With that agenda, on October 5, British Columbia and Ottawa both delivered a clear message: no more government money for Moli. In fact, they said the battery blow-up amounted to an "adverse material change" in the company's affairs. On that basis, they stopped their second loan—which hadn't yet arrived—to the company.

With no money and no orders, Wynne-Edwards began laying off staff. He let fifty-six people go at the end of September. That news was kept from Keevil. At this point, it was unclear how much the entrepreneur knew about Moli's state. He had been partially briefed at the end of June and knew there had been a problem with the battery pack in Japan. But the Moli scientists had reassured him that everything was under control. "He didn't know about the collapse, because he was dying," explains Wynne-Edwards. "And we kept the newspapers, radio and TV and telephones from him."

On October 9, 1989, Dr. Norman Bell Keevil, Sr., died. That was also the end of the line for Moli, as far as the Keevil family was concerned. "As soon as the old man died, Teck had no synergy with Moli," says Wynne-Edwards. On October 13, Moli laid off another sixty-three employees; staff levels had been halved. The next day, Wynne-Edwards flew to Japan for meetings with Mitsui and NTT. The NTT point man at Mitsui, a former NTT employee placed at Mitsui on an exchange basis ("rather like the diplomatic corps," says Wynne-Edwards), quickly took the Moli CEO to see the chairman of NTT. "The loss of face between Mitsui and NTT over the product recall was enormous, and one of the things they were most anxious for me to do was to apologize to NTT," says Wynne-Edwards.[12]

Wynne-Edwards had gone to appeal to the Japanese for support. He offered them unlimited technical and financial access to the company, if they would help with a restructuring. By October 20, he was back in Vancouver with a proposal from Mitsui. At the same time, he struggled to find other potential buyers for the company. North American battery companies had for years made derisive jokes about coming in and picking up the pieces when Moli fell apart. They suddenly weren't interested. Neither were the Europeans. Says Ito: "A lot of people were just interested in the technology at a bargain price." The Japanese sat back and waited. By early 1990, Moli had no other hope.

The Japanese were shocked that the Canadians, particularly the Keevils at Teck, didn't rally round. The Japanese nurse their sick companies. Ito recalls, "Quite frankly, if some other outfit had taken over this organization, we'd be just as happy to have a minor interest in the company." Ito says the lack of interest is tied to the unfortunate short-term North American philosophy about business. "The Japanese saw it as an opportunity, but the Canadian investors saw it as a disaster," agrees Wynne-Edwards. "It makes a lot of statements about cultural makeup. You have to admire the Japanese."

Finally, in February 1990, Wynne-Edwards issued termination notices to the employees, and the province brought in accounting firm Deloitte & Touche as its receiver. Moli Energy, suspended from the stock exchanges, was an insolvent shell of a company. The assets were transferred to a new

---

12 NTT wasn't the only customer. NEC used the Moli battery in its lap-top computers. "I would shudder when I saw their ads," recalls Wynne-Edwards, "because the Moli battery was in there, thinking what could happen to a person with this thing in their lap." Luckily, there were no accidents.

The Holy Grail Technology   221

company, Moli 1990 Ltd. Ottawa tried to resist the move for a while, claiming that the technology was pledged against its loan. But that didn't last for long. "Basically, Ottawa caved in," says Deloitte & Touche's John Bottom.

Moli kept negotiations open with the Japanese, however. The British Columbia government was still looking for a solution that would keep the technology in the province, keep the British Columbia plant open, keep the jobs. In the meantime, both Teck and Mitsui gave the company money to keep a skeleton staff—the Keevil family at Teck in particular knowing they'd never see the money again.

Mitsui represented a consortium, including electronics manufacturer and Moli client NEC and Japanese battery manufacturer Yuasa Battery. Dealing with the Japanese was, Wynne-Edwards recalls, "a fascinating and exhausting process. The Japanese work differently. They query and they query and they query and they query pieces of information." They keep asking until they understand completely. "It's the key to the Japanese success." A very different approach, certainly, from the almost willful blindness exhibited by the Canadian managers at Moli toward the battery's defects.

From Ito's perspective, it was a matter of satisfying all sides all over again that the company could make a workable product. "It wasn't an easy job to convince Mitsui," he says. "I had to sweet-talk them." But ultimately, they wanted the product and the people at Moli. "When we go into a joint venture we're not influenced by the size of the company or the wealth of the company," says Ito. "But we always look at the staff. If a company doesn't have dedicated people, we shy away from them." They didn't want Wynne-Edwards, however. Instead, they would appoint their own CEO from Japan—Michi Tsunoda, who led the negotiations for the Tokyo investors. Ito, on his way to retirement, remained involved, however.[13]

British Columbia Ministry of Finance official Ken Davidson represented the province, with John McKircher of Russell Dumoulin handling the legalities. "This was no sweetheart deal," Ito insists. Mitsui, he adds, felt an obligation to follow through and properly develop a product it had marketed to clients. Still, it was clear that the Japanese had all the cards. By spring, they had the company. Essentially, the Japanese paid five cents on the dollar for one of Canada's few innovative technologies. The assets were

13 Ito, now retired, is still involved with Moli as part of his duties as a consultant for Mitsui Canada. The Japanese believe that the executive who begins a project is responsible for it until its conclusion.

placed in the new company, which has no obligations to public share-holders. There was a lot of outrage in the local press at the time of the deal, and a bit of national coverage. But it was nothing compared to, say, the coverage of the Mérieux purchase of Connaught Biosciences the previous autumn. Yet Connaught was not a company that was at the cutting edge of its field, and Moli was. Batteries are obviously not as sexy as genetically engineered virus cures. Of course, as Ito says, "talk is cheap, it's the money that counts."

And the Japanese could have simply worked on the technology in Japan. On the other hand, there was all that one-of-a-kind equipment just sitting there in Canada, and it would have been prohibitively expensive to re-produce it. "I think they were fairly shrewd, difficult negotiators," John Bottom says with a laugh. "They struck a very hard deal." Whether it was a good deal, he says, is beside the point. "It was almost the only deal."

There were a couple of other interested parties. A former employee claimed to represent a Taiwanese group. And an American said he was looking at Moli on behalf of the United States government. Bottom seems doubtful of that claim. "I don't know what he was. I guess he was, for want of a better term, a scientist." Neither, however, came up with a "mean-ingful offer." Neither was really interested, for instance, in keeping the company in British Columbia. And the few key remaining staff—including Brandt—were getting feelers from other potential employers. "If they'd lost those people, the whole house of cards would have fallen," says Bottom. "The concept is of such a specialized nature, all you'd have ended up with would have been scrap value for all the money invested."

Moli's spending wasn't all that out of line. Large companies traditionally expect to spend ten to twelve years and $200 million on innovation of this nature. Moli had invested most of that time and money; it needed an extra $35 million by Wynne-Edwards's estimate, to make its goal. "The Japanese saw a major innovation 100 yards down the track," he says. "You could see the end of the line and they bought all that for $5 million." Plus, of course, a commitment to be good corporate citizens of the province of British Columbia. Bottom says that British Columbia did all the right things as well; the jobs and community building have given British Columbia its money back many times over. But the province certainly couldn't sink any more money into the project.

The life, death, and rebirth of Moli Energy is, sadly, no surprise. Too many small research-based companies have faltered in Canada for lack of funding and management skills. Moli, with Keevil's backing ensuring a stock issue and some corporate support, was in a better position to succeed than many others have been. But even when investors decide to support a cutting-edge technology, in this country they demand too much from it, too soon. Keevil and the Moli managers' reaction to demands from government and investors to show results was natural. Unfortunately, the government was supporting Moli for the wrong reasons—jobs—rather than to develop a product.

The most upsetting part of the whole episode is that with just a bit more support, Moli could have been one of Canada's real success stories. We can produce innovative products in this country, but we have to make a real investment commitment to them.

That is what the Japanese do—and that's Japanese companies and investors, not the Japanese government. The Japanese also don't abandon a company that needs help. The small Canadian investors holding worthless Moli stock are by no means at fault; however, the larger corporations should have rallied around Moli. Alcan, for example, could have afforded to be more supportive. The Japanese deserve all the money that they make off Moli in the years to come. Bottom reflects, "It's a case of the Japanese coming and saving the day."

These days, Ito and the Moli people won't talk in any detail about what they're doing. But they've closed down, as Wynne-Edwards originally proposed, and are doing tests and more tests, as well as new product research. Some in Japan, but mostly at the Maple Ridge plant still. The Japanese have half a dozen consultants there, quality-control people from the battery company, NEC Corp., and Mitsui. They were scheduled to be finished by August; that was extended to the end of 1990. By July 1991, they still weren't ready. One estimate has the Japanese spending at least another $50 million on testing. A company official will say only "double-digit millions." It's a lot of money for an uncertain return, says Bottom. "I'm still not sure Moli has a future."[14]

If it doesn't, it won't be for lack of trying. "It will take two to three years to make sure that the battery performs exactly as the brochure reads," says Ito. The Japanese will settle for no less. "We have to make sure," Ito adds. "It cost us a lot of money with this accident in Japan. We don't want to repeat the whole thing. The insurance rate would go up and our reputation would go down. So for the next generation of batteries in Japan, we want to make sure that there is no mistake." That's good. At Moli, there has been one too many mistakes already.

14 The Japanese purchase of the company's assets won't be finalized until August 1992.

CHAPTER NINE

The Mean Season

M ichael Wilson was not a happy camper. It wasn't easy being finance minister in the autumn of 1990. He had been called as good as a liar by the public for refusing to admit there was a recession until September—and then saying it was something most Canadians wouldn't be affected by. Canadians were blaming a high dollar and high interest rates—his fault from a political standpoint—for making the Free Trade Agreement a failure. And nobody had time for his explanations. Worst of all, he was becoming known as the minister responsible for the GST. The new goods and services tax was loathed with a passion by voters; it hung like a limp noose around his and Brian Mulroney's necks, waiting only for an election that promised to turn into an execution.

This day in November 1990, however, Wilson was speaking to a sympathetic audience. The Canada-United States Business Association was an organization full of Tories; in fact, the room was dotted with old friends and fund raisers. They were all happy to have Michael back in Toronto, in the business community where he had matured and where he felt most comfortable. They all clapped politely after Wilson gave a remarkably dull speech on how the GST fit into the same grand Tory agenda as free trade: structural reform for Canada.

But the press who had come to the lakefront Westin Harbour Castle hotel to hear Wilson didn't buy the Tory rhetoric. After the speech, they didn't allow the suits much time to cosy up to the minister. They rushed Wilson in their usual manner, in what's known as a scrum but which more closely resembles animals devouring fresh meat. Most of the talk was GST; that, at least, Wilson was used to. He didn't, however, want to discuss all the business executives who couldn't be with him at the pro-free trade luncheon because they had to stay in the office and try to deal with companies that were going out of business.

Wilson keenly resented the implication that it was his government's policies that had pushed these businesses to the brink. He took it personally. After all, Canada was suffering through a recession, as businesses had before, he said petulantly. They would bounce back. How could they bounce back when they would be wiped out by American competitors? the journalists cried. "I believe in Canada," Wilson said lamely. "I believe that our companies can be competitive." But no answers, no solutions. As his handlers hustled him off, it was clear that Wilson had retreated behind a wall. A wall of ideology.

By this time, Wilson had been warned by the country's bankers that things would get worse, not better. In late September, five or six weeks before the Harbour Castle speech, Wilson had called a private dinner meeting for the chief executive officers of the large banks at the Sutton Place Hotel to meet with Michel Camdessus, managing director of the International Monetary Fund. For an hour before the IMF chief arrived for dinner, the bank heads told Wilson what they were seeing in the trenches—trends that wouldn't show up in the statistics for months but that were already obvious. "We told him about the increases in bankruptcies in Ontario, for example, before it was in the *Toronto Star* or the *Globe*," recalls Dick Thomson of the Toronto-Dominion Bank.[1]

This, after Wilson had been denying the undeniable for months. Canadians had been waiting to hear the "R-word" escape from his lips. Only a week before the bankers' meeting, in fact, he'd done the deed. But Wilson had blithely assured Canadians that "we're on the borderline," and "if there is a recession, it's going to be a shallow recession." Canadians would hardly feel a mere "technical recession," he added. "There's such a little bit of difference between going below the line and going above the line . . . you wouldn't notice the difference as a Canadian."

But Canadians did notice. They noticed factories closing and jobs disappearing. They knew the government didn't have any answers, or at least none that it wanted to admit. But they needed a scapegoat. So by and large

---

1 Thomson, whose bank would be the worst hit by the downturn in Ontario, was ribbed by the other bankers for attending in black tie; he had to slip out to accompany his wife to the annual Opera Ball.

they blamed the Free Trade Agreement (FTA) for the misery in Canada during 1990 and 1991.

The Tories had made a deal with the United States, the conspiracy theory ran: sign the Free Trade Agreement, they'd told the Americans, and we'll keep the Canadian dollar high—high enough that you'll find it easy to come in here and scoop up business. The idea was ludicrous, but it gained credence in larger and larger circles in the country during 1990. So much so that in early December 1990, discredited former Tory cabinet minister Sinclair Stevens landed on page one of the *Toronto Star* with his version of the theory. Stevens claimed that during the free trade negotiations completed while he was still a minister, just such a deal had been made. Nothing on paper, mind you. More of a wink and a nod.

The media lapped it up, even though Stevens hadn't been around for much of the free trade negotiation. Five years earlier he had been hanged in effigy by the same media and subsequently had been excoriated by a commission of inquiry for using his public position to interest Bay Street in helping him out with his personal financial affairs. Former cabinet minister Pat Carney, who had been the one making the free trade deals at the time Stevens was around, denied the story vehemently. But those who wanted to believed it anyway. And there were a lot of them. Everyone knew, they added, that Mulroney would rather be an American than a Canadian. Look how much time he spent in Palm Beach.

Besides, there really wasn't any other explanation that made sense to a lot of people as to why the Tories were insisting on such a rigid high-dollar, high-interest-rate policy, which resulted in American businesses being able to push into Canada while Canadian business floundered.

The Free Trade Agreement became the natural scapegoat for just about everything that went wrong in Canadian life. It made sense. People were losing their jobs because Americans were closing their branch plants in Canada and importing goods from head office, or expanding their operations into Canada and undercutting Canadian firms. Either way, Canadian companies were going out of business. Fewer people had money to spend, and retailers were suffering. The economy was spiraling downward. Opposition member Sheila Copps was mouthing a standard line when she said of rising unemployment figures that "this country is heading toward deindustrialization." Royal Bank of Canada economist Edward Neufeld estimated that by spring 1991 the FTA had been wrongly blamed for the loss of 90,000 jobs.[2]

---

2 In fact, most of these lost jobs could be blamed on such causes as the shift from a

Wilson and John Crow, governor of the Bank of Canada, had a number of set lines to explain their monetary strategy. First and foremost, they were fighting inflation. They wanted to kill it dead, so that it couldn't come back to haunt them in the future. Secondly, they had to keep the dollar high in order to attract the foreign money needed to pay for the government deficit. And that was hard to come by in 1990 for a number of reasons: other countries needed more money at home and were also offering higher interest rates; also Canada was considered more unstable as a result of Meech Lake, so investors weren't as comfortable buying government bonds. A higher rate was needed to entice them.

Nonetheless, the actions they had taken to fight inflation were rigid and regressive, particularly after the economic downturn began. During the summer of 1990 Canada suffered through an all-time high in real interest rates. Since the beginning of 1986, the dollar had risen by 21 percent against the American dollar. And this when businesses were struggling to stay alive.

In early 1991, *Globe and Mail* economics columnist Peter Cook described the Bank of Canada and the finance department as the places "where the recession was authored." Cook claimed in a telling piece that the high-dollar, high-interest-rate combination had jolted the economic ecology of Canada. Economists have borrowed the term "hysteresis" from physics to describe a wrenching shock to the system that does lasting damage. Cook compared the shock effect in Canada to Britain's tight-money policy of the early 1980s, which entrenched unemployment, or the Americans' high-dollar policy of the mid-1980s, which allowed foreign firms to gain an unrecoverable advantage in high-tech sectors such as machine tools, automobiles, and computer chips. His article, titled "The Hollow Economy," was an indictment of the Bank of Canada's policy and the government's agreement with it.

Business certainly thought the government was being too rigid about inflation and carrying its tight-money policy too far. And business was particularly resentful because it was the group that had supported free trade. The Business Council on National Issues, through an affiliated group co-headed by Donald Macdonald and Peter Lougheed, had launched an unprecedented two-year lobby effort in support of the Free Trade Agreement. They pulled out all the stops for the election campaign, running

---

manufacturing to a service economy, taxes, labor costs, financing costs, interest rates, and the Canadian dollar. A Royal Bank survey of companies that were leaving Canada ranked these reasons as primary in their decision to move. Free trade was lumped in with eight other factors that had affected their decision.

expensive scare-tactic ads and recruiting non-partisan heavyweights into their camp.

Yet when free trade arrived, they were caught flat-footed. A real bitterness developed between business and government as the recession arrived and businesses began to flounder or move to the United States. Business leaders who had preached at the government about high debt had not reduced their own companies' debt. And they needed more money to expand their production for export. All their plans to compete aggressively under the FTA had been made with the Canadian dollar at 75 cents U.S.

Ontario was worst hit by the recession after its boom years in the stock market and real estate. It had a record number of bankruptcies during 1990 and 1991 and many entrepreneurs lost their companies. "Soft receivership" became a favorite term around accounting firms, as banks placed workout specialists into companies such as Magna International and Denison Mines. Certain sectors were just falling apart. The steel industry, for one, was in a shambles. Dofasco had bought Algoma in 1988; it abandoned the company in 1990. "If the executives running Canadian steel mills were Japanese," wrote Peter C. Newman, "they would have committed hara-kiri long ago."

Of course, this had happened before; in a resource-based economy everyone was used to cycles. And there had been seven good years to prepare for the lean ones. In fact, in their ivory towers in universities or at banks and think-tanks, economists could cite statistics that showed this recession was no worse than any other, as recessions go — better than the 1981-82 brand, for example.

But no one felt that way about it. It was as if the nastiness in the country over Quebec and the Senate and Oka and the GST had seeped through to color everyone's feelings about the recession. That and fear. Native instinct was telling everyone that this recession was different. Business and labor became one voice in confirming that suspicion. The Canadian Manufacturers' Association spoke out: half the jobs lost, it said, including those in low-tech factories producing furniture, textiles, and auto parts, were gone forever. For once, the Ontario Federation of Labour was more optimistic, saying at least 20 percent of 150,000 lost jobs will never return. "Obviously Canada cannot hope to be competitive in the longer run if we lose our industrial base today," warned Bank of Nova Scotia chairman Cedric Ritchie, "yet that is what is happening."

Meanwhile, the anti-free trade forces were saying I-told-you-so. They could point to plant after plant closed, office after office transferred, empty warehouses and firesale bankruptcies. The Canadian Labour Congress began compiling a list of jobs lost to the United States. It counted 70,000 after one year, 226,000 after two. Council of Canadians leader Maude Barlow published the list of companies that had gone under or moved away and the numbers of employees out of work as an appendix to her 1990 anti-free trade book, *A Parcel of Rogues.*[3]

The anti-free trade movement felt all its predictions had been justified: Mulroney and his gang of thieves had sold the country down the river to the Yanks for some as-yet-unrevealed personal gain. In October 1990, Barlow told the *Washington Post,* "People now see that Canada has been sold out for pure greed."

The Pro-Canada Network[4] had its own lexicon for all this: multinationals talking of shifting operations south were practicing "free trade blackmail" and the Free Trade Agreement was "a corporate bill of rights." A headline on their January 1990 publication hit the mood of the country spot-on. It read: "Free Canada—Trade Mulroney!" The article ran in part: "The Tories have cut back on unemployment insurance, health, education, regional development, and just about everything else. And Brian Mulroney takes the U.S. side on everything from agricultural trade to El Salvador. Coincidence? We don't think so." To this group in particular, everything— from cuts in grants to women's groups to a proposed restructuring of unemployment insurance—was part of the free trade plot to make Canada part of the United States.

Both the business types and the anti-free trade groups were wrong. Oh, they had a right to be angry at Ottawa. After all, Brian Mulroney had campaigned in 1988 on the pledge that the FTA meant jobs, jobs, jobs, when his own internal studies showed that wasn't the case. The agreement would create a few extra jobs in the long term simply because it removed barriers to trade. But that wasn't why Canada was asking for the FTA. Canada needed free trade in order to keep on the good side of the United States at a time when the United States was becoming protectionist.

Mulroney had also promised special assistance to people who lost their job as a result of the FTA—and he hadn't delivered. But no matter what the

---

3 Key Porter, 1990.
4 This is an amalgam of labor, environmental, and women's groups that includes farmers and churches as well. The Council of Canadians helps distribute its publications. In spring 1990 the group changed its name to Action Canada Network in English, Réseau Canadien d'Action in French in order to be more flexible in the unity debate.

anti-FTA groups claimed, the plant closings and company transfers couldn't all be blamed on the trade deal. Instead, they were the result of a complicated range of causes, and many would have happened with or without free trade, given the recession. There could have been more if the United States had begun, in the absence of a trade deal, to shut us out.

As for the business community, it was caught by its own underlying smugness. For years it had campaigned for free trade; lobbied for free trade with the United States; said it was ready for the agreement. But it hadn't prepared its own companies for the competition. It had too much debt and its costs were too high to compete effectively. This wasn't all the fault of high rates or a high dollar, but of bad management. And this was the group that had criticized Ottawa for years for not dealing with the deficit; now it was crying because Ottawa was trying.

The largest companies weren't really affected by high Canadian rates. They did most of their borrowing on foreign markets anyway.[5] In fact, their foreign borrowing in part kept the dollar up at 85 to 87 cents U.S.[6] Smaller and medium-sized businesses had a right to cry uncle. But business had simply overestimated its own worth and underestimated the competition.

Some businesses weren't affected by the FTA but by other types of deregulation. The airlines and the truckers come to mind. Rhys Eyton of Canadian Airlines International and Jack Fraser at Winnipeg-based conglomerate Federal Industries had been two of the most vocal proponents of the FTA. By 1991 Eyton was cowering at the specter of open competition in his own industry, while Fraser was trying to sell a trucking company that he had bought only two years earlier.

Two years after the Free Trade Agreement was signed, a Royal Bank of Canada study showed normal "recessionary" job loss; a rise in foreign investment and some new jobs (for example, in the food processing and chemical sectors)[7] because of the FTA; and a loss of manufacturing jobs in part because of the ongoing shift from an industrial to a service economy. That particular trend had been publicized to death during the early 1980s, but now everyone had forgotten about it.

The companies leaving the country didn't blame the trade agreement. Instead, they cited—in order—high labor costs, high taxes, high interest

---

5 See Chapter One.
6 They borrow in a foreign currency, then convert that money to Canadian dollars, keeping up the demand for Canadian dollars.
7 Certain jobs were created as a result of foreign companies (not necessarily American) moving to Canada.

rates, and the high Canadian dollar. The dollar was a big part of labor costs, of course—40 percent of the increase in wages since 1985.

Still, the government also had some pretty serious charges to answer. It had long known that the country's economy needed structural reform. Free trade was to be part of an upgraded and more efficient economy, a shift to "knowledge jobs." That was the idea when it was first suggested by Donald Macdonald's Royal Commission on the Economic Union and Development Prospects for Canada in 1985. But the rest of the suggestions from the Macdonald Commission had been ignored and free trade was instituted on its own.[8]

Ottawa had also long known about the deficit, especially by the time it was negotiating the Free Trade Agreement. So the government knew it would need a tight money policy, but it had never realized that tight money would be particularly damaging as the Americans took advantage of open borders and Canadian companies needed to do the same. This could be nothing but willful blindness.

Ottawa had not provided enough transitional money for workers in need. But even worse, its initiatives for retraining workers who had lost their jobs were ineffective given the number of people out of work. It had been reducing its support for research and development spending. And it had no concept of where business should be heading. It had no strategy to complement a trade deal upon which it had staked Canada's prosperity in a one-issue election campaign in 1988. Mulroney's own National Advisory Board on Science and Technology took a few layers of skin off the government's hide for just that lack of foresight in a "secret" but widely leaked report in late 1990. The poor business climate increased the danger of the country "de-industrializing," it said.

All through 1990, Ottawa seemed unable to react to the economic disaster. Mired in its constitutional failures, it was unable to cope with anything else.

---

8 Macdonald urged at the time that his blueprint—drawn up after three years of intense study—be implemented as a whole. His other economic suggestions included an emphasis on education and retraining. He proposed that a free trade agreement be tied to training programs and mobility grants for workers, a guaranteed minimum wage to replace our patchwork of social benefits, a cut in the unemployment insurance fund, and the establishment of a transitional fund to retrain workers displaced by free trade. He also advocated a realignment of Canadian marketing boards and incentive bonuses to increase worker productivity.

Then, suddenly, it had to deal with a crisis originating in Washington.

Just when Canadians thought matters couldn't get much worse, the United States revealed a new agenda. The United States was happy enough with its deal with Canada, despite its own recession, a financial institutions crisis, and a disintegrating industrial sector. It was happy enough, in fact brave enough, to do it all over again, this time with Mexico, a nation with a substantially lower cost structure, lower wages, fewer regulations for business, and lower taxes.

The United States had its own reasons for doing this. Those same reasons didn't apply to Canada. But Mulroney's team was going to have to put the best face on a second, unwanted trade agreement. It had no choice but to follow Washington's cue.

The anti-FTA, Mulroney-and-business-sold-out-the-country-for-personal-gain theory immediately falls apart when it comes to naming the members of the cabal on the American government side.[9] Most Americans don't care enough about Canada to conspire to take it over or knock it off as business competition. When the country is brought to their attention, they blithely and consistently make two major errors about Canada. First, they assume that since Canada is roughly the same physical size as the United States (bigger, actually) and has roughly the same standard of living (arguably higher), Canada is an economic equal. Second, they think that Canada believes it is an economic equal.

Such ignorance extends to the administration and the Congress, including some highly paid policy advisers. There is, of course, a small group of Canadian experts. President George Bush is fairly knowledgeable himself. But even those familiar with Canada and the ideological battle underlying the 1988 "free trade" federal election haven't given much thought to Canada's reaction to the reality of free trade with the United States. American ambassador Edward Ney knows that Canadians are blaming the FTA for all their economic woes, but practically no one else connected to Washington does. Those who do just don't seem to care. Which explains why the American politicos didn't worry much about the Canadian reaction to a potential United States-Mexico trade deal. They were a bit

---

9 The only name anyone would ever offer was James D. Robinson III, chairman of American Express and a big free trade supporter. He gained a Canadian bank shortly after the FTA was signed—see Chapter One.

frustrated that Canada took so long to make up its mind. But it didn't matter a whit to their game plan.

George Bush is definitely a president for the 1990s. All that kinder, gentler nation stuff showed that he understands that Americans these days care more about the quality of their life — the environment, urban issues, areas in which they can make an impact. The Gulf War proved that he wasn't a wimp and that America was still *the* superpower, able to handle any number of international initiatives at once: in November 1990 Bush went straight from a visit to the Saudi Arabian desert to a cowboy-gear summit with Mexican President Carlos Salinas de Gortari.

Salinas had been asking for and getting Bush's ear a lot during the previous two years. One of Bush's "great nation" platforms had been an Initiative for the Americas, which envisioned that one day a free trade zone would stretch through North and South America. Salinas wanted to make that day happen very soon in Mexico. At first American trade experts didn't take his bid for free trade with Washington very seriously. But by March 1990, when Bush publicly confirmed that they were going to push for a United States-Mexico deal, it became clear this was an important item on his administration's agenda. In June, a formal announcement was made: once the GATT talks were finished, Mexico was next at the trade table.[10]

This was a surprisingly generous decision on Bush's part. After all, 1990 was not a stellar year for either the American economy or international trade matters. The victory in the Gulf had not yet restored the American psyche to its full power of positive thinking. A rare black-and-white cover on *Time* magazine's October 15, 1990, issue said it all: the famous shot of Harold Lloyd hanging from a clock above a mass of urban sprawl. The title: "High Anxiety." Iraq was pegged at that point as "the catalyst that brought the world's economic weaknesses to bear all at once." During the previous three months, the United States had lost nearly 500,000 jobs. Stock markets were worse than unstable. Oil prices were escalating erratically. The Americans couldn't even take unalloyed pleasure in the Japanese financial crunch; they needed money and the Japanese weren't lending.

The economic pressures were telling on the nation, according to *Time*. Americans had less confidence in the country's future than they had had

---

10 The GATT talks broke down in December 1990; at the time of writing, there were still ongoing negotiations to revive them.

since the rust-bowl recession of 1982, and the weak economy was being blamed for "a national sense of uncertainty and malaise." Said economic guru Robert Reich: "We are skating on what may seem to be firm ice. But it is thinning rapidly, and we really don't know how thin it is." Like Canada, the United States was not prepared for and not coping well with radical and rapid changes in the nature of its economy.

Yet Bush chose to negotiate a trade deal with Mexico for reasons that, while related to economics, were not purely economic in origin. Free trade was partly a way to ensure that a neighbor kept his social and political problems to himself. By encouraging job creation in Mexico, for example, Bush hopes to stem the flow of illegal immigrants to the United States.[11] Bush also hopes to get a better handle on cross-border drug trafficking— and to coerce Mexico into doing the same.

There are trade advantages to the deal, but they're mostly longer-term. As Mexico prospers, its 85 million people will become a big market for American goods. Right now, Mexicans spend only U.S. $300 annually per capita on American products; Canadians spent U.S. $3,000. With free trade, larger American companies will feel more secure in locating in Mexico and taking advantage of cheap labor; the United States will also be able to be more confident of Mexican oil exports. And with Salinas, a Harvard-educated economist, pushing through widespread reforms to turn a socialist country into a capitalist one, Mexico has already been rated a rising star by the 1,500 executives polled at a recent World Economic Forum in Geneva.

The gains will not, however, be spread evenly throughout the United States. Texas, with its immigration problems, stands to gain, while Illinois will likely lose auto-parts jobs. Some areas of American agriculture will be hit by the deal; there will be pressure on labor unions to cut wages; smaller companies will find it harder to compete with cheaper Mexican goods without being able to take advantage of expansion opportunities there. But Bush wanted free trade badly and was prepared to take on organized labor to gain approval for a deal with Mexico. As Ambassador Carla Hills told the House Ways and Means committee in early 1991, the pact "would be a cornerstone of the president's vision of a hemispheric zone of free trade."

It's easy to understand why Salinas asked Bush for the deal.[12] Inspired by the Canada-United States pact, Salinas wants open borders to export many

---

11 By 1988, there were 1 million illegal Mexicans working in the United States.

12 The United States cannot by law initiate a free trade deal; the other country must approach it, as Canada did.

of the same type of products to the United States that Canada sends: cars, auto parts, machinery, steel, cement, petrochemicals, textiles, and furniture. Mexico became the outsider staring in after the 1988 FTA. Salinas also wants to encourage foreign investment so that Mexico's plants will be upgraded. He doesn't want his country to be ignored amidst the excitement about the developing Asian nations and Eastern Europe. With free trade, certainly, the studies all predict that Mexico will be the big winner in jobs, trade, and investment.

For Canadians, Mexico's motivations don't really matter. As caring citizens of the world, we should wish Salinas well with his rebuilding. As citizens of Canada, we must realize that the only thing that matters in this case is Washington's commitment to the pact. That is clearly strong. Bush pulled out all the stops to ensure that the Mexico deal was placed on the Congressional "fast track." In technical terms, this means that the administration has two years to negotiate a deal and that once it's negotiated, Congress can only approve or disapprove. No amendments allowed. In practical terms, however, the late May fast-track vote was viewed as a yes or no for Mexico.

Bush visited with key Congressional leaders at the White House, and his cabinet lobbied over breakfast, lunch, and dinner. Carla Hills spoke with 150 Congressional members — including two-thirds of the Senate — personally; she finally went hoarse a couple of weeks before the late May vote. A special Bush trade adviser returned from GATT trade talks in Geneva to stickhandle the vote through the House Ways and Means committee. Bush's chief lobbyist was working on Mexico full time.

And most important of all, in early May Bush gave Congress a detailed strategy paper forestalling as many criticisms as possible. His "Action Plan" called for transition periods in some sectors of up to twenty years before tariffs disappeared. He said there would be strict "rules of origin" on products so that other countries couldn't funnel their goods through Mexico; as much as 75 percent of a product — parts and labor — would have to originate in Mexico, as compared to 50 percent for Canada. There would be money to help American workers "adjust" when they lost their jobs in low-tech industries. There would be improvements to working conditions, labor standards, and occupational health and safety laws in Mexico. No product would be allowed into the United States unless it met American environmental standards. And there would be negotiation on toxic waste.

The latter provisions successfully divided the anti-fast-track coalition of environmentalists and labor unions. Congress approved a continuation of the administration's negotiating rights for two years on May 25, 1991, six days before the June 1 expiry. A deal could be ready by the end of 1991.

While Bush was playing the great statesman, Brian Mulroney and his Canadian cabinet were left in rather less flattering roles: puppets on a string. The Pro-Canada group could—and did—happily quote American futurist Peter Drucker: "In North America the only question is whether Mexico will join in; Canada has basically already integrated with the U.S."

Everything that the anti-FTA groups had said about Canada signing over its foreign policy to the United States seemed to be coming true in early 1990, whether it was External Affairs minister Joe Clark playing the macho warrior in pale imitation of George Bush's Gulf War stand, or International Trade minister John Crosbie being caught off-guard by the March 1990 Bush-Salinas public announcement. Bush and Salinas had been making noises since 1988, so Crosbie couldn't have been completely unaware of the likelihood of a United States-Mexico trade agreement, but it certainly appeared that he and his department were. There was public dithering for six months. Then in September, Crosbie formally requested a seat at the table. At that moment, it seemed that Canada might have to force its way in.

Canada had no choice in the matter. It had to be at the negotiating table. If it stayed out of the agreement, both the United States and Mexico would gain at Canada's expense. Mexico would be able to offer other countries the same access to the American market that Canada was flogging to investors in Tokyo and Hong Kong, London and Bonn. And Mexico would be pushing aside Canadian products—the two countries overlap on 60 percent of exports to the United States. Canada had to protect what territory it could.

There were reasons why neither the United States nor Mexico would want Canada at the table. Mexico sees Canada as a potential ally in dealing with the United States, but it isn't worried about its ability to negotiate on its own. And Mexico wanted a deal with the United States. It didn't want to be forced to deal with certain matters simply because they were on the Canadian agenda. For example, Mexico doesn't want to let the United States or Canada have any special access to its oil resources. Its laws don't allow any foreign ownership in the oil business, and any suggestion that this stance be renegotiated is seen as a strike at the country's sovereignty. But Canada has already promised to supply the United States with oil in a time of global crisis and will insist that Mexico do the same.

As for the United States, if it had two separate deals it could play off one against the other. Academics call this the hub-and-spoke theory. It's always better to be the hub with two spokes, rather than one point of a triangle. But the United States didn't really care that much either way; if Canada wanted in, fine. Which, of course, was immediately just fine with Mexico too. As Hills told the Ways and Means committee, there were more lofty goals at stake: "Whether we go at it in one bite or two bites is less important than that we achieve our vision of this hemisphere being a free trade hemisphere."

On February 5, 1991, Ottawa was officially included in the upcoming talks. The pace picked up immediately. A week and a half later, Crosbie jetted to Mexico City for a special North American Free Trade (NAFTA) conference. He told reporters there Canada's participation came with "no strings attached." Except that Canada, as the latecomer, had agreed not to delay the show. By March, the three governments had worked out nine discussion areas. Banking and transportation, not part of the Canada-United States deal, were among the sectors listed, as well as agriculture, autos, auto parts, petrochemicals, and insurance. The other two points involved the rules of play: the rules of origin question (which could be called the Tokyo rule), and the levels of reduction for tariffs and non-tariff barriers to trade.

Salinas came to Canada to sell the deal as part of his almost constant hopping to and from Washington during March, April, and May. But Canadians weren't buying the idea of Canada competing for jobs with a Third World country. With the Canadian economy—arguably the Canadian nation—falling apart at the seams, it seemed incredible that Canada now had to open its doors to the competition of cheap labor and goods from Mexico. A Gallup poll in early March 1991 in the *Toronto Star* showed that Canadians didn't want this new deal: 63 percent of those polled said it would hurt more than it would help the economy. Only 28 percent of Canadians said it was a good idea, versus 72 percent of Americans and 66 percent of Mexicans polled. Perhaps most significantly, 54 percent of the Canadians believed that the United States will benefit the most from any deal.

Carla Hills's bellicose attitude toward Canada certainly cemented that type of anti-United States thinking. Hills began saying that with Canada at the table, any section of the Canada-United States deal was potentially up for renegotiation—any section that the United States didn't like, that is, such as Canada's protection of its cultural industries. Of course, Hills had just seen so many of her own nation's cultural industries sold to the Japanese that she may have felt perfectly justified in that request. And she was playing a typical game of political posturing for the home audience to make it clear that the Americans planned to be tough talkers at the bargaining table. But it was the most insensitive remark she possibly could have made. Historically, Canada had been formed by a disparate group of peoples who had in common a wish not to be American, and the sacrosanct nature of our cultural industries is one of our few remaining barriers. Her comments certainly played right into the hands of the anti-free trade groups in Canada and set off speculation that Canada might have to abandon the talks.[13]

There was also the likelihood that other matters would land on the negotiating table. The auto pact, negotiated in 1965, had been left as is in the FTA. It called for minimum Canadian content levels in North American cars; that would have to change. Moreover, the United States isn't happy with Canadian generic drug laws and might well be talking about intellectual property rights in terms of drug patents for its large pharmaceutical companies. The textile industry, already hit by free trade, could expect more blows from Mexico. Canada's best hope of protection from further scrutiny by the United States was the push for a quick deal acceptable to all three countries. But in spring 1991 the United States government's former deputy negotiator during the United States-Canada talks wasn't optimistic about Canada's position. William Merkin, now a Washington trade consultant, told *Maclean's* magazine, "You come into this negotiation and you'll be told: 'Okay, Canada, you wanted to be involved. Well, here's what it's going to cost you.' It's going to be very painful."

Pain we don't need. Nor fear-mongering. We're scared enough as it is. By early 1991, Canadian confidence had sunk so low that we were afraid of competing with a Third World nation. And this sorry state had come to pass under a federal government that had pledged in 1984 to concentrate on Canada's economy. A government so pro-business it was regularly accused of being in bed with business. A government that, although it had paid lip service to all the right ideas, had never instituted them. A government

13 Later, in July 1991, Hills sounded more conciliatory, saying culture and the auto industry will not be up for negotiation.

seemingly incapacitated by debt, unable to formulate an economic policy. A government that hadn't realized how uncompetitive Canadian business was when it launched its drive for free trade.

Because its own economic policies had misfired, Ottawa hadn't been answering the charges that free trade was causing the economic angst in Canada. It had ammunition: a $3-billion increase in trade with the United States since 1988 and a net gain of 240,000 jobs in Canada since 1989 as well as 136,000 more jobs in the first nine months of 1990, despite the government's own harmful tight-money stance. But by 1991, the upcoming Mexico negotiations made it vital that it take a stand on the economy.

With their fortunes at such a low ebb, Mulroney's Tories needed a miracle. They needed a way to show that free trade was a good idea without dwelling on their own disastrous economic management of the country since free trade.

And the Tories think they have it. A unique, an astounding, a mind-blowing solution. Economic policy. Not industrial strategy, that dirty socialist-sounding word. But a complete re-examination of Canada's economic underpinnings. An attempt to understand why it is that we measure ourselves using the same yardsticks as an underdeveloped nation, yardsticks such as the cost of our labor and our resources. Why we don't have a hope of competing on the basis of technology or research or high productivity or innovation. Although the government's motives are questionable, it has the right idea.

Michael Wilson is the key. In April 1991, Mulroney finally moved him out of Finance, but he remained the key economic minister: he was given the portfolios of Industry, Science and Technology, and Trade, and the chairmanship of the cabinet committee on economic policy. From that position, the game plan went, he would begin to deal with the underlying economic issues during the summer and autumn. But first he must make the best of the Mexico talks.

Wilson's transformation from recession minister to recovery minister was showcased on the muggy Wednesday afternoon of June 12, 1991. It was not an auspicious occasion. Wilson walked into the media den at the Sutton Place Hotel in downtown Toronto with Carla Hills and Mexican negotiator Jaime Serra Puche and took his place at the podium. The room had a smattering of diplomats and a few of the trappings of multilateralism, including English, French, and Spanish translators. Behind the trio was a row of diplomatically arranged flags: Canadian, Mexican, American.[14]

That morning, the trio had met for the official opening of the North American free trade negotiations. While they kept the press corps waiting for about forty-five minutes, this was the real reason for the meeting. The negotiators had spent the morning discussing the fact of the negotiations, rather than anything of substance. Now they would pose, smile, and draw a few lines in the sand to ensure that they received good reviews for strong performances on opening day.

Serra was adamant that Mexican oil was not open for negotiations. Culture he didn't care about. Hills and Wilson did, however; she restated her position that Canada's protection of cultural industries should be open to renegotiation in this new round of meetings, while Wilson said stolidly that it most certainly wouldn't be. Aside from that, Hills wasn't giving much; as she deftly told a reporter, "I didn't come to this press conference to negotiate the North American Free Trade Agreement."

None of the Canadian questions had any positive slant to them. They were all about jobs already lost during two years of the Canada-United States free trade, the potential environmental dangers in dealing with Mexico, the danger of opening our border to a low-wage country. It seemed inevitable, then, that like an echo of a past deed that he couldn't escape, Michael Wilson would be faced with the conspiracy theory. Right out in the open, so that negotiators and camera crews from all over North America knew what Canadians really thought about all this free trade stuff. The reporter backed into the question. Would Canada be negotiating an agreement on currency levels with Mexico, he asked, "like the behind-the-scenes agreement between Canada and the United States?" Wilson's answer was quick and dismissive. "There is absolutely no agreement between the United States and Canada."

Clearly that was not the real question. The reporter, and all the other Canadian reporters, wanted to know why the Canadian government had put the country in such a terrible economic bind. And until the Tories explained that adequately, a lot of people were going to cling to the ridiculous but appealing theory that the country had been sold down the river to United States interests. That was the shadow that Wilson would

---

14 The three countries' negotiators sat discreetly behind the politicians: Julius Katz for the United States, John Weekes for Canada, and Herminio Blanco for Mexico.

have to defeat with an explanation of the past and a vision of the future. Before 1991 is out, Michael Wilson might be thinking fondly of the good old days when he was held responsible only for the budget, the dollar, and the GST.

CHAPTER TEN

The Prosperity Campaign

The sense of betrayal felt by ordinary Canadians about the federal government's economic policies has hit Wilson where it hurts most: in his own riding.

The night after the high-powered inauguration of the North America Free Trade talks, the Etobicoke Centre Federal P.C. Association held its annual meeting in the larger of two basement meeting rooms in the Pentecostal Church of St. Wilfrid, on Kipling Avenue in suburban Toronto. About eighty stalwart supporters perched on ancient plywood stacking chairs in a room brightened by yellow, orange, and red portable baffles and studded with painted yellow metal poles. There was an air of easy camaraderie in the room, the type of feeling that comes from election battles fought by a loyal corps of foot soldiers; although the group included P.C. youth and senior citizens, it was clear that most of these people knew each other.

After the evening's business was disposed of, Wilson spoke to them of the party's "clear sense of direction as we move down the road to the next election." He talked of the marriage of national unity and competitiveness as election issues, and how he was handling the economic platform by launching a cross-country debate on issues such as education, research and development, and the country's economic future. Then guest speaker Gilles Loiselle, Wilson's former junior minister of finance and more recently head of the Treasury Board, spoke of Canadian unity from the Québécois perspective.

I slipped out the back as the applause for the speakers shifted into end-of-evening handshakes and coffee. Down the hall, the atmosphere was radically different. A woman was leaving the church's smaller meeting room to go outside for a cigarette.

"What's your meeting?" I asked. "Narcotics Anonymous," she replied. "Michael Wilson's down the hall," I offered. "No kidding!" She blasted with a hoarse guffaw—a laugh that contained no happiness. "You mean nobody's assassinated him yet?"

This is a strong reaction to the man who has been tagged over the years as the most consistently believable Tory cabinet minister, particularly since no one could possibly argue that Wilson is in league with business to destroy the country for his own personal gain. He gave up a career at brokerage house RBC Dominion Securities[1] that former partners and friends estimate would have earned him as much as $15 million had he stayed for the bull market and bank buyout of the 1980s. That opportunity is gone now; he's fifty-four years old, and no one is going to write him a check for $15 million in return for his stewardship of the country's economy.

When Wilson is asked about the animosity he faces from Canadians at large, his press aide, John Fieldhouse, quickly jumps in with a positive story. Why, just the other night, someone came up to the minister at the airport and told him what a great job he was doing. Wilson is more willing to admit to some boos in the crowd. "In politics you know that at any one time in a three-party system, you're always going to have more than half the people who would vote against you. Even in my riding, in 1984 when we had the biggest win, I guess I had 55 or 56 percent of the vote. But that's very unusual."

Why put up with it—with anger over the GST and blame for both the deficit and the tight-money policy he adopted to combat inflation? Why shoulder the blame for the fallout from free trade, including the widespread belief that he's been in on some sort of conspiracy to keep up the value of the dollar so that Americans can benefit from free trade at Canadian expense? A man can take only so much beating up for the faults of a nation, after all.

There's the usual politician's ego involved here. But there's been something more driving Michael Wilson during his seven years of shepherding the Canadian economy. His belief in the federal government's economic policies borders on religious mania. There is no room for dissension. Backing high interest rates and a tight dollar was absolutely the right way to

---

1 It was just Dominion Securities when executive vice-president Wilson stepped aside in 1979 to run for Parliament.

get through the 1990 recession, Wilson says: "If anything, the Governor [of the Bank of Canada, John Crow] has indicated that maybe [money] should have been a little tighter." Wilson maintains that his government has done enough about research and development and training during its tenure, although study after study states that Canada has serious, systemic problems in both areas. And this is not political grandstanding. These are articles of faith. Michael Wilson sees himself as a missionary in the Church for a Better Canada. "What keeps me going," he says, "is that I know I want to change things, to improve the livelihoods of people who live here. It's a challenge, because I know that part of this is changing people's attitudes, outlooks, and perceptions."

He adheres to his credo. Wilson has made interminable speeches about productivity since the early 1980s—and he'll quote from them without prompting in conversation. He began talking seriously to Mulroney about switching from Finance to the Industry and Trade portfolios in the summer of 1990, but the move has been on Wilson's private agenda since the summer of 1983. After losing the Conservative leadership race to Brian Mulroney, Wilson discussed his future with a senior government bureaucrat who over the years had become a personal friend.

At that time, Wilson had two jobs in his sights: Finance and Industry. At Finance, he would fight the deficit. At Industry, he would concentrate on what he had dubbed the "ITTT pillars"—investment, technology, training, and trade. Assuming the Tories won the September 1984 election, he asked, which job should he be lobbying for? The bureaucrat said Finance: the macroeconomic problems had to be fixed before the microeconomic ones could be dealt with.

In mid-1991, Wilson staunchly believed that he had set the country on the right economic track. With Don Mazankowski committed to executing Wilson's game plan at Finance, he could move to Industry and work on the microeconomic problems. When it's pointed out that there are other ministers in the Conservative cabinet who could, perhaps, have been working on those microeconomic problems in the meantime, Wilson's answer is a bit defensive. "But I don't get these jobs because I want them. I get them because there's someone else up there who wants to put me in those positions. So clearly the prime minister supports the direction that I have been going in, and this is a collaborative thing." It's essentially an admission that he doesn't think anybody else could do the job.

Given the belief that he's carrying the weight of the country's economic future on his shoulders, it's natural that Wilson didn't like Canadians telling the Spicer commission that they were unhappy with the government's performance on issues such as free trade and the GST. "I'd just like to say one more thing, get something off my chest," Wilson said during an interview at his downtown office-away-from-the-office a couple of weeks after his constituency meeting.[2] "People say, 'This government has no economic policy.' I wish I knew why, because this has been a government that has had a consistent economic policy since we first got in." The plan was outlined in the Tories' November 1984 Agenda for Economic Renewal paper—and was based on his beloved ITTT pillars. "And now here we are in 1991, about to have a consultation paper on investment, science and technology, training, and trade."

Where Wilson sees consistency, however, others see inaction. The lack of coordinated policy on the "microeconomic" items such as research and development, training and investment in innovation suggests, in fact, that Wilson might be right: he might be the only Tory minister with the vision and the capacity to do the Industry job.

On the other hand, any attempts his predecessors in Industry—Sinc Stevens, Don Mazankowski (who did the job until Mulroney could replace Stevens), Michel Côté, Robert de Cotret, Harvie Andre, and Benoît Bouchard—may have made to reposition Canadian industry and labor into a more workable economic format may have simply been defeated by the system. The reality is that Ottawa is a place where the process of government usually outweighs any individual effort. And the wheels of change turn slowly. Michael Wilson could jump to Industry in 1991 confident that he could get to work on the microeconomic issues of the day because the Industry ministry was ready and waiting for a new leader. It had taken most of the Tory tenure in government to get it that way.

The Industry ministry used to be a powerhouse in Canadian government.[3] Then, in 1982, Pierre Trudeau and his Clerk of the Privy Council, Michael Pitfield, disembowelled the ministry, taking away the international trade function and adding responsibility for regional economic development (DREE). The renamed DRIE—the Department of Regional Industrial Expansion—was essentially the government's pork-barrel ministry, used

2 The office, shared by Toronto-area cabinet ministers, is used by only Wilson and External Affairs minister Barbara McDougall these days.
3 It was known as Trade and Commerce until 1970, when it was renamed Industry, Trade and Commerce.

for funding politically motivated regional development projects. By mid-1987, when the Tories took away the regional development mandate again, the department had turned into, by one mandarin's account, "the department of industrial basket cases." It continued to handle ad hoc bailouts, often of companies to which it had earlier given grants or loans. He adds, "No successful company dealt with us."

The bureaucrats began creating a new mandate for the department to go with its new name: Industry, Science and Technology (IST). By the end of 1988, it had been reborn with new legislation as a ministry that would encourage wealth creation, rather than dealing in wealth redistribution. A department more interested, for example, in what could be done about low literacy levels in New Brunswick than in throwing money at the province.[4]

This meant, in the opinion of the department's own senior officials at least, that its job was to intrude on other departments' turf. In worrying about competitiveness, they wanted to look not just at science and technology, but at trade, financial markets, the environment, and crown corporations. They divided Canada's future into five "building blocks" in the summer of 1989: markets; people; science and technology; financing innovation; and the business climate. Then they began talking about how to tackle the basic problems in each of these areas. They talked with private-sector groups, with labor groups, and, most surprising of all, with other government departments. They contacted Energy, Mines and Resources; Labour; Environment; Trade; and Finance.

Wilson's finance department was very interested. Labor costs were helping to create inflation and hurt productivity. Finance bureaucrats were hearing international concerns about productivity at OECD hearings and from high-level advisers such as former trade negotiator Sylvia Ostry. And of course, they were waiting to see the impact of free trade. "We've dabbled on the edges of structural policies through the latter half of the 1980s," one Finance official explained. "People began to realize that the government was behind the game in terms of globalization." A senior IST official adds that when Ottawa began looking at the issues, it was hoping to help industry cope better with the expected recession than they had in 1982.

That was an opportunity sadly missed. But finally, in November 1990, special teams of bureaucrats from Wilson's finance department and from IST began working on a master plan for long-term economic renewal in

---

4   There are still funds for regional development; they have been spliced off into independent Atlantic, Quebec, and Western redevelopment funds, each administered in its region.

Canada. The only question that nagged at them was which political master would execute the agenda. When Wilson switched to Industry the next spring (and added Trade to his responsibilities), the answer was the most natural one. As Giles Gherson said in the *Financial Times* in late April 1991, "Wilson's cabinet switch is less a case of him trading down from the Finance hot seat than Industry and Trade trading up to him."

A week after he took the job, his old employees at Finance and his new employees at IST had completed a 30,000-word draft of their plan for economic renewal. They called it The Brick, and it was just about as heavy as one: 190 pages of weighty matter. Finally, the government had set out in detail the reason why it had chosen to fight inflation instead of stimulate employment. For wider consumption, they had a more digestible document, nicknamed The Key: fifty or so pages of the most important points — the document they expected would become the basis for any debate.

But there was still much to be done before the paper could be released. After all, this was an inter-departmental matter; there was turf at stake. And the negotiating, the compromising, the fine-tuning were all closely monitored by the prime minister's people — because by the time the bureaucrats at IST had discovered the issue of competitiveness as the hook for their born-again department, the issues involved in The Brick had taken on a much higher political priority. Michael Wilson's appointment to Industry was no coincidence, although it was blessed with the luck of happy timing. The Brick was about to become the basis for the economic portion of the Tory national unity election platform.

The autumn 1991 debate on unity and prosperity that Wilson had outlined to his constituents in the Etobicoke church basement was being carefully orchestrated by Mulroney's handlers. Even the loyal Tories knew it wouldn't be an easy sell. But Mulroney's politicos were desperate when they began casting around for answers a year earlier, after the failure of Meech Lake and the debacle of Oka. The public didn't like politicians in general, and they really didn't like Mulroney. They had just thrown out David Peterson in Ontario in part because of his association with Mulroney in pushing the now-dead Meech Lake Accord. During 1990, there was a lot of talk in the party and in public about Mulroney stepping aside before the next election.

The prime minister, however, had no intention of doing that. He had been hated before, after all, and won. In February 1987, he had been at 22 percent in the popularity polls. The next year he had won a one-issue election campaign based on Canada's economic future.

But by 1990 that one issue had turned against him. Behind the stonewalling on the recession and the dilly-dallying over its reaction to the United States-Mexico free trade negotiations, the Tory government was clearly panicked by the beating that Canadian business was taking from American competitors. The politicians and the bureaucrats knew what they wouldn't admit: the businesses that were going under or moving away were gone for good. And even worse, their polls showed that the ordinary guy in Elliot Lake and Hamilton knew the truth as well: Canadians couldn't compete on labor costs, taxes, and cost of living with areas of the United States and Mexico.

In fact, an October 29, 1990, *Globe*-CBC poll showed that the public was "deeply worried about the economy, pessimistic about future prospects, and mad as hell at the government's prescription," according to *Globe and Mail* columnist Jeffrey Simpson.

The polls showed the Tories something else, however. Something that made them sit up and take notice. The same Canadians who were turned off by politicians wanted leaders. And while in the autumn of 1990 they were fed up with Meech Lake and Quebec (or in Quebec, with Canada) and the Senate and the whole political process, and they didn't like the GST and free trade, Canadians knew the country had some basic economic problems, like too much debt. They trusted the Tories to handle the economy more than many of the other issues facing the nation. Most of all, they wanted a concrete plan to fix the problem. And they didn't believe the opposition parties had that plan.

There was more than a hint that if the Conservatives could carefully marry Canada's economic future to the national unity issue, Mulroney might just be able to win again. It sounded like insanely wishful thinking, but it was the only hope they had. Don't forget, this was a government with a 16 percent popularity rating. (It would fall to 15 percent by the summer of 1991.)

The government's new, proactive 1990s look made its debut in the February 26, 1991, budget. The budget didn't offer much—no false promises, at least—but Wilson had to admit that the deficit was about $30 billion again, for all the scrimping and saving and cutting and misery endured by the country. And he made some very positive forecasts about rates, inflation, and the deficit, leaving observers with a "same time next year" feeling about the whole exercise.

But the budget also mentioned the new agenda and the idea of dealing with the country as we found it, not as we "might wish it to be." About resilience, resourcefulness, action, and "facing up to economic reality." About what the Tories had tagged "the prosperity challenge." Wilson said that ordinary Canadians would be canvassed about Canada's economic problems and potential solutions as part of "a national effort to build a new partnership for prosperity" as soon as a special discussion paper was released late in the spring.

The next step came in April 1991, when Mulroney shuffled his cabinet. Joe Clark became the super-minister for national unity. And buried under all the hoopla about the power of western ministers, Michael Wilson became the super-minister for economic management. Don Mazankowski in Finance was another sign of the importance the PMO was placing on all this: as deputy prime minister, Maz would be working closely with Wilson. But Clark and Wilson were the point men for the party's election formula: Unity plus competitiveness equals prosperity.

Prosperity is one of those lovely words that nobody can disagree with. Not as pushy as, say, competitiveness. Not as elitist as globalization. A word that speaks of home and family, of plentiful harvests and satisfied appetites. Of getting back to basics and having the economic stability and clout to be able to deal with challenges. Of a nation where people can afford to be generous with one another.

It's also a lovely word for political manipulation, in that it can evoke all those emotional images while actually meaning something quite different. For the Tories, the prosperity campaign has two components: competitiveness and education. Everything could be wrapped up in this tidy package, from a national securities commission to the elimination of inter-provincial trade barriers to national standards for education. All these things also fitted in neatly with the national unity theme.

The party faithful were told of the strategy in small rallies across the country, like the Etobicoke annual meeting. While Clark was stumping for national unity, Wilson would be pushing prosperity. The two would make it clear that only the Tories had the answers on both issues— all the while consulting the public on their thoughts. Then, jumping off from the

Quebec referendum, the Tories would run their "prosperity" election campaign.

It sounded pretty incredible even to some of the party faithful; this after all was a government reviled. Its economic record was appalling. And Brian Mulroney had unfortunately used the word prosperity a few times before in his electioneering, most notably in 1984 when he told Cape Bretoners that he planned to "inflict prosperity on Cape Breton," a threat Cape Bretoners are still waiting to see carried out.

But many bought in. They had been hoping for a strategy, any strategy. And they realized that like any organization, the party had its mixture of selfish plans and genuinely selfless policy goals. The competitiveness crusade made sense, as well as fitting in with Tory beliefs about the way markets operate.

The May 1991 throne speech contained seventeen mentions of prosperity in a twenty-five-minute address. It had been carefully drafted by Mulroney's chief aides. The theme was "A Learning Culture." No ideas yet; those were to come from the background paper. In the meantime, the throne speech didn't call for much from business—just 2.5 million new jobs in the next nine years. That's actually about on target in historical terms. But it did say that job training would quadruple by the end of the decade— although again, it did not say how, except to note that it would be without large doses of government money. This the government called "a turning point in Canadian history." The reviews were mixed.

Still, as he left for his sales trip to Hong Kong and Tokyo in May,[5] Mulroney told the *Toronto Sun*'s Michel Gratton that he felt "the poison" was leaving the body politic. The *Toronto Star*'s Carol Goar, who is the best in the country at gauging Ottawa's mood, said that despite unemployment and plant closings and truckers blockading Parliament Hill in anger over their diesel taxes, Mulroney was right. The mood, she added, had shifted to "a mixture of weariness, pragmatism and grim determination."

The background report was set for June release. It was late, of course.[6] But the preparations for the autumn cross-country consultations with business,

---

5 See Chapters Six and Seven.
6 When this book went to press, it had not yet been publicly released. In July, however, Wilson began circulating a "pre-consultation" draft version of The Key to his provincial counterparts and to business and labor groups, entitled, "Prosperity through Competitiveness."

labor, academics, and the general public went ahead, with Tony Eyton, former Canadian ambassador to Brazil and consul-general to New York, seconded from the trade ministry to set up a new competitiveness secretariat.[7] Eyton, reporting directly to Wilson, would coordinate the report's release and the consultation to follow.

The Brick and The Key contain fewer answers than questions about the directions the country should take during the next decade. (It is assumed, of course, that the country will remain as some sort of federation.) Six areas have been set out for the year-long discussions: Canada's access to export markets; education and training (including, as Wilson likes to point out, all of his ITTT pillars); the business environment, including taxation and regulation; science and technology; research and development; and finally the investment climate for new ventures and industrial innovation. The report brings no big promises. A senior industry bureaucrat was blunt about that: "There can't be any expectation that we've got the answers to this thing. We're not smart enough and we're not rich enough." And even if they had the money, it would be difficult to make the right decisions about how to spend it, he adds—for instance, should research and development take precedence, or work-force retraining? "If we took the competitiveness problem and tried to throw $10 billion at it, I don't know how we'd spend the money."

But the competitiveness consultation leaves a lot of big questions for the country to grapple with. The same senior industry official admitted that Canadians are facing "a pretty scary four years." He's hoping that a sense of direction will emerge from the cross-country consultation and the electioneering. He's counting on dedication and moral fiber to pull Canada through.

Wilson, who has plenty of both those qualities to complement his missionary zeal, is confident that business will show some moral commitment to country, a commitment it hasn't shown in recent years in dealing with its own well-documented shortcomings in research and training. "What is happening today?" asks Wilson rhetorically during our late June discussion. "Businesses are scared. And there is much concern on the part of labor— workers know that they need a greater amount of skills training. There's a

---

7 Eyton is also Senator Trevor Eyton's younger brother and first cousin to Canadian Airlines International chairman Rhys Eyton.

sense of urgency. It's important to get on with this and get out across the country and press upon people the problems and then maybe they'll get on to it. But it's not going to happen overnight."

While Canadians must be concerned about keeping our industries, Wilson warns that we can't hold on too tightly through regulations and financial restrictions. "We don't have a ringed fence around this country." Instead, he argues, "we must create an environment" that's attractive to business—without a wholesale reduction in taxes or living standards.

"If people see we're not as a country addressing the competitiveness issue and they see us drifting on the biggest political issue of our lives—the unity of the country—and the integrity of the country seems to be slipping and deteriorating, then yes, it's a natural thing for people to say, 'Well, I'm not sure that this is the place that I want to have my savings invested.' So people are going to start to drift, and put a plant in the States or put a plant in Europe—wherever."

Animated, his large hands grasp at air as he attempts to mold the complicated issues into neat sentences. "But if we can demonstrate that we're not going to be overwhelmed by these issues . . . that yes, we are taking you seriously, yes, we do have the will, political and business, to deal with the issues then . . . they are going to get drawn back into the country and be a very active and supportive part of it."

As he leads me into the anteroom after the meeting, I catch a sideways view of his next visitor: Olympia & York Developments' Albert Reichmann. I can't help wondering, as the door closes behind the minister and the multibillionaire, whether their conversation will touch on the commitment of Canadian business to more support for research and training and more innovative types of investment in Canada. Can Mike Wilson proselytize in high places and "change the attitudes, outlooks, and perceptions" of the business community? I can't help worrying that this is wishful thinking.

A Splash on the Map

*Canada is not coming apart on the issue of
patriotism, but because of economics. I know of
no case in which people rioted for lack of poetry.*
— Bill Norgate, 4 Office Automation Building,
Burlington, Ontario, in a letter to the
editor of *Canadian Business* magazine

R eporters, political aides, and diplomats shifted anxiously in their
seats. The press conference to kick off the North American Free
Trade negotiations[1] had been called for 2:15 p.m.; it was now 2:35 and
battery-operated translating devices hung heavily from lapels all over the
room. Camera operators, anxiously checking their film packs in preparation for the moment when Carla Hills, Michael Wilson, and Jaime Serra
Puche would mount the dais, began shifting the heavy camera equipment
from shoulder to shoulder.

In the front row, *Toronto Sun* journalist Dick Chapman, a gregarious
general assignment reporter with a lively mind and a keen sense of the
moment, was fretting about more than just the wait. He didn't like anything
about this free trade idea. Chapman leaned forward to talk to one of the TV
technicians. "It's the end of the country," he declared. "The map won't
have any meaning."

Chapman tied the trade question to the national unity debate. It just
wasn't right, he said, any of it. Regions within the countries grabbing more
power; Quebec's threat to separate; and now more free trade. With most of
their economic ties to the south, what would give Ontario any incentive to
support the Maritimes in future? "Individual regions," Chapman worried

1 See Chapter Nine.

out loud, "will be making decisions that have nothing to do with the color of the map."

It was the map allusion that caught my attention. I had been captivated by the map metaphor in an essay that Eugene Forsey finished slightly more than two weeks before his death in February 1991 at the age of eighty-six. Forsey made a forceful argument that in order to function as a country, Quebec must be in or out. "I am not interested in a Canada that would be just a splash on the map, with a six-letter word scrawled across it," Forsey wrote. "The only Canada I want to preserve is a Canada that can do something: for its own people, for the hungry two-thirds of the world, for the survival of the planet; not a phantom that can only watch helpless as we all tumble down a steep place to destruction." He was making a constitutional argument, but it is also a powerful summation of our economic state.

Chapman is also worried that we're all tumbling down a steep place to destruction. The only answer he can see for the economy is to re-erect trade barriers. Let's admit that we can't compete with cheap foreign labor, he says; stop allowing less expensive foreign goods free access to our markets. After all, he says, look at the jobs that had already been lost since free trade was instituted. At this point, I had to jump into the conversation. "We don't want those jobs anyway," I offered. Chapman turned around and glared at me. "That's easy for you to say, but what about the guy in Windsor or Brantford who's lost his job and doesn't have any hope of another one? The job looks pretty good to him."

I didn't have an easy comeback. There isn't one. Hundreds of thousands of people have lost their jobs in recent months; many of them have been lost because of free trade — because a Canadian firm couldn't compete and shut down or a Canadian firm relocated to the United States. Some of them won't be replaced because a company, either domestic or foreign, chooses to expand in the United States rather than in Canada. For those people, Canada is experiencing the modern-day equivalent of the Industrial Revolution.

But that isn't the fault of free trade. The United States-Canada trade deal simply speeded up the job losses; one Ottawa mandarin estimates that many jobs that would have been lost during the next five years were instead eliminated more quickly, more dramatically. We just can't compete with the low wages; we need jobs that require an educated work force. Like me, the Ottawa policy adviser can look on these losses from the comfort of his or her ivory tower. From that perspective, it looks like a good thing that the recession and the free trade fallout have brought on a sense of economic crisis in the land. Now, the adviser thinks, Canadians will be willing to face some hard truths about the nation's future. The only big worry left is that if better times return, we'll be able to postpone dealing with reality a bit longer. That's something Canada's political masters are ensuring won't happen, by placing competitiveness front and center on the nation's agenda.

Most of the academics across the country are sounding the same note. This has been a hot season for competitiveness studies. Beside the government's Brick, during early 1991 there were eight other studies of Canada's competitiveness completed or ongoing at about the same time.[2] Their basic conclusion: we are in trouble.

Only one of them had as much clout as the government study, however. And it was controversial for two reasons: it was being done by an American; and if he remained true to form, it would be negative. Michael E. Porter, economist, professor of business administration at Harvard University, author, and competitiveness guru, had already given Canada the brush-off in his 855-page seminal work, *The Competitive Advantage of Nations*.

Porter detailed and analyzed the reasons why certain firms in certain countries compete so well internationally in his best-selling 1990 book. Then he used his findings to figure out why companies cluster to grow and do research and make money, since huge companies that compete worldwide are often located in the same city, and why they grow in some centers and countries and not in others.[3]

His few comments on Canada were dismissive at best, damning at worst. He put Canada in the same category as Australia, as a "prosperous nation with bountiful resources" that is in fact on a par with Third World and socialist countries in coping with today's competitive world. He also compared Canada to OPEC nations such as Kuwait and Saudi Arabia—countries living off their wealth rather than building for the future. "Few nations with truly abundant natural resources have achieved sustained prosperity in this century of knowledge-based international competition," he warned.

In August 1990, the Canadian government and the Business Council on National Issues hired Porter for the princely sum of $1 million to expound

2 Appendix A lists the major studies and briefly summarizes their findings.
3 Porter and associates studied ten countries: the United States, Japan, Germany, Italy, Sweden, Korea, Denmark, Switzerland, Great Britain, and Singapore.

on the state of Canada's economy and trade picture.[4] They wanted him, of course, to be more positive about Canada. That wouldn't be easy. In Porter's neat little economist models, there are four stages of economic development. If things work well, a country progresses from an economy dependent on cheap labor or cheap resources, to one driven by investment, to one enlivened by innovation. That's the best place to be; after that, people become too wealthy and complacent and decline sets in. Canadians, in Porter's judgment, jumped straight from dependence on cheap resources to wealth-sated decline.

Through 1990 and 1991, Porter fit twenty-seven Canadian industrial sectors into his aptly named "diamond" model.[5] Porter's results were reviewed several times by a special government-industry-expert board. Almost everyone monitoring the study had an ax to grind. Some academics had their noses out of joint that an American was being paid a cool million to do a job that they felt had already been done time and time again by Canadian economists. Labour ministry representatives were very interested in Porter's negative findings on the role of foreign capital. Right-of-center members of the committee were pressuring him to change his tune on that and say that Canada must look at North America as its home market. Ottawa bureaucrats had an interest in ensuring that his findings dovetailed with their own discussion papers.

His detailed study is due for publication in the autumn of 1991. But Porter really said it all in his book's brief dismissal of Canada. We have few companies with a solid home base. We haven't provided the money and ensured the rivalry to make our companies innovative and productive. The country is in trouble because Canadians have taken our prosperity for granted. Now that we are losing our nation's wealth, we must take decisive action.

Whether the voice speaking hails from Ottawa, academia, the *Sun* newsroom, or any of the many Canadian communities whose residents told the Spicer Commission on Canadian Unity that they are unhappy with our

---

4   The government paid $400,000, the BCNI $600,000.
5   He identifies four important, interconnected factors that determine a company's success: resources, such as labor or raw materials—what economists call "inputs"; company structure and strategy; corporate rivalry; and demand. Two outside factors—chance and government—can be helpful or harmful, but are not, Porter found, essential elements in creating a competitive company. If a company has all these needs met, it has what Porter calls a home base. From there, it can conquer the world.

country's structure and economic outlook, the message is the same: let's move, let's get on with it. Let's rebuild Canada. The blind negativism of 1990 has for the most part been washed out of the system. Outside Quebec, people are willing to work on the country's structural problems, and even in Quebec there is an acknowledgment of the need for some kind of shared economic structure.

Happily, we have a lot of material to work with. Michael Wilson points out that the Industrial Revolution metaphor is too sweeping when talking about the economic transformation that must take place. Canada does have resource wealth and an industrial base; Canadians are well educated by international standards; we have many of the basic building blocks for a different type of economy. We must not, however, reach for a more prosperous Canada as if it were a shiny bauble at the top of the Christmas tree that we can grab if we only stretch a bit higher; we must build it by stretching our minds to encompass a new vision of the country.

We've now viewed Canada's business strategies and economic puzzles from a number of angles. We have seen a patchwork of the nation's business ventures and investment strategies during the past few years. There have been tales of individual achievement and systemic failure; takeover battles and companies going belly-up; high-stakes negotiations and international diplomacy; government deal making and deal breaking; entrepreneurial gambles and savvy management moves; successful foreign investments, and less inspired ventures by foreigners into Canada and by Canadians abroad. But this has not been just another guided tour to the lives of the rich and famous. We can take from these examples of Canadian business life some lessons, some ideas, and some examples of how to reshape our country's business landscape.

First, we looked at how different companies and industries have developed strategies to compete. Some, like the banks, were successful. Some, like Connaught Biosciences, were doomed by lack of money and lack of globally competitive innovation. Others, like the airlines, are now at a turning point that will be determined by management's vision and carefully crafted government regulation. We found that our companies need not only a strong home base, but also access to foreign—particularly American—markets to prosper in the future.

Then, like detectives, we followed the money. We looked at how Canadian family groups such as the Reichmanns view their investments, and how foreign investors such as British Gas can look at an Ontario gas utility and see a very different prospect from that seen by Toronto-based real estate developers. We also explored the investment philosophies driving Asian money, both that of Hong Kong families, such as Li Ka-shing and his Canadianized sons, and of the big-league lenders and investors who control the flow of money from Japan to North America and the rest of the world. We saw much that was surprisingly good about our traditional bogeyman, foreign investment, but a discouraging lack of initiative by the managers of our indigenous pools of capital. It became clear that in order to build a strong and progressive country, we need a commitment by our companies to investment and innovation.

Finally, we came home again to dissect the Canadian reaction to free trade with the United States and the proposed agreement with Mexico. Most important, we looked beyond free trade at the underlying factors that have made Canada unable to cope with a knowledge-driven world economy, let alone compete effectively on the basis of innovation and technological achievement. We also gained an understanding of the political response to this crisis of confidence in the Canadian nation, a crisis that is prompting widespread discussion of our economic as well as our political future.

It became clear that grass-roots involvement is essential; all Canadians, we now know, must work together to create an environment that will enable companies to be prosperous. This involves some sacrifices on our part. At the same time, this community of Canadians must include our business leaders, and they too must make short-term sacrifices in order to build the knowledge-based resources that will ensure business remains and grows in Canada.

The experience of Toronto-Dominion and other Canadian banks in the United States corporate lending market clearly shows that our companies can deal on an equal footing with top-rung foreign competitors. But it also showed that our companies must recognize their limitations; it was only after the bankers realized they couldn't be global competitors that they were able to become North American forces. TD's success in New York is due in good measure to an early pullout from other foreign markets and a strategy of specialization within the American corporate market in areas such as communications lending.

It's heartening to see Canadian business competing effectively in a sophisticated, knowledge-intensive industry such as financial services. The banks couldn't have done this, however, without a strong home base. Their recognition of this and their move into the stockbrokerage business in the mid-1980s, although it was expensive for many of the firms, was the only strategy that could assure them that base. They avoided large-scale foreign brokerage takeovers, which could have resulted in an erosion of their dominance of the Canadian financial services arena. It's also interesting to note that so far, the competition within the banking business in Canada has not resulted in any mergers among the six large banks. Their competitiveness at home prepared them for the cutthroat atmosphere of Wall Street and corporate America.

While it benefits Canadians to have a strong, stable financial system that is developing new markets for its wares, we must be worried about the effect of globalization of financial services on our native capital market. This is not being caused by the banks' forays abroad; the banks are but a link in the chain of international finance. They followed their corporate clients into equity financing and into foreign financial markets. The cause of that flow of companies away from Bay Street to foreign financial markets is the lack of capital in this country. Because money is more expensive and less easily available here, we can't hope to compete as a financial source for the nation's businesses—let alone our own governments.

The truth is, Canada has been built on foreign capital. We must recognize this fact. And while we have to strive to keep our capital markets as competitive as possible for entrepreneurs and growing businesses that are not yet able to attract money in the world's first-tier financial centers, we shouldn't bemoan the continued and inevitable enervation of Bay Street.

We should worry more about what finding funding abroad does to the attitudes of companies toward their homeland. We don't have to fret, however, about losing the loyalty of our banks. The Canadian corporate bankers now think of themselves as bankers to a North American market, but they still have a strong retail deposit base to remind them of their roots in this community.

The dilemma facing the Tory cabinet about the Open Skies talks is the same one that confronts us all when we consider cross-border shopping and the benefits of freer trade. As consumers, we benefit from being able to buy the best products at the best possible prices. As employees, we realize this type of competition means that we must be more productive in order to ensure that our companies can provide a fair share of those products in our own and other markets.

It used to be that airlines were regarded as more than just a consumer service. Having a national airline that linked our disparate communities overrode purely economic considerations. This doesn't seem to be the case any longer—at least judging from Ottawa's sale of Air Canada and from Canadian consumers' demands for more choice when booking domestic or international flights. Yet there are still traces of this vestigial desire for an airline that mirrors our traditional belief in the sanctity of our transportation links.

Add to that the fact that airlines provide not only the type of sophisticated training grounds that we need to foster a pool of skilled talent for computer-related industries, but also a boost to the development of our tourist industry, and there's an argument that we need to have an airline with a domestic bias. Enough of an argument, at any rate, to make Ottawa very careful about the ongoing Open Skies talks. These are a difficult set of negotiations; if the government doesn't improve our carriers' access to the United States market, the Canadian airlines won't survive on our small market base alone. But if it gives the American carriers too much access to Canadian routes, Air Canada and Canadian Airlines International could lose their home base—and in that case they certainly won't survive.

The term "flag carriers" originated in the transportation business from ships that displayed the emblem of their home nation, and it transfers neatly to the red maple leaf emblazoned on Air Canada's tail fins. But the idea that we need to foster "national champions" in industry goes well beyond the airlines; it is one of the most controversial business issues in this country. There are arguments both for and against the idea. Many Canadian business people believe that we should be nurturing particular companies, which will then be able to grow to international size and be, like Air Canada in transportation or Northern Telecom in telecommunications, the nation's representatives in the international economic wars. This is, however, an argument against competition. Michael Porter, for one, states strongly that stifling domestic competition doesn't create international winners. On the contrary, the more competition there is in an industry, he says, the better the domestic companies become. And when companies become competitive at home, they are able to take on the world. The banks are a good example of this idea.

The Air Canada tale certainly demonstrates the problems of protecting certain companies and industries. Claude Taylor, in his crown corporation cocoon, didn't understand how far behind its international competition Air Canada was when the airline was sold by the government to individual investors in 1988. Now he's struggling to make the company competitive while dealing with bad economic conditions and the fickleness of diplomatic negotiations.

The Canadian Airlines approach to global competition has been to seek alliances with foreign companies. This has been one of the most talked-about management strategies for Canadian companies competing abroad. It has not, however, produced a rash of notable success stories yet. And there have been a few trip-ups; Molson Companies, for one, was caught in the middle of 1990 when its Australian ally suddenly ran out of money. The fact is, alliances cannot be counted on to boost a company that is not itself competitive. Marketing or product development deals with foreign companies will not be the savior of Canadian business. And the trade-off must be recognized: alliances involve a loss of control over a company's destiny.

The airlines question is a microcosm of the two roads Canadians can take: the traditional Big Government approach, which demands money and usually produces substandard companies; or the more recently adopted free market approach, which leaves Canadian companies open to foreign competition and at times sacrifices our sense of community.

Right now, the government is debating the question of whether the telecommunications industry should be deregulated. The issues are exactly the same as those that faced the airline industry a few years ago: consumers are demanding better service and better products; but the protection of the telecommunications business has allowed Canada to develop expertise and an internationally competitive technological edge.

There's an interesting corollary here, however, particularly in light of the implicit protection that the airlines are asking of the citizenry of this country. One of the heroes on the go-global circuit is Northern Telecom. It has been able to develop its internationally competitive technology because majority shareholder Bell Canada Enterprises has had a protected telecommunications monopoly. That gave it a tremendous advantage when the United States deregulated its giant telecommunications market.

Yet Northern, in recent years, has become less and less Canadian. The chief executive is American and he has transferred many executive functions outside the country. It is questionable whether Northern is a Canadian company in an operations sense. Although Bell and Canadian pension funds and insurers own a sizable chunk of its stock, it has located a number of research facilities outside the country, and many of its day-to-day decisions are made in the United States. While I don't advocate wholesale interference in company policies, Northern is an example of a company that has in effect distanced itself from its home base, even though its development was supported by government policy that favored its corporate parent at the expense of the Canadian community at large.

That doesn't mean we should try to fence Northern in. We can't ask for foreign investment yet discourage our own companies from investing abroad. We simply need to recognize that making policy compromises for the sake of nurturing "national champions" doesn't guarantee those companies' long-term commitment to Canada.

If we opt for national champions, there is the inevitable question of which companies to choose for national support. Connaught Biosciences is the perfect example of a company chosen in good measure for its image rather than as a result of a realistic assessment of its chances of surviving and prospering. The company was nurtured for decades: by the university and then by the government. There were undoubtedly better bets around. And in part because of these relationships it was never able to develop into a competitive pharmaceuticals company.

There's still a debate in the scientific community over the value of Connaught's research discoveries. Even if we accept the company management's assessment of Connaught's standing, its record is not outstanding: a few good products, but not enough to ensure that the company would be able to develop cutting-edge medicines in future years. And even if it had the products, it wouldn't have been able to bring them to market because it didn't have the money.

Yet Connaught became the symbol of Canada's lost technological opportunities. David Peterson used to hold up the vaccine manufacturer as an example of misguided federal funding policies. "We tend to cultivate our most innovative and promising companies—like Lumonics and Connaught Biosciences—only to sell them off to the highest bidder," Peterson moaned to a group of electronics manufacturers in October 1989, when Ciba-Geigy and Institut Mérieux were battling for ownership of Connaught.

The technological opportunities have been lost for much more basic reasons. Canadian governments and especially Canadian industry don't spend enough on basic research and development. The federal government spends about 1.3 percent of the country's gross domestic product on R&D.

That's half the percentage shelled out by Germany, Great Britain, Sweden, or Japan. And our commitment dropped slightly during the 1980s.

Historically, however, that hasn't translated into more research in the pharmaceutical industry, for one, by foreign-owned companies in Canada. Quite the reverse. Canadian-owned firms spend about 10.7 percent of their sales on R&D; foreign-owned firms spend 2.6 percent in Canada, although, of course, they may also be transferring technological innovations from related companies outside the country as well. In recent times, the federal government has been putting the squeeze on the essentially foreign-owned pharmaceutical industry here to improve those numbers. In return for stronger patent protection, Science Minister William Winegard is demanding that the firms increase their research to domestic levels. Institut Mérieux, in order to win Connaught, had to agree to much bigger research commitments.

In other businesses, the Canadian-owned firms don't have such a stellar track record in research. Only six Canadian industries qualify as research- and development-intensive, and in every one of those areas, for a fifteen- year period ending in 1984, Canada was the only one of eight North American and European countries that consistently imported more product than it exported.[6] And in those areas in which research was being done, it wasn't being translated into developed products that could compete internationally.

That, too, is not surprising. After all, research takes money, lots of money. Canadian companies don't have this money, and many can't afford to borrow it. But worst of all, managers are afraid to make the commitment to initiatives that don't show immediate payoffs, because shareholders demand results every three months. That doesn't allow companies to buy into or fund a company with a strong R&D program.

To his credit, Peterson did recognize that much of the fault for foreign sales of Canadian technology firms lay with the lack of interest in high technology among the captains of Canadian industry. There are pools of capital in this country, both family-based and institutional, but they won't invest in our future. Former Connaught Biosciences head Brian King knows; they all turned him down. "How many new businesses have any of the big pools of capital in this country spawned in the last twenty or thirty

---

6 The industries are: engineering and scientific services; aircraft and parts; telecom- munications equipment; other electronic equipment; computer services; and electronic parts and components. The countries: the United States, Germany, France, Sweden, Great Britain, the Netherlands, Japan, and Canada. This is the latest available data.

years? I don't think there are too many," he says plaintively. "They've bought and sold and rationalized a hell of a lot of things, but how many new businesses have they created?"

One of the family-based Canadian industrial groups that politely turned Connaught away at the door was the Reichmanns. Like many other family-controlled Canadian companies, they're simply not interested in funding companies that specialize in technological innovation or research and development. This is not their type of gamble. Instead, as we found when looking at the Reichmanns' less-than-perfect record of diversification during the 1980s, these family companies tend to favor traditional natural resource industries.

While wealthy families are only one element of the Canadian corporate ownership structure, they are an important one. Many of the country's largest companies are controlled by family groups. And these groups are among those who argue that Canadian business needs size to conquer, although by increasing the size of their own businesses they have failed to prove that they can win market share abroad. The Edper group, controlled by Peter Bronfman and his executive suite, is a good example of the need for more productive management. *Report on Business* magazine editor David Olive recently tagged Edper as the Canadian equivalent of a Japanese *keiretsu*. Olive pointed out that the Canadian group has squandered its opportunities because it didn't understand enough about or concentrate enough on the actual operations of its various business interests.

Canada's large firms concentrate on financial dealings at the expense of developing competitive operational structures. The largest Canadian companies are also the least innovative: small companies spend 12 percent of their profits on research and product development; medium-sized firms reinvest 10 percent of the profits in those endeavors; large companies spend a paltry 0.9 percent of profits on R&D. These numbers belie the traditional explanation that Canadian companies spend less on innovation because it costs them more to borrow money: large companies can always borrow cheaper money from abroad.

Even in our traditional specialty areas such as metals, paper and printing, chemicals, and automotive parts—industries with a strong representation from family groups—Canadian companies haven't even been importing the latest industrial technology for use in our plants: in 1989 fewer than half of

Canadian manufacturers were using technological innovations such as robotics, computer-aided design, or laser technology.

We hear that there is a solid R&D base in our pulp and paper and mining sectors, that technology is being developed here that is being adopted around the world. But both pulp and paper and mining rank near the bottom of the undistinguished Canadian record for R&D as a percentage of corporate sales.[7] The mining industry spent 0.6 percent of the amount it raised through product sales on R&D; the pulp and paper industry spent 0.3 percent. So it didn't surprise me to find out that 60 percent of Ontario's newsprint machines are more than six decades old. No wonder foreign factories can make things more cheaply.

This pattern of steering clear of innovative ventures is not going to change, judging from recent investment decisions. During the 1980s diversification into new businesses was going to make companies like Olympia & York safe from the cycles of its real estate business. Instead, it taught the Reichmanns that if you don't understand a business, you shouldn't be in it.

The one point that sets family-controlled firms such as the Reichmanns' and the Bronfmans' apart from large, broadly owned public companies is that they have their own private, family-oriented agenda as well as a corporate strategy. In a way, that removes them even further from the decisions that affect the rest of Canadians. Although the Reichmanns have inspired a generation of Canadian entrepreneurs, they have not demonstrated a commitment to help their fellow Canadians build a strong, competitive community.

This commitment is becoming a critical element of our rebuilding process. A recent report by the prime minister's advisory board on science and technology discussed the need for "technological transformations in traditional resource and manufacturing industries such as steel, auto parts, and forest products"—the last being a sector in which the Reichmanns and the Edper Bronfman group both play a dominant role. That transformation, according to the scientists and researchers who wrote the special study, is critical to retaining exports, generating income, and maintaining our standard of living.

Foreign investment has built this country. It has also been reviled for most of our history. In future, it will be more controversial than ever. Between

7   Using 1987 numbers, the latest available.

1983 and 1988, the flow of foreign investment increased by 20 percent annually worldwide; the flow of trade rose by 5 percent, by contrast.

There are sound arguments against foreign ownership: companies tend to spend money on research and innovation in their home country. That certainly has been the Canadian experience when foreigners have set up branch-plant operations here. And certainly this is one of the findings of Michael Porter's international study. Foreign money doesn't invest in innovation, he says; countries should not encourage foreign mergers or takeovers.

The United States has a much more positive experience with foreign-owned firms doing domestic research. That leads American economists such as Robert Reich to argue that we are moving to an era of "transnational" companies that will do research wherever there is an attractive environment. He may be right; it could be that Canada needs to foster that innovative environment that is now so sadly lacking (rather like W.P. Kinsella's story of the farmer who built a baseball diamond after he heard a voice saying, "If you build it, they will come").

Our experience with the telecommunications sector supports Reich's thesis: in an area in which we have the domestic base to provide skilled labor and support systems, research and development is almost as high a percentage of sales among foreign-controlled firms as among our domestic favorites such as Northern Telecom.

Our experience with British Gas is also a story of hope and good intentions. It presents a credible argument that it is better to have a foreign investor willing to spend money on research as the owner of a company than to have one of the country's wealthy family groups, a group that had little intention of encouraging innovation at a company that was essentially merely an underperforming segment of its investment portfolio.

Perhaps we should be developing policies to attract more of a research orientation among all firms. That, however, opens the Pandora's box known as Industrial Strategy. Canadian governments should stay firmly out of the business of running businesses. It's questionable whether they should even target national champions. And despite the NDP's successful deal making with British Gas, they should be very careful when cutting deals with the private sector. They have too dismal a record of choosing losers.

The Reichmanns are international investors with a Canadian base; the Lis are Hong Kong-based investors with Canadian holdings. Yet the same people who thrill to details of the Reichmanns' billion-dollar developments overseas cry foul when Li Ka-shing wins the Vancouver Expo lands development project. There is something very wrong here. Li's aims, it would seem, are very much like the Reichmanns': security for his investments, a future for his children—quite possibly but not necessarily in Canada.

As we saw, Li's experiences with Canadian investment have been mixed. He has learned that Canadian resource companies don't offer a steady return. He has been patient about his investment in Husky Oil; his money allowed the company to buy new properties and to restructure its holdings at a difficult time in the oilpatch's history. Yet after months of indecision, Li's partner, Nova Corp., has placed its holding in Husky up for bidders. Li Ka-shing and his son, Victor Li, have been criticized for their real estate purchases in Vancouver—although they did nothing that a local developer wouldn't do. On the other hand, Li's venture into the United States with Gordon Investment Corp. has so far yielded no exciting investments south of the border.

Foreign investment does lessen our sovereignty. But we need the money. And we need the skills that foreign investors bring, particularly the Hong Kong "astronauts" who are looking at eventual resettlement here. Besides, once we admit that we have no control over the spending habits of our own families and institutions, how can we demand that control over outsiders? We must simply work to link companies operating in this country to our community.

As for our attitude toward immigration, we should be deeply ashamed of ourselves. An October 1990 poll by the *Globe and Mail* and the CBC showed that only 16 percent of Canadians wanted to increase immigration levels. This is an utterly wrong-headed, prejudiced attitude, especially from a frontier nation. Whether the immigrants have money or not, they should be welcomed. We need them.

Before we make up our minds on any of these issues of innovation, investment, and competitiveness, we should look at our economic system. What sort of business model are we working from? How can we change it?

There are good arguments that the traditional economic view of the world needs updating. Canadian economist Richard Lipsey is among those making that argument; he's involved with a think-tank that is rethinking conventional economic approaches to include a role for technologically inspired innovation and one for community-centered goals such as family, religion, and patriotism as valid, non-monetary motives for investment. One of Lipsey's think-tank colleagues, professor Paul Romer from the University of California at Berkeley, recently declared that ideas and technology must be at center of policy making. Now that the capitalism-communism debate has been settled, he added, the next debate is over the best type of capitalism. "Anybody who is familiar with the experience of South Korea or Japan or even Quebec can't help but be struck by the extent to which the notion of group identity affects attitudes toward policy, toward economic growth."

Canada — except for that unified business-government axis in Quebec — is a mix of European social-democratic capitalism and the American free market approach. We have become more American in recent years; it is this that the anti-free trade forces abhor. They have some reason: the American model is too short-term, too cutthroat for our tradition of cooperative nation building. Besides, the United States has many of the same problems that we have in terms of dying industries and industrial sclerosis. Its education problem is substantially worse. But a reliance on the European model is also dangerous; too much government in business has in past meant mismanagement and unnecessary expense.

We need to take a closer look at the Japanese way of doing things. We certainly don't want their rigidity or their repressiveness or their chauvinistic social mores. But they have managed to work together—government, business, labor, and the public—toward a common economic goal, with spectacular success.

I am no Japan expert by any means. But even my brief experience with that country left me in awe of their ability to find the essence of a subject and master it. Robotics didn't make the auto industry; it was teamwork and innovation that pushed Japan ahead. These are qualities worth imitating. Perhaps the best solution is our version of the California Roll—taking the best from the American and Japanese models and building on our traditional European-derived social-democratic base.

At the same time, we can learn from our previous failures to convince the Japanese to invest in Canadian industry and technology. We must be able to guarantee access to the American market in order to gain their investment money; and we can't expect joint ventures when we don't have the basic technological tools to build the partnership. When we do have those tools, however, it seems a good bet that the Japanese will be interested. We do still have the most uniform education system in North America, a fact they appreciate.

And as the cautionary tale of Moli Energy showed, when we offer them a technology with potential, the Japanese don't hesitate to get involved. Moli, unfortunately, is all too typical of small, innovative Canadian companies that risk everything on each new technology—and are vulnerable to any mistake. Moli's former chief executive Hugh Wynne-Edwards is a member of Mulroney's scientific advisory board, and Moli was one of the companies the board studied before it released its report on the state of Canadian technological competitiveness in 1991. Wynne-Edwards detailed the company's problems with capital and its disastrous rush into full-scale production of a flawed product. He also spelled out how the Japanese clients were the only ones willing to step in and buy the company, even at five cents on the dollar.

The science advisers' report, when it was published in the summer of 1991, zeroed in on the lack of capital as the single largest problem for emerging technology-intensive firms like Moli. We live in a knowledge-driven era, but knowledge isn't an asset on an accountant's or a banker's ledger. Since cash flow depends on the product's uncertain chances of acceptance by the marketplace, these companies rely on equity investors. In recent years, however, poor returns have turned venture capital away.

"More likely," the report says, start-up money will come "from relatives, friend, colleagues, and angels—investors [like Norman Keevil, Sr.] who believe in the management of the firm or the product to be developed. Often the amount of money from acquaintances is inadequate to the task. The fledgling firm, if not stillborn, starves."

If the company does make it past this stage, it can founder on a simple lack of communication. As with Moli, key decisions can be put down to a lack of understanding between the financiers or investors and the technology's inventors-cum-corporate managers. "This lack of understanding, on both sides, creates a self-perpetuating cycle of failure, twin vicious circles of undercapitalization."

The group offered the usual disappointing suggestions for government funding through the tax system and through a new merchant bank. But it also suggested a $1-billion government "risk-sharing fund" for use by firms with sales of less than $50 million annually. These companies could borrow up to half the money they needed to develop an idea and repay the loan "eventually," from the proceeds of product sales.

Even more interesting was the suggestion that the seed money for this fund could come from a penalty tax on pension funds that do not invest at least 1 percent of their assets in technology-intensive firms. The group calculates that it could raise $1.8 billion from the $179 billion in trusteed pension plans. The penalty tax—calculating that 10 percent of the 1 percent minimum investment was not in fact invested according to this prescription—could raise $180 million a year.

That $179 billion accounts for much of the money behind our industrial structure—much more than the fifty richest families in the country combined. A quarter of that sum was invested in Canadian stocks. That means that pension funds own about one-third of the stock of companies listed in the TSE 300. Another large portion is invested in Canadian corporate bonds. And the payoffs from investment mean that these gigantic piles of money are growing almost exponentially: by 1994 the funds could have as much as $350 billion in their coffers. That amount equals the entire present value of the Canadian capital market.

Fund managers, however, don't invest in innovation or make long-term commitments to companies. Instead, they're pushing for short-term performance. Fund managers justify this attitude by pointing out that they need to provide the most money possible for the country's pensioners. Concentrating funds on regional development can be dangerous to those counting on the money—Alberta's Heritage Fund has shown that through a series of dismal corporate investments in the province. (There was a fair amount of pork barreling involved in that instance, however.) And it can be counterproductive when funds try to foist their social agenda on the companies in which they invest.

Still, pensioners need to look at what their corporate funds spend money on. I'm not suggesting wholesale revolution here. But we always hear that we have bankrupted this country and that our children and grandchildren will pay. Maybe the grandparents could pay closer attention to the investment policies of their pension funds. Or, as the science advisers concluded, "Pension funds must be asked to participate in the financing of our economic future."

That future remains a big question mark. In good part because, as the report also concluded, "By any measure, Canada's science and technology performance is below the level required to sustain living standards at the level of the leading industrial countries." Of course we still have wealth, and we can continue to live off it. As one stockwatcher said to me recently, analysts are calling for Inco to be the stock of the 1990s. But that's not the point. What happens when Inco or Alcan or forest products or oil can't carry us? What will we have built? How susceptible will this country be to shocks from the rest of the world?

Michael Wilson has a favorite saying these days. "The first hundred years we lived off our resources," he tells me. "The next fifteen years we lived off our credit. Now we've got to live off our imagination, our energy, our skills, our initiative, and good hard work."

The Canadian response to the Free Trade Agreement with the United States, however, doesn't augur well if we're switching from resource and credit dependency to stand-on-our-own initiative and elbow grease. We're familiar enough with the United States market to know its needs and its strengths; after all, three-quarters of our trade is done with the United States. But we were caught off guard by the fast-paced realignment of industries after the Free Trade Agreement took effect. Several bureaucrats in Ottawa admitted to me that they expected Canadian companies and foreign subsidiaries to expand south of the border. They were shocked by the number of companies that simply closed up shop here.

This does not mean that all the lost jobs add up to a deindustrialization of Canada. We needed to lose some of them; they were going anyway. In fact, we must be careful not to subsidize dying industries. During the next nine years, we could lose half our auto industry jobs. Perhaps we should let them go; perhaps we shouldn't be in that business if we don't have the technological capacity to compete. We don't want jobs for the sake of having jobs. That type of industrial policy has long since been proven to be short-sighted, expensive, and pointless.

But here's a pleasant surprise. Despite all the moaning about lost jobs and lost opportunities, in 1990 we somehow managed to export more to the United States than ever before. And that's with a high Canadian dollar and high corporate interest rates and a recession on both sides of the border. So much for the conspiracy theory that our government had sold us out.

Yet our fear-ridden attitude toward free trade is understandable. The Free Trade Agreement was negotiated with Canada in a defensive position. We were afraid of an aggressive movement toward protectionism in the United States. This was the wrong attitude to take going into an international negotiation. All our economic postures during the 1980s, such as deregulation and privatization, were defensive. We were either reacting to strong international forces or trying to recover from bad government mismanagement that had overwhelmed us with debt. We still have the debt.

But the economic moves of the 1990s must be aggressive, proactive, dynamic, and at the same time reflective. A tough order.

As a nation, we've always looked for comfort and security from our elected leaders. Now we must accept that there are no instant or magic solutions. We are leaning toward populism right now in how we are governed, our constitutional structure, and our political parties. But we can't afford to make the mistake yet again of choosing people who tell us only what we want to hear.

Instead, we need to think seriously about issues such as research and job training. Our governments spend about $45 billion on education annually and another $5 billion on adult retraining. Industry, however, hasn't been doing its part. Canadian companies spend half the amount on training as the United States; one-fifth the amount spent by Japan; one-eighth the amount spent by Germany. The average Canadian worker has seven formal hours of training annually. Japanese workers have 200 hours of on-the-job training, Swedish workers 170 hours.

We're not that productive; we were recently ranked fifth among twenty-four countries by the Organization of Economic Co-operation and Development. Part of the problem here is psychological. We feel alienated by the changes in the nature of our work. The corporate juggling act of the past decade has undone lifelong commitments and rewarded loyalty with a pink slip. In part, we have blamed this company-vs.-labor scenario on technology and trade pressures, when it is really a problem of commitment and communications. We need to become committed to our work, and to learning and advancing technologically. And our companies need to commit to us on a long-term basis.

The most volatile issue for the future is the decision facing Canadian businesses: leave, or stay and make a commitment to Canada. There is reason to hope that they will choose the latter option. After all, this is a great place to live—we are second only to Japan in standard of living, according to a recent United Nations study. We still get high marks for our education and health systems, despite their drawbacks. Much higher, according to a UN spokesperson, "than [the country's] rank in terms of income should give it."

The general populace must forge a consensus with business over our future. We can't separate business from the rest of our policy making. We can't allow business to operate in one realm and the rest of Canadians to believe different myths or operate from a radically different policy perspective. The two hands must work together to fashion our future. That means a commitment from business not to operate for short-term profit goals only. And a commitment from the rest of society to accept that business and government can work together without there being some secret conspiracy to do us all out of something.

Tax policy is another matter. We have a huge national debt to pay off and we can't ignore that fact. However, we should try to make the concessions that our airlines and our truckers and our other industries need in order not to lose their businesses because of uncompetitive pricing. As for our personal tax level, that is offset by a larger social net than many other countries offer. Businesses should not expect any big breaks either, since the country pays for health care and transportation and there is no need to subsidize housing, for example, as there is in Japan. Our tax rate is higher than in the United States, but lower than in Japan, Germany, and Britain. Taxes may be one factor in pushing a business out of the country. But if we offer well-trained people and an exciting climate of research and innovation, I believe that will entice businesses to come here.

Where does that leave our politicians? Certainly the Tories are doing the right thing in pouncing on productivity and competitiveness, even if it is a last-ditch attempt to restore their fortunes. As for the other parties, we must demand that they respond with their own economic solutions. We don't want solutions that pander to Bay Street or unions or Newfoundland or British Columbia, but solutions that talk of our united future.

Let's not let the politicians get away with using our real economic worries as a stick with which to beat Quebec. The economic truth is that Quebec can make it alone if it chooses to do so. It will also pay a price that it isn't now admitting: it will have to negotiate itself into the North American trading bloc and deal with a $100-billion debt. Try selling that to the Japanese. Quebec's deficit will be bloated because it will have to pay foreign investors high interest rates. And it won't be receiving any transfer payments from Ottawa. But if the people of Quebec are willing to pay that price, they can do it.

Instead of fear mongering, we should concentrate on an arrangement that benefits all of us. I prefer to concentrate on a vision of a united Canada. Whether in this constitutional structure or another, we all face the same economic problems. There are arguments for decentralization—as long as regions are willing to take on responsibility for themselves without the present system of cross-subsidization. But no one will benefit from a multi-tiered system of fiefdoms hugging power to themselves, which makes it expensive and inefficient for investors and companies to operate—and difficult for Canada to represent its parts internationally. We can function under a more decentralized structure—any country can. It would be more difficult, and we should admit that.

Most important, we must realize that Canada cannot just "muddle through." If we leave matters to chance or think that things will take care of themselves, the country will lose control of its destiny. Our options will disappear. And in five years' time we will be much worse off. In this fast-paced information-based world, where natural resources have lost their magic, that type of national disintegration could happen very quickly.

Global politics is about control, pure and simple. So is global economics. The fall of the Berlin Wall and all the accompanying power shifts in Eastern Europe and the Soviet Union clearly demonstrated that economics is now the governing force for the world. We all look to Europe when we talk about globalization because of the way the European nations in the EC have redefined their sovereignty in economic terms. But eastern Europe has turned that redefinition on its head; it now signifies not only those linked together, but those shut out of the arrangement.

And we are certainly not alone in our fears and our desire to withdraw from each other and the world economy. *Toronto Star* columnist Richard Gwyn, who has in the past written so eloquently about the Canadian political psyche, is now reporting on the changes in the new Europe. In mid-1990 he made a trip to Lake Couchiching to tell a Canadian audience about a frightening movement he sees gathering force there: tribalism. "The nineteenth-century version of the nation-state has collapsed," Gwyn notes, because "the nation-state cannot protect its citizens from the global economy. What is left between an individual and the wide world is the tribe." The Berlin Wall is gone, but Gwyn says the people still live in fear. This time, they fear their neighbors' economic successes. "There is a great danger that Europe will set out to replace the Wall with an economic and innovation barrier."

I visited Berlin's famed American crossing point, Checkpoint Charlie, while conducting interviews in Europe for this book. There, for a few deutschemarks, chisels could be rented so that tourists could knock off their own pieces of the Wall. People had set up stands out of the backs of their cars and on tiny tables, offering packaged pieces of rock, guards' caps, all sorts of mementoes of the recent, yet already distant, past. The Wall was built to keep people from fleeing to capitalism; its dismantling was the scene of raw capitalism of the sort that would make Hong Kong proud.

I went home clutching a few rocks purchased at one of the stands. Now I'm trying to knock a few holes in the walls Canadians have built, both to isolate ourselves within Canada and to provide some sort of psychic barrier from the big, bad world. I see us all—Wilson the politician, Chapman the reporter, Taylor the airline chief, the laid-off workers, the scientists, the ardent, old-line nationalists like Maude Barlow, Ontario energy czar Marc Eliesen, young Richard Li, Bob Blair in the oilpatch, the money makers at Gordon Investment, the diplomats, bureaucrats, natives, sovereigntists, you, me, even the poets—as a thin, straggling line of Canadians, stretched across the country, using whatever tools we have to tear down our barriers and build a new Canada together. We may have different approaches to our country's future and lean toward different solutions. But it's heartening to know that by force of will, no barrier is too daunting to be overcome.

APPENDIX

Major Academic and Industry
Studies on Competitiveness

1. Business Council on National Issues/Government of Canada. American
Economist Michael Porter, author of *The Competitive Advantage of Nations*, is studying twenty-seven Canadian industrial sectors to determine
where Canada stands in terms of international competitiveness—and what
factors benefit or inhibit the development in Canada of globally competitive companies. The report is due to be published in autumn 1991.

2. Kodak Canada Inc. *Fast Forward: Improving Canada's International
Competitiveness*, by Alan M. Rugman and Joseph R. D'Cruz, University of
Toronto. Part of a series on globalization being funded by Kodak. Premised
on the idea that Canada is regressing in terms of international competitiveness. Published January 1991. According to this report, in order to
be competitive, Canada must:
a. reduce fiscal deficits;
b. change the country's protectionist mindset;
c. balance manufacturing and service activities;
d. find a less interventionist role for government;
e. develop policies for better education and training.

3. National Advisory Board on Science and Technology. Prime Minister
Mulroney appointed this board in 1987 to advise him on how to improve
the relationship among science, technology, innovation, and competitiveness in Canada. The report runs to sixteen volumes. Dozens of
academics and other experts were involved in each area. The board's study
was based on the premise that Canada is not "meeting the competitiveness
challenge." The report states that "Canada is a nation at risk." Published
March 1991. Its findings include:
a. Innovation, as much as natural resources, drives the global economy.

b. There is a strong link between long-term economic prosperity and quality of life.

c. A competitive economy demands private-sector leadership.

d. Governments, educational institutions, and individuals must work with the private sector to create an environment where innovation can thrive.

e. By any measure, Canada's science and technology performance is below the level required to sustain living standards at the level of the leading industrial countries.

f. Canadian industry conducts little research and development for two equally important reasons. First, the economy is dominated by industries with intrinsically low ratios of R&D spending to output. Second, goods-producing industries in Canada tend to perform less R&D than similar industries in other highly developed countries.

g. Adult training is our greatest area of untapped potential.

h. Investment in training should be initiated by employers but supported by government.

i. The relatively high cost of capital in Canada threatens all industries.

j. Technology-intensive firms in the start-up or early phases face severe difficulties in gaining access to capital.

4. Economic Council of Canada. In early 1991, Prime Minister Mulroney asked the Economic Council of Canada to undertake a study on competitiveness. It is due to be published in 1993, with a preliminary study expected by the end of 1991.

5. C.D. Howe Institute: *The Innovative Society: Competitiveness in the 1990s.* By Bryne Purchase. The report's aim was to look beyond the recession to the competitiveness issue. 1991 Policy Review and Outlook published January 1991. Its nineteen recommendations included the following:

a. Ottawa should continue its tight-money policy as long as necessary to control inflation.

b. Canada should be part of the North American Free Trade Agreement negotiations.

c. Foreign investment in Canada's innovative businesses should not be discouraged.

d. Targets for research and development and innovation should be regionalized and set up with a broader range of factors, and should be results-oriented.

6. Coopers & Lybrand. *Reshaping Canada to Compete*, by Maureen Farrow. Former C.D. Howe chairman Maureen Farrow coordinated a study which interviewed more than 100 influential Canadians in labor, government, and business. Published January 1991. The study focused on four problems facing Canadian society: the internationalization of business; the erosion of market competitiveness; pervasive global and domestic structural change; and the leadership crisis in Canada. The report found that in order to deal with these problems, business and government must:
a. formulate a competitiveness strategy for the 1990s;
b. build a government-business trade initiative that is responsive to globalization;
c. establish a new interprovincial-federal policy called the G-12, which would include Ottawa, the provinces, and the native peoples;
d. complete constitutional discussions quickly; overhaul Canada's governmental structure and costs.

7. Canadian Manufacturers' Association. *The Aggressive Economy: Daring to Compete*. The theme of this study is that in order to compete globally, Canadian business and government must have competitiveness as its central economic goal. Published in the summer of 1989, the report made the following recommendations:
a. Education must be better integrated with national economic goals.
b. The tax system should encourage investment. There should be generous tax incentives for investments in plant and equipment, and more attractive R&D tax credits.
c. R&D spending must be focused, and keyed to commercial results. Innovation in industry, new product development, and new processes must be emphasized. Canada should follow the example of the Japanese, who are "masters at identifying the most important parts of competitive leverage."

8. Conference Board of Canada. The 1990 annual report established competitiveness as the theme of the coming decade.

INDEX

Spiegel, Thomas, 157
Stackhouse, John, 69
Steinberg family, 121
Stelco Inc., 212
Stevens, Sinclair, 55, 88, 226, 245
Stewart, Walter, 117
Stiles, Jim, 211-12
Strong, Maurice, 88
Structual Impediments Initiative, 189-91, 193, 195
Sumitomo Corp., 183
Summerville, Paul, 188, 197
Suzuki, Akira, 195
Swissair, 55, 64

Takeshita, Noboru, 185, 190, 200
Taylor, Claude, 48-54, 57-59, 64, 68-73, 75-77, 260-61, 275
Taylor, Paul, 29
TDK, 210
Teck Corp., 200-1, 210, 212-13, 216, 220-21
Teleglobe Inc., 55, 66
Telesis, 148
Tembec, 34
Terry, Edith, 180, 192, 205
Texaco Inc., 114, 165, 167
Texasgulf, 88
Thatcher, Margaret, 5, 56, 112, 123
Thomson, Ken, 131
Thomson, Richard, 16-19, 22-23, 25, 35, 42, 43, 45, 46, 225
Toda, Makoto, 197-98
Toigo, Peter, 172
Toronto-Dominion Bank, 14-27, 33-37, 40-47, 125, 140, 147-48, 225, 258
Tory, John, 131
Trans-Canada Airlines, 51, 53
TransCanada PipeLines Ltd., 33
Trizec Corp., 113, 122, 126

Troper, Harold, 178
Trudeau, Pierre, 2, 80, 88, 184, 245
Trump, Donald, 194
Tsunoda, Michi, 221
Tsutsumi, Yoshiaki, 194
Turbo Resources, 167
Turner Broadcasting System, Inc., 34
TWA (Trans World Airlines), 61

UNICEF, 91
Unicorp Canada Corp., 136-37
Union Bank of Switzerland, 33
Union Gas, 134, 136
United Artists, 35
United Nations, 272
University of British Columbia, 209, 211
University of Calgary, 83, 100, 162, 168, 180
University of Saskatchewan, 131
University of Toronto, 78-79, 81, 86, 104, 108-109, 210, 277

Vander Zalm, William, 172-73
Varity Corp., 12, 144
VenTech Healthcare Ltd., 101
Via Rail Canada Inc., 59
Volcker, Paul, 5
Vuitton, Louis, 188

Walwyn Stodgell Cochran Murray, 31
Ward, Max, 58
Wardair, 58, 62
Warner-Lambert Co., 82, 85
Watkins, Mel, 139-40
Weekes, John, 240
Wesley, Malcolm, 134, 140, 142, 145-47
Westcoast Energy Ltd., 134, 137